Salutation to
MAHARSHI PATANJALI

योगेन चित्तस्य पदेन वाचां,
मलं शरीरस्य च वैद्यकेन।
योऽपाकरोत् तं प्रवरं मुनीनां,
पतंजलिं प्रांजलिरानतोऽस्मि।।

Yogena cittasya padena vacham
malam sarirasya cha vaidhyakena
yopakarottam pravaram muninam
patanjalim pranajaliranato'smi

(Let us bow before the noblest of sages Patanjali, who gave Yoga for serenity and sanctity of mind, grammar for clarity and purity of speech and medicine for perfection in health. Let us prostrate before Patanjali.)

Salutation to **GURU'S**

Swami Shivananda

T. Krishanamacharya

Shriram Sharma

Acharya Mahaprajna

Maharshi Mahesh

K Patabhi Jois

BKS Iyengar

Swami Ramdev

Sri Sri Ravi Shankar

Dr HR Nagendra

Acharya Balkrishna

Dr. Yogi Bikashananda

Swami Dharmanand

Prof. Dr. JPN Mishra

Dr B.B. Goyal

Dr Anil Bansal

I dedicate this book to these Gurus from whom I derived inspiration to work on Yoga. I resolve to continue my endeavours in this noble path of service to humanity.

SEVEN
SECRETS OF
YOGA

[Shatkarmas, Sukshma Vyayam, Asana,
Bandhas, Mudras, Pranayam, Meditation]

Yogaguru Mohan Karki
NDDY, ND, DNY, MA (Yoga & Science of Living)

Publishers

**THE YOGAGURU PUBLICATION
DELHI (INDIA)**
Contact : +91-9911-316-600 | 9911-316-685
E-mail: theyogaguru.mohan@gmail.com
www.tygyoga.com | www.theyogaguru.com

ISBN : 978-93-5196-010-2

Published by :

The Yogaguru Institute
Delhi (India)

Phone : +91-9911316600
+91-9911316685

Website: www.tygyoga.com | www.theyogaguru.com
E-mail: theyogaguru.mohan@gmail.com

© Publisher

Price : ₹ 455/-

Edition : 3rd 2019

Typesetting by :

Vinod Yadav, Delhi

Printed by :

Literacy House, Mehrauli, New Delhi

FOREWORD

When a person having experience in a field resolves to pick pen and writes down his experience in shape of a book, it becomes pleasing for readers to go through the same & easy to derive benefits from it.

Sh Mohan Karki is an experienced Yoga teacher and practitioner. He adopt Yoga & has been insensibly practicing it for quite along time. He organises Yoga classes and teaches Yoga to people. He, so far, held thousand of Yoga classes in which thousands of people participated & got benefited.

It is good to see a book titled "Seven Secrets of Yoga Science" by Sh. Karkj. The journey through this title gives glimpses of his experience and insights towards Yoga. The book encapsulates, Self restraint (Yama), Scriptural rules (Niyama), Posture (Asana). Breathing (Pranayama), With drawal of senses from their subjects (Pratyahara), Concentration (Dharna), Meditation (Dhyan) & Transidental Meditation (Samadhi), with the primary knowledge of Satkarma, Bandha, Mudra & Chakras. Sh Mohan Karki's style of elaboration is simple, scientific and lucid, which will prove to be boon for the readers of his book.

Now a day, when our lives are full of tension & puzzles leaving us to lead disease stricken lives in various ways, the above-said book may be inspiring for people to adopt yoga in their daily lives regularly entailing them to happy healthy lives. A healthy person by contributing his optimum virtues and talents to his family, society, national and world will prove to be a living as set, which this world desperately spires to.

I, extend my good wishes for Sh Mohan Karki & pray to God that his book may be amilestone in dissemination of Yoga for healthy & happy life of a yoga practitioner.

(Acharya Balkrishna)
University of Patanjali
Vice-Chancellor / Secretary General

FOREWORD

For a long time till my college days I always thought Yoga was boring. I used to believe it as a tool for elders to cure diseases and then I met Mr. Mohan that changed my perception. Look how our first meeting happened. I was sitting in a room full of strangers, feeling alone and awkward, here comes a person with a friendly smile. This was almost a decade back when I first met Mohan Ji. I went to attend a workshop and found him there attending the same. I was new to the place and did not know anyone there. I looked around with a hope to find some acquaintance and found this gentleman looking around in the same manner. That was our first meeting and as the workshop progressed we came close to each other and became friends.

Generally I do not open up with anyone easily but Mr. Mohan's deep knowledge about yoga and naturopathy took my attention and we became friends forever. After the workshop we use to sit together and discuss a lot of things about yoga and practiced different yoga postures together. As our practice went a step further and we started feeling a lot of positive effects of yoga in our life, we thought to spread the awareness and benefits to everyone and started The Yogaguru.

With the help of Yoga Mr. Mohan has treated many patients having chronic problems like Insomnia, Diabetes, Asthma, Hypertension etc. to spread the awareness he wrote this book with his vast experiences and extensive research. This book is really helpful to have a basic knowledge about yoga, especially for beginners and it is a helpful tool for people who want to be Yoga teachers. This book explains many forms of Yoga, basic yoga postures, body cleansing techniques, Pranayamas – Breathing and Meditation formats.

Mr. Mohan's book, I know will enable many to become the Yoga Instructors like Mr Mohan. These instructors, our society needs the most for obvious reasons like life style diseases, obesity, with expectation of a better & toned body, flexibility, strength, and stamina etc. Best Wishes.

SHAILENDRA SINGH
President, Holistic Healthcare Foundation Society

PREFACE

ॐ संगच्छध्वम् संवदध्वं
सं वो मनांसि जानताम्
देवा भगं यथा पूर्वे
सज्जानाना उपासते।।

May you move in harmony;
May you speak in unison;
Let our mind be equanimous like in the beginning;
Let the divinity manifest in your sacred endeavours.

I started to work on this book from 2007 while preparing contents for our website www.theyogaguru.com. The major contents were added while designing Yoga Teachers Training Manual for the Yoga Teachers' Training that we conduct in Holistic Healthcare Foundation. I could reorganize this while finalizing the contents for www.tygyoga.com. My experiences while practicing and teaching yoga assisted me enormously to make this book more practical. In this journey, I received feedback and support from thousands of students and friends. This encouraged me to work tirelessly for several years that made it possible to bring this book as finished product which is now available for all aspiring Yoga enthusiasts.

I hope and trust that this book will be one of the most useful books for those who want to understand applied Yoga in detail. I have explained the major tools of yoga viz. Sukshma Vyayam, Shatkarma, Asana, Pranayama, Bandha, Mudra, Chakras, and Meditation. Understanding the Scientific and Spiritual aspects of Yoga will help you to apply and achieve the desired results. I have made necessary efforts to meet the requirements of all readers. After reading this book, you will be your partial doctor. This will help you to lead a healthy life with minimal use of chemically derived medicines and prevent numerous side effects of these medicines.

Practicing yoga will produce natural medical stimulus resulting in excellent health benefits. Explanations about therapeutic applications make it more useful for those who want to practice yoga as a therapy. It will be of immense value to Yoga Students and Teachers.

This book can be a great gift that you can give to your friends and family. I hope all students and Teachers of Yoga will generously support our mission to spread this message of Ancient Indian Wisdom to many Homes, Gurukuls, Libraries, Fitness Centres, Schools, Colleges and Universities.

I sincerely dedicate this book to all my Gurus (I believe my Parents are my first Guru). I derived all the encouragements from my Guru's guidance and blessings to keep going despite obstacles and hardships. I am indebted to all my students. Your faith in me made me more responsible. Optimistic results achieved by students while practicing yoga with me gave me much needed confidence to make yoga teaching as a major goal of my life.

I thank my friend and Co-founder of Holistic Healthcare Foundation Shri Shailendra Singh and my wife Neha Karki for the support they have been providing me. I thank Manoj Khadka and Ramesh Khadka for assistance in typesetting this book. I thank Chaman Rawat, the Director of GR Printers for page setting, designing, printing related advice and support.

Last but not the least, your efforts to spread the Ancient Indian Wisdom which is scientific and useful for all, will be highly appreciated. Yoga can give Holistic Health to all practitioners. Spreading Yog Sciences benefit all in creating a beautiful, happy, healthy, joyous, peaceful and prosperous world all together.

OM

MOHAN KARKI

The Yogaguru Institute
New Delhi, India

Contents

INTRODUCTION TO YOGA

Yoga is an ancient wisdom with scientific validations for overall development. It can help improve all the dimentions of personality that includes Physical dimension (Annamaya Kosha), Energy Dimension (Pranamaya Kosha), Mental Dimension (Manomaya Kosha), Intellectual Dimension (Vigyanamaya Kosha) and Spiritual Dimension (Aanandamaya Kosha). We can understand yoga as a science of consciousness as well which can give us access to conscious self as well as subconscious self.

Yoga is to unite. It represents the union between Jeevatma (soul) and Parmatma (super soul), Shiva and Shakti, Prakrit and Purush, Sun and Moon, Ha and Tha, Eda and Pingala, exhalation and inhalation, blood and semen, positive and negative energy, sympathetic nervous system and parasympathetic nervous system, as well as North and South pole of the magnetic energy; thus it can bring balance in everything that exist in this universe.

Yoga is a universal science which goes beyond all barriers of gender, sex, cast, creed and religion. Household people should understand it as a discipline to improve or develop one's inherent capacity in a balanced manner to achieve desired success in life through perfection. It is a way of conscious evolution and holistic realization. Above all, yoga is a process which can free us from the grip of senses. We can acquire the biggest tool for helping us to live our lives more meaningfully & with awareness. In this context, we can also see yoga as a way of life or science of living which can help us to achieve balance between materialistic and spiritual life. Practice of yoga helps us to acquire holistic health which covers physical, mental, emotional, behavioural, socio-economical and spiritual health all together.

DEFINITIONS OF YOGA

Yoga is skilfulness in action. Practicing yoga generates moral and mental cultivation which further imparts good health (Arogya), contributes to longevity (Chirayu) and total intrinsic discipline. It leads a person to perennial peace and happiness with experience of union between individual soul and super soul (universal soul or GOD).

योगश्चित्तवृत्तिनिरोधः॥

Yogah Chitta Vritti Nirodh. (P.Y.S 1.2)

According to the Patanjali's Yoga Sutra "the mentioned union is possible through the control of whirls of mind."

समत्वं योग उच्यते॥

Samatvam Yoga uchyate (Bhag. Gita 2.48)

Yoga is a state of balance in all situations sorrow or happiness, success or failure, win or loss.

Balance/equanimity is called Yoga.

योगः कर्मसु कौशलम्॥

Yogah Karmasu Kaushalam (Bhag. Gita 2.50)

Cessation of mental modifications is Yoga Control of whirls of mind makes a person balanced.

Samatvam Yoga Uchhyate in every situation whether pleasure and sorrow, success and failure.

Samatva and Chitta Vritti Nirodh bring perfection or skilfulness in action as mentioned by lord Krishna in Bhagvat Gita.

JOURNEY FROM HERMITS TO SCIENTIFIC EXAMINATION

Great sages and saints found yoga thousands of years ago. Earlier it was restricted only to hermits, sages and saints but nowdays it can be seen commonly in our everyday life. It has aroused a worldwide awareness and acceptance after scientific evaluation in the laboratory of modern science with proven effectiveness. Yogic science and its techniques have been re-oriented to suit modern sociological needs and life style. There are thousands of cases cured by yogic therapy, which were considered incurable by allopathic medicine.

Experts of various branches of medicine including modern medical sciences are realizing the role of these techniques in the prevention of disease, mitigation (control), cure of disease and promotion of health.

Yoga plays three types of role in health-care viz. promotion of health, prevention of diseases and cure of different types of diseases. If we use it as a therapy, it works, first of all, as preventive treatment of forthcoming ailments.

It helps in the process of blood circulation, energy formulation and vitalization of organs that promotes good health. It improves immunity and resist diseases; as a result, it brings curative effect. There are various diseases which can totally be cured with yoga. Practice of yoga awakens the latent energy. The awakened energy works as resistance power by increasing immunity of the body. As a complete physical, mental, emotional, behavioural and spiritual drill, it increases tolerance, efficiency and stamina. It makes the body so strong that cold and heat; pain and pleasure; ups and down etc. can do no harm.

Last but not the least, better co-operation and coordination among thoughts, speech and action is the most important gift of yoga practice. It is a tool for success in a competitive world. It works as an excellent antidote to today's silent killer- stress, tension and psychosomatic diseases as well.

4 TYPES OF YOGA

Yoga is a science of consciousness. It is a tool to free ourselves from the grip of senses to live life meaningfully. There are four major types of yoga which use different path to achieve the state of ultimate bliss. Raja Yoga uses mind control through training of Asthanga yoga for achievement of liberation. Gyan Yoga uses knowledge and wisdom for realizing the ultimate truth about the essence of self. Karma Yoga uses selfless action as a path to achieve liberation. Bhakti Yoga uses path of devotion as well as channelization of energy to realize transcendental and divine nature inherent in every human being. There are other types of yoga as well which are understood as a substitute or part of Raja Yoga i.e. Hath Yoga, Nada Yoga, Kundalini Yoga, Swar Yoga, Tantra Yoga, Laya Yoga and Kriya Yoga etc.

(1) Karma Yoga

Karma yoga teaches us to perform all duties without lust and greed. One should consider there duty as divine action; performed with whole hearted dedication by shunning away all desires. It will lead to perfection with success and happiness. According to Sankhya philosophy nature is composed of three forces (called in Sanskrit): Sattva (equilibrium), Raja (activity) and Tamas (inertness). Tamas is typified as darkness or inactivity. Rajas is activity expressed as attraction or repulsion and Sattva is equilibrium of the two. Karma yoga teaches you to deal with these three factors by teaching what they are and how to employ them.

Principles of Karma Yoga

There are certain principles of Karma Yoga which are fundamental to follow:

Do your Duty with Right Attitude and Right Motive: It is not what you do that counts; but your real motive behind it. As Swami Sivananda said, "man generally plans to get the fruits of his work before he starts any kind of work. The mind is so framed that it cannot think of any kind of work without remuneration or rewards". But Karma Yoga believes in dutifulness. God will decide the return. We must perform our duties. The person who shuns away duty falls down in a dark hole of mess. Your duty is towards god or self or the inner teacher who teaches you through all the specific circumstances of your life as they appear.

Do your best and result will follow: Realize that you are not the doer but only an instrument. God is the doer of everything. The way to realize this truth is to constantly work for the sake of work and let go of the result, good or bad. Attachment binds the individual but detachment dissolves the Karmic seeds. An action without personal motive or expectation is called Niskam Karma, which do not bring karma sanskara or bondage; thus they can be called as liberating karma.

According to the Law of Karma, the result of every good or bad work will come to you without fail. Some actions bring results immediately and some may take time. Do good work to derive good result; as you sow, so you will reap. Results will ultimately come for sure. So, don't waste your time and energy on expectation; just do your duty with right attitude and right motive.

Follow the discipline of job: Each job is a teacher of some sort. It is better to know that there is no superior or inferior job. You can learn different skills doing different jobs. Each job has different requirements in terms of time, degree of concentration, skills, experience, emotional input, physical energy and will power. If you know a better way to serve, you must use it. You can achieve the best possible result with an honest effort to do our best. Do not hold back because of the fear of effort or because of the fear of criticism. Do not work in a sloppy manner just because no one is watching or because you feel the work is not for you. Give your best. Try to do such actions that can bring maximum good and minimum evil.

Serve the God or the self in all: You naturally expect care and loving response from others. As we expect, so we should treat others with love, affection, care and respect, regardless of their position in life. We achieve self transformation with actions.

(2) Bhakti Yoga

The term Bhakti comes from the root 'Bhaja' which means to be attached to God. Bhakti is intense devotion towards God. Bhakti yoga is a system of intense devotion with emphasis on complete surrender to divine will, leading to freedom from egoism, humble and unaffected by the dualities of the world. This much dedicated Bhakti can free you from all types of pain and sorrows leading towards happiness. Shraddha (reverence) and Vishwas (faith) are the incipient stages of devotion. They develop into Bhakti. Faith is the most important factor in the path of devotion. As a famous Indian proverb says, When bhakti enters food, food becomes prasad; When bhakti enters hunger, hunger becomes a fast,; When bhakti enters water, water becomes theertham; When bhakti enters travel, travel becomes a pilgrimage; When bhakti enters music, music becomes kirtan; When bhakti enters a house, house becomes a temple; when bhakti enters actions, actions become services; When bhakti enters in work, work becomes karma, & most importantly; when bhakti enters a man, man becomes human.

The qualifications for the attainment of Bhakti: Pure loving hearts, faith, innocence, simplicity, truthfulness, Vairag (detachment) and Brahmacharya (celibacy). The one who follow the path of Bhakti is called Bhakta (devotee).

There are 4 categories of Bhaktas (Devotees)
1.	Arta (the distressed)
2.	Jigyashu (the curious)
3.	Artharthee (the desirous of wealth)
4.	Gyani (desirous of the absolute knowledge)

There are nine tools of Bhakti Yoga:
(i)	Sarvan (Hear the Lilas of the Guru/God)

(ii)	Kirtan (Sing the praise of the Guru/God)

(iii)	Smaran (Remember the name of the Guru/God)

(iv)	Pad Sewa (Worship the lotus feet of the Guru/God)

(v)	Archana (Offer flowers to the Guru/God)

(vi)	Vandana (Prostrate yourself before the Guru/God)

(vii)	Dasya-Bhava (Do service unto the Guru/God)

(viii)	Sakhya Bhava (Make friendship with the Guru/God)

(ix)	Atma-Nivedan (Do total unreserved surrender to the Guru/God)

Obstacles to Bhakti Yoga

Lust, Anger, Greed, Moha, Pride, Jealousy, Hatred, Egoism, Desire for power, Name, Fame and hypocrisy are the obstacles in the way of Bhakti Yoga.

How to overcome the obstacles to Bhakti Yoga?

The obstacles can be replaced with sincere intention to erase. Lust can be removed by entertaining pure thought; Anger and Hatred by love; Greed by Charity, Honesty and Disinterestedness; Moha (attachmente) by Viveka (knowledge); Pride by Humility; Jealousy by Magnanimity or Nobility (Mudita) and Egoism by Unconditional or unreserved self-surrender to god.

Pray frequently like Prahalad, Sing his name like Radha, Weep in solitude like Mira on account of Viraha

Agni, Kirtan like Gauranga and Repeat his name like Valmiki and Kalidas. Never sit idly praying to God but be up and keep working as God helps those who help themselves. Do the best and leave the rest to God. Kindle the light of love in heart. Love all including every creature by cultivating universal and cosmic love.

(3) Gyana Yoga

Gyana yoga teaches to discriminate the self and non-self to acquire the knowledge of one's spiritual entity through the study of ancient scriptures, literatures, Satsang (company of saints, wise, intellectuals and laureates) and practice of meditation.

Sadhana Chatushtaya

The qualities and qualification required for success in Gyan Yoga are collectively called as Sadhana Chatushtaya.

1. Viveka (discrimination between the real and unreal)
2. Four Stages of Vairagya (non attachment)
    i. Yatmana (endeavouring)
    ii. Vyaterika (separation)
    iii. Ekendriya (One organ of sense- mind)
    iv. Vasikara (Subjection or complete control of 5 senses organ and 5 action organs and mind)
3. Shatsampathi (six attributes):
    i. Shama (calmness)
    ii. Dam (self-control)
    iii. Uparati (Detachment or self withdrawal)
    iv. Titiksha(endurance or patience)
    v. Shraddha (faith or sincerity)
    vi. Samadhan (not losing the sight of goal) and
4. Mumukshuttva (intense desire for liberation)

3 Stages of Gyan Yoga Practice

i. Sravan (listening)
ii. Manan (contemplation)
iii. Nidhidhyasana (repeated meditation or attaining oneness with reality)

(4) Raj Yoga

Raj yoga is one of the most popular yoga form which helps in achieving ultimate liberation through training and programming of the mind. There are many yoga forms like-Laya yoga, Kundalini yoga, Hatha yoga, Mantra yoga, Tantra yoga etc. which are the part of Raj yoga.

Astanga Yoga

Astanga yoga propagated by Maharshi Patanjali for all-round development of human personality is a foundation for Raj yoga. It is popularly known as Raj yoga. The ultimate goal of yoga is to get self-realization or get enlightened. Maharshi Patanjali wrote Yoga Darshan in 3000 B.C. Yoga Sutra includes 195 sutras devided into 4 chapters.

1. Samadhi Pada (51 sutras)
2. Sadhana Pada (55 sutras)
3. Vibhuti Pada (55 sutras)
4. Kaivalya Pada (34 sutras)

There are eight steps (folds) of yoga which is called Ashtang Yoga as mentioned by Patanjali in his book 'Yog Sutra'. This can be achieved only after practicing the process step by step. First five of them are called Bahirang Yoga (Yama, Niyama, Asana, Pranayama and Pratyahara) which are practiced for physical and mental development through outer purification. The last three (Dhrana, Dhyana and Samadhi) are considered as Antarang Yoga for mental, emotional, behavioural and spiritual development through inner purification.

According to Sage Patanjali, continuous practice of yoga with self restrained perseverance is important to achieve the ultimate goal. The modifications are restrained by perseverance and detachment.

अभ्यासवैराग्याभ्यां तन्निरोध:

Abhyasa Vairagyabhyam Tannirodhoh (P.Y.S. I.12)

(1) Yama (Behaviour)

There are 5 social codes of conduct of yogic behaviour mentioned in Patanjali's yoga sutras.

अहिंसासत्यास्तेयब्रह्मचर्यापरिग्रहा यमा:

**Ahimsasatyaasteyabrahmacharya aparigraha Yamah
(P.Y.S. 2.30)**

Non-violence, Truthfulness, Non-covetousness, Abstinence and Non-possessiveness are Yamas.

(A) Satya (Truth): Be truthful to yourself. You can never lie to yourself. If you are not truthful to yourself it will haunt you again and again. Being honest to self is a prerequisite to achieve peace within and awaken the hidden capacities.

(B) Ahimsha (Non-violence): Ahimsha is essential to achieve peace within and outside. In yoga, ahimsha means following non-violence in action, speech and even in mind. As you love your life, so does every living being. They love their lives and want to live more. So never indulge in violence, never encourage violence and never approve violence done by others.

(C) Asteya (Non-stealing): Not to steal is the literal meaning of Asteya. In yoga, it includes not to deprive the right of others as well.

(D) Brahmacharya (Celibacy): Brahmcharya literally means celibacy. Observing celibacy or preserving sexual energy helps you to flow it upward to awaken upper body energy centres. Sexual energy is the essence of energy that our body produces after a long process of producing RAS, RAKT, MAAS, MEDA, ASTHI, MAZZA and finally SUKRA. SUKRA energy when preserved and flown up helps to produce OJAs. OJA helps to improve our energy field that in return helps to increase our capacity to influence the energy of the surroundings wherever we go. Secondly, Brahmacharya is made of two words, Brahma (the creator), and Acharya (the knower). Observing Bramhcharya with the help of self study, Sadhana, detachment and satsang helps the Sadhak to march ahead on the right path.

(E) Aparigraha (Non-hoarding): Aparigraha literally means non-hoarding. Desire of achieving more is natural. Being a victim of desire or being a slave of desire leads you to disaster. It is essential to have control over desires to achieve silence within to have crystal clear perception. So, that one can march ahead to achieve self mastery.

(2) Niyama (Rules)

There are 5 individual codes of conduct or rules and regulations mentioned in Patanjali's Yoga Sutra.

शौचसन्तोशतप:स्वाध्यायेश्वरप्रणिधानानि नियमा:

Shauchsantoshtapah Swadhyayaeshwarapranidhanani Niyamah (P.Y.S. 2.32)

Cleanliness, Satisfaction, discipline, self study and surrender towards are observances.

(i) **Sauch (Cleanliness):** Sauch literally means cleanliness which includes physical and mental cleanliness.

(ii) **Santosh (Contentment):** Santosh literally means contentment. Being content with what you have and who you are is very important to preserve your energy so that you can use it for the right purpose of life.

(iii) **Tapa (Dutifulness):** Tapa literally means right endeavour or dutifulness. It is essential to achieve what you want in your life.

(iv) **Swadhyaya (Study and regular practice for self improvement):** Swadhyaya literally means self study. In yoga, self study means to study your own self with the help of Contemplation, Study of Literature, Satsang and Sadhana.

(v) **Ishwarpranidhan (Complete Surrender in God):** Ishwarpranidhan means complete (undoubted) faith and surrender to God. It is very essential to have faith in

God (generator, operator and destroyer of the universe) especially when you face tricky or unresolved questions in your life.

(3) Asana (Postures)

Asana is the systematic process of physical exercise to maintain fitness of the body through proper circulation. According to Gherand Samhita there are 8.4 millions asanas as there are 8.4 millions of species of living creatures in this universe. Among them 84 are the best and among 84 asanas; 32 have been a found very useful for mankind from health perspective. There is fundamental difference between other exercises and yoga. You feel tiredness after practicing exercise i.e. gym, aerobic etc. but you feel relaxed after 1-hour of yoga practice. If you are feeling tiredness after practicing yoga you should realize that you are practicing wrongly. Sage Patanjali clearly mentioned that "STHIRA SUKHAM ASANAM" which means practice of different postures in which you sit comfortably for a long time without any difficulty is called asana.

स्थिरसुखमासनम्

Sthirasukhamaasanam (P.Y.S. 2.46)

Asanas can be classified into the following categories:

(A) On the basis of position:
- Standing (Utthit) Asana
- Sitting (Badda) Asana
- Lying (Shupta) Asana

(B) On the basis of movement:
- Static Asana
- Dynamic (moving) Asana

(C) On the basis of Effects
- Meditative Asana
- Flexibility Building Asana

- Strength Building Asana
- Relaxation Asana
- Therapeutic Asana etc

(4) Pranayama (Yogic Breathing)

Pranayama is the scientific process of controlled breath. Breathing is the doorway to supply Oxygen and to remove carbon-dioxide. We receive pranic energy or vital energy or cosmic energy and divine power along with the inhaling breath. While exhaling, we throw out all types of toxins that include carbon-dioxide, other poisonous gases, forbiden matter and negativity. It makes our body relaxed and healthier than before. This process helps us to get rid of all types of diseases.

तस्मिन् सति श्वासप्रश्वासयोर्गतिविच्छेदः प्राणायामः

Tasmin Sati Swas Prashvasyor Gati Vichhchheedah Pranayamah (P.Y.S. 2.49)

Regulating the flow of breath is Pranayama. Practice of Pranayama can remove the blocking barrier of the flow of prana and life force.

ततः क्षीयते प्रकाशावरणम्।।

Tatkshiyate Prakasshawaranm. (P.Y.S. 2.52)

According to Patanjali Yogsutra, the practice of Pranayama regulates the flow of five pranic forces (Pran, Apan, Saman, Udan, Vyan) that improves the functions of the body, mind and spirit. The Chitta has its own nature, all knowledge. It is made of Sattva particles, but is covered by Rajas and Tamas particles which can be removed by practicing Pranayama.

(5) Pratyahar (Control of sense organs)

Pratyahara is derived from two Sanskrit words, Prati and Ahara. Ahara means food, or anything taken into ourselves and Prati a preposition meaning away or against. Together they mean, weaning away from Ahara or ingestion.

स्वविषयासप्रयोगे चित्तस्वरूपानुकार इवेन्द्रियाणं प्रत्याहार
Svavishayaasamprayoge Chitta Swaroopanukara
Ivendriyanam Pratyaharah (P.Y.S. 2.54)

Withdrawal of senses (pratyahara) is that by which the senses do not come into contact with their objects and follow as it were the nature of the chitta. Pratyahara (withdrawal of the senses) is a bridge between the Bahiranga (external aspects of yoga): Yama, Niyama, Asana, Pranayama and the Antaranga (internal aspects of yoga) namely dharana dhyana and Samadhi. Having actualized the Pratyahara, the practitioner is able to effectively engage into the practice of Samyama.

At the stage of Pratyahara, the consciousness of the individual is internalized. As a result, sensations from the senses of taste, touch, sight, hearing and smell don't reach their respective centres in the brain. It takes the Sadhaka (practitioner) to subsequent stages of Yoga, namely Dharana (concentration), Dhyana (meditation) and Samadhi (mystical absorption) being the aim of all Yogic practices.

Methods to Practice Pratyahara

One of the most common practices for Pratyahara is Pranayama, wherein we automatically withdraw from the external and bring our focus inwards towards our breath as connection with the external senses and stimuli are all gradually severed. Yoga Nidra is another method used to aid in the development of Pratyahara. Concentration on a point between the eyebrows (Ajna Chakra or the third eye centre) can be another method of Pratyahara. Practice of Tratake can be another great practice to achieve Pratyahara. Another common technique for inducing Pratyahara is to first reduce physical stimuli and then practice the perception of senses, such as hearing. The mind has a natural tendency to roam between the sensory inputs. It gets forced to turn inwards when there is no longer any other thing to do, significant sensory input. Japa is another good method to achieve Pratyahara.

(6) Dharana (Concentration)

Dharana is translated as collection or concentration of the mind or the act of holding, bearing, wearing, supporting, maintaining, retaining, keeping back (in remembrance) of a good memory etc. Dharana is built by refining Pratyahara further to ekagrata or ekagra chitta (single pointed concentration and focus). In Dharana, the mind thinks about one object and avoids other thoughts where as awareness of the object is still interrupted. Dharana is the initial step of deep concentrative meditation. The difference between Dharana, Dhyana, and Samadhi is that in the former, the object of meditation, the meditator, and the act of meditation itself remain separate.

देशबन्धश्चित्तस्य धारणा

Deshbandhashchittasya dharana (P.Y.S. 3.1)

Concentration is the confining of the chitta within a limited area.

(7) Dhyan (Meditation)

Continuous flow of the contents of consciousness is Dhyana. In Dhyana, the meditator is not conscious of the act of meditation (i.e. is not aware that s/he is meditating) but is only aware that s/he exists (consciousness of being) and aware of the object of meditation. Dhyana is distinct from Dharana in which the meditator becomes one with the object of meditation. Dhyan is an instrument to gain self knowledge, separating maya (illusion) from reality to help attain the ultimate goal of moksa (liberation).

तत्र प्रत्ययैकतानता ध्यानम्

Tatrapratyayaiktanata dhyanam (P.Y.S. 3.2)

Continuous flow of the contents of consciousness or effortless concentration is dhyana. According to Patañjali, this is one method of achieving the initial concentration. In deeper practice, the mind gets concentrated between the eyebrows and begins to automatically lose all locations and focus on watching itself. Eventually, the meditator experiences only the consciousness of existence and achieves self realization. Swami Vivekananda describes the process in the following way, 'When the mind has been trained to remain fixed on a certain internal or external location there comes to it the power of flowing in an unbroken current, as it were, towards that point. This state is called dhyana.'

According to Gheranda Samhita, there are three types of Meditation: Sthula, Jyotirmaya and Sukshma Dhyana.

1. Sthula Dhyana (Gross Meditation): It is absorptive contemplation on a divine form, more specifically, the image of personal god (ishtadeva), or that of one's religious preceptor (guru).

2. Jyotirmaya Dhyana (Effulgent Meditation): It is focusing on the individual soul (jivatma) or on the supreme Self, radiating light (tejomaya brahma) in the cavity of the heart. With practice, the sadhaka is able to see flashes of light in the primal sound reverberating within him. Sometime, focus is made on luminous objects, like the flame of a candle or an earthen lamp (diya), or the sun, moon or a star, as advised by the guru.

3. Sukshma Dhyana (Subtle Meditation) : It is made on something abstract, like a mantra, geometrical form (yantra), inner music (nada), the vital being (prana), or the serpent power (kundalini shakti) that lies coiled up at the base of the spinal column. It is best performed in shambhavi mudra, with eyes half-open, and focused within. According to Gheranda Samhita, jyotirmaya dhyana is a hundred times better than sthula dhyana, and sukshma dhyana a million times better than jyotirmaya dhyana.

(8) Samadhi (Communion)

This stage includes a range of the highest spiritual achievements from the first Samadhis to the mergence with the primordial consciousness and with the Absolute. Samadhi gives one a vivid novelty of bliss.

In the Bhagavad Gita, Krishna speaks about Samadhi and about two principal stages of Nirvana:

I.	Nirvana in Brahman, the Holy Spirit
II.	Nirvana in Ishvara (the Creator)

Nirvana requires not only meditative skills but also ethical preparation (destroying the lower self in every possible way and replacing it with the collective self first and then with the universal Self or Paramatman). This is the only way one can connect to the unlimited Divine Power.

तदेवार्थमात्रनिर्भासं स्वरुपशून्यमिव समाधिः

Tadevaarthamatranirbhasam Svaroopashoonyamiva
Samadhih (P.Y.S. 3.3)

That state becomes Samadhi when only the object appears without the consciousness of one's own self. When one has so much intensified the power of dhyana, as to be able to reject the external part of perception and remain meditating only on the internal part, that state is called Samadhi. It means in the process of intense concentration only the object of concentration remains and the consciousness as a contemplator, is merged in the consciousness of the object alone.

There are two types of Samadhi

1. Samprajanata Samadhi: The state of Samadhi in which consciousness of object of concentration remains is called amprajanata Samadhi.

2. Asamprajanata Samadhi: State of Samadhi with complete cessation of all types of mental modifications (internal or external) is called Asamprajanata Samadhi.

Nine Antarayas (9 Obstacles in Yoga Practice)

We must understand that, essentially, the obstacles are not the problem. The problem is how we react and respond to the obstacles. When they come up, most people use them as an excuse to stop practicing. We have to have faith in the importance of effort. The main purpose of spiritual practices is to make us aware of the mind. In this way, even when there are obstacles, our efforts can benefit us. In these situations, stay calm and persevere. All progress proceeds by rise and fall.

व्याधिस्त्यानसंशयप्रमादालस्याविरतिभ्रान्ति

दर्शनालब्धूमिकत्वानवस्थितत्त्वानि चित्तविक्षेपास्तेऽन्तरायाः

Vyadhi Styana samsaya pramada alasya avirati bhrantidarsana alabdhabhumikatva anavasthitatvani cittaviksepah te antarayah (P.Y.S. 1.30)

1) **Vyadhi:** Physical illness
2) **Styana:** Lack of enthusiasm
3) **Samsaya:** Doubt
4) **Pramada:** Carelessness

5) **Alasya:** Laziness
6) **Avirati:** Desire for sense objects
7) **Bhranti Darsana:** False knowledge, wrong understanding
8) **Alamdha Bhumikatva:** Inability to concentrate
9) **Anavashitattva:** Instability, slipping backwards from ground gained

अत्याहार: प्रयासश्च प्रजल्पो नियमाग्रह:।

जनसंचयर लौल्य च शड्भियोगो विनश्चित।।

Atyāhārah prayāsaścha prajalpo niyamāghrahah janasangaścha laulyam cha shadbhiryogo vinaśyati (HYP1.15)

Overeating, Over Exertion, Excessive Talking, Adhering to Rules- Too Much!, Excessive Public Contact and Fickle mind are the barriers to success in yoga.

उत्साहात् साहसाद् धैर्यात् तत्वज्ञानाच्व निश्चयात।

जनसंगपरित्यागात् शड्भिर्योग: प्रसिद्ध ।।

Utsāhātsāhasāddhairyāttattvajñānāścha niśchayāt janasa ngghaparityāghātshadbhiryogah prasiddhyati (HYP1.16)

Utsaha (Enthusiasm), Sahas (Courage), Dhairyata (Patience), Tatwa Gyan (Right Knowledge) Nischya (Determination) and Janasang Parityaga (Avoiding Excessive Public Contact especially bad company) all together help to achieve success in yoga.

मैत्रीकरूणामुदितोपेक्षाणांसुखदः खपुण्यापुण्यविषयाणं
भावनातश्चित्तप्रसादनम्

maitreekarunamuditopekshanan sukhaduhkhapunyapunyavishayanan

bhavanatashchittaprasadanam (P.Y.S. 1.33)

The mind becomes purified by the culmination of Maitri (Feeling of Amity), Karuna(Compassion), Mudita(Goodwill), and Upeksha(Indifference).

APPLICATION OF YOGA IN MODERN AGE

Yoga is widely applied in different fields for the achievement of respective goals. It really gears up our life when applied regularly in different fields from healthcare to education, from self development to social upliftment. The only need is to practice it in a disciplined manner to achieve the optimum health called holistic health. If you perform properly designed set of asanas you should start achieving heightened physical and mental energy by the end of your practice. This will help you to forget your everyday problems and will bring you into a neutral state of mind. Do not look upon Yoga as something beyond you or as calling for any extraordinary efforts. You can remain in your stage of life, carry on your work and at the same time embark on the Yogic path. Any effort in the direction of Yoga never goes in vain. You will realize thereby the fruits of even a little Yogic practice. Yoga can help you to improve holistic health. It can improve your quality of life and increase your longevity. It can be applied to different areas of life.

Yoga can be applied in every field of life. Some of the fields where it can be applied are as follows:

1.   Healthcare (Health Yoga)

2.   Yoga for Stress Management

3.   Yoga for Fitness, Flexibility, Strength and Stamina

4.   Yoga for Efficiency Enhancement

5.   Yoga for Spirituality

6.   Yoga for Global Peace

7.   Yoga for Corporate (Corporate Yoga)

8.   Yoga for Pregnancy (Pregnancy Yoga)

9.   Yoga for Kids (Kids Yoga)

YOGA THERAPY

Therapeutic yoga is designed for people with ailment, which can be treated with yoga therapy. The duration would depend upon the ailment. Yoga therapy with other alternate therapies is practiced to give permanent relief. It is scientifically tested and proved as highly effective for certain ailments. An integrated and systematic approach to yoga has a positive effect on holistic health. Holistic health includes physiological, mental, emotional, social as well as spiritual wellbeing. Health Yoga is very effective in dealing with psychosomatic problems. If practiced thoroughly on a long-term, it can give a significant effect on a person's health both as a preventive measure and a curative measure, with added side benefits.

A. PRINCIPLES OF YOGA THERAPY

Yoga therapy has been scientifically proven to be effective to overcome diseases. It is a technique that helps overcome all types of problems if practiced appropriately.

1. Proper cleansing or detoxification of the body
2. Proper exercise (for proper activation of joints, proper circulation of blood, proper detoxification and nourishment of the systems within)
3. Proper relaxation and sufficient sleep (for healing, maintenance and rejuvenation)
4. Proper diet (for proper nourishment)
5. Positive thinking

Scientific research has shown that various diseases can be treated through yoga therapy. According to research done by CCRYN, Ayush Department, Government of India, the following diseases are amenable: Bronchial Asthma, Nasal allergy, Chronic Bronchitis, Diabetes, Thyroid problem,

Obesity, High and Low Blood Pressure, Heart diseases (HD), Migraine, tension, headache, anxiety neurosis, Depressive Neurosis, Rheumatism, Back pain, Arthritis, Gastritis and Peptic Ulcer, Chronic Diarrhea and Dysentery, Irritable Bowel Syndrome (IBS), Ophthalmic Disorders (short sight & long sight astigmatism, squint eyes, initial stages of cataract and glaucoma) and Mental Retardation etc.

B. TOOLS OF YOGA THERAPY

Science of Yoga is like an ocean. There are so many things to explore and experience. It is a fitness tool for a fitness freak; it is a challenge for an adventurist; it is a therapy for people who are suffering from ailments; and it is a Sadhana of self realisation for the spiritual seekers.

Here are some tools used in yoga as therapy.

1. SHATKARMA

धौतिर्बस्तिस्तथा नेतिस्त्राटकं नौलिकं तथा ।

कपालभातिश्रैच्तानि षट्कर्माणि प्रचक्षते

Dhautirbastistatha Netistratakam Naulikam Tatha
Kapalabhatiscaitani Satkarmani Pracaskate||HYP 2.22||

Shatkarmas are 6 yogic detoxification techniques given in Hath Yoga Pradipika and Gherand Samhita which includes: 1. Neti 2. Dhauti 3. Wasti 4. Nauli 5. Kapalbhati 6. Trataka

षट्कर्मनिर्गतस्थौल्यकफदोषमलादिकः।

प्राणायामं ततः कुर्यादनायासे सिद्धयति

Satkarmanirgatasthalyakaphadosamaladikah
Pranayamam Tatah kuryadanayasena Siddhyati (HYP 2.37)

Having removed over weight (fatness), imbalance of Kapha humour, impurities etcetera through the practice of six cleansing processes, afterwards success in Pranayama is effortlessly attained.

2. YOGIC SUKSHMA VYAYAM (MICRO EXERCISES)

Yogic Sukshma Vyayam are micro exercises to activate every joint of the body for proper activation of the whole body so that blood circulation happens in every part of the body and keep the nervous system vibrant. Proper blood circulation will ensure the supply of nutrition and oxygen to every cell of the body on the one side and facilitate the detoxification of cellular and metabolic wastage on the other site. Proper nourishment and detoxification is a foundation for good health.

3. ASANA

Asana is a very prominent part of this practice. Many people who are into yoga are mainly practicing asana alone believing it to be a complete yoga. It is not so. Asana is just a part of 8 folds of yoga suggested by Maharshi Patanjali. It helps to improve alignment of the joints, strengthen the muscles and improve efficiency of the internal system of the body thus helping the body, mind, emotion and intellect work in harmony that leads to holistic health.

4. MUDRA

Science of Mudra is based on 5 element principles and it uses bioelectric current to influence the energy mechanism that helps us improve the quality of life from bad health to good health, from good health to better health and from better health to perfect health.

5. PRANAYAMA

Practice pranayama as one of the most effective tools to bring therapeutic effects in physical, mental and emotional state of the body. There are various techniques of pranayama i.e. Udgit, Bhastrika, Anulom-Vilom, Nadisodhan, Surya Bhedi, Chandra Bhedi, Shitkari, Shitali, Ujjai, Bhramari etc.

6. BANDHAS

Bandhas are energy locks which help to stop energy leakages and move upward which will ultimately help the practitioner to achieve holistic health. There are 3 main energy locks suggested in classical texts:

1.   Mula Bandha (Root lock)

2.   Uddiyan Bandha and

3.   Jalandhar bandha.

7. MEDITATION

Meditation is the practice that leads to the liberation of mind. It will make a person free from stress and its manifestation. It leads a person from bad health to good health, from good health to better health and from better health to perfect health.

SOME USEFUL YOGIC MANTRAS FOR MEDITATION

Guru Mantra (गुरू मंत्र)

Guru Brahma Guru Vishnu Guru Devo Maheshwara
Guru Sakshat Param Brahma Tasmai Shri Gurave Namah.

गुरूर्ब्रह्मा गुरूर्विष्णुः गुरूदेवो महेश्वरः।
गुरूः साक्षात्परब्रह्मा तस्मै श्री गुरूवेनमः।।

Translations: (Guru is verily the representative of Brahma, Vishnu and Shiva. He creates, sustains knowledge and destroys the weeds of ignorance. I salute such a Guru.)

Gayatri Mantra (गायत्री मंत्र)

Om Bhuur Bhuvah Svah Tat-Savitur Varennyam
Bhargo Devasya Dhiimahi Dhiyo Yo Nah Prachodayat.

ॐ भूर्भुवः स्वः तत् सवितुर्वरेण्यं।
भर्गो देवस्य धीमहि। धियो यो नः प्रचोदयात्

Translations: (We meditate on the transcendental Glory of the Deity Supreme, who is inside the heart of the earth, inside the life of the sky and inside the soul of the Heaven. May He stimulate and illuminate our minds.)

Mahamrityunjaya Mantra (महामृत्युंजय मंत्र)

Om Trayambakam Yajaamahe Sugandhim Pushtivardhanam
Urvaarukamiva Bhandhanan Mrityor Mukshiya Mamritat

ॐ त्र्यम्बकं यजामहे सुगन्धिं पुष्टिवर्धनम।
उर्वारुकमिव बन्धनान् मृत्योर्मुक्षीय मामृतात्।।

Translations: (Om, We Worship the Three- Eyed One (Lord Shiva), who is Fragrant and who Nourishes all beings. May He liberate us from fear of Death for the sake of Immortality.)

Prarthana Mantra (प्रार्थना मंत्र)

*Om! Asatoma Sadgamaya, Tamasoma Jyotirgamaya,
Mrityorma Amritam Gamaya, Om Shanti, Shanti, Shantihi!*

ॐ असतो मा सद्गमय, तमसो मा ज्येतिर्गमय।
मृत्योर्मा अमृतंगमय, ॐ शांति, शांति, शांति ॥

Translations: (Om, lead me from the unreal to the real. Lead me from darkness to light. Lead me from death to immortality. May there be peace everywhere.)

Sangathan Mantra (संगठन मंत्र)

*Om Sahana Bhavatu, Sahanau Bhunaktu Saha Veeryam Karvaa
vahai, Tejaswee Naava Dheeta Mastu Ma Vidvishaa Vahai,
Om Shanti Shanti Shanti*

ॐ सहनाववतु, सहनौभुनक्तु सहवीर्यम् करवावाहे।
तेजस्विना, वधीतमृस्तु मा विदविशाव व है ॐ शांति, शांति, शांति ॥

Translations: (May the Lord protect us both, may He nourish us both, may we work together with great vigor (divine strength). May we both acquire brilliance of our intellect through our studies, may we not hate each other. Let there be peace, peace, peace.))

Prarthana Mantra (प्रार्थना मंत्र)

*Tvameva Mata cha Pita Tvameva, Tvameva Bandhus cha
Sakha Tvameva, Tvameva Vidya Dravinam Tvameva, Tvameva
Sarvam Mama Deva Deva.*

ॐ त्वमेव माता च पिता त्वमेव। त्वमेव बन्धुश्च सरखा त्वमेव।
त्वमेव विद्या द्रविणं त्वमेव। त्वमेव सर्वम् ममदेव देव।

Translations: (You alone are my mother and my father. You alone are my friend and my beloved companion. You alone are my knowledge and my wealth. O Supreme Lord, you alone are everything for me)

Shanti Mantra (शांति मंत्र)

Om Sarve Bhavantu Sukhinah Sarve Shantu Nir-Aamayaah Sarve Bhadraanni Pashyantu Maa Kashcid-Duhkha-Bhaag-Bhavet Om Shaantih Shaantih Shaantih

ॐ सर्वे भवन्तु सुखिनः सर्वे सन्तु निरामयाः ।

सर्वे भद्राणि पश्यन्तु मा कश्चिदुःखभाग्भवेत् ।

Translations: (May all possess happiness. May all be healthy (free from all diseases). May all see beauty. May there be good fortune and no misery anywhere. May there be peace everywhere.)

Shanti Mantra (शांति मंत्र)

Om Dyau Shanti Rantariksham Shantih Prithvi Shanti Rapah Shantih Roshadhayah Shantih Vanaspatayah Shantih Vishwed Devah Shanti Brahma Shantih Sarvam Shantih Shanti Reva Shantih Sa Ma Shanti Redhi Om Shantih Shantih Shantih Om

ॐ द्यौः शान्तिरन्तरिक्षं शान्तिः,

पृथ्वी शान्तिरापः शान्तिरोषधायः शान्तिः।

वनस्पतयः शान्तिर्विश्वे देवाः शान्तिर्ब्रह्म शान्तिः,

सर्वम् शान्तिः, शान्तिरेव शान्तिः, सा मा शान्तिरेधि,

ॐ शान्तिः शान्तिः शान्तिः

Translations: (May there be peace in heaven. May there be peace in the sky. May there be peace on earth. May there be peace in the water. May there be peace in the plants. May there be peace in the trees. May there be peace in the Gods. May there be peace in Brahman. May there be peace in all. May that peace, real peace, be mine)

Shanti Mantra (शांति मंत्र)

Om Purnamadah Purnamidam Purnat Purnamudachyate
Purnasya Purnamadaya Purnameva Vashishyate
Om Shantih Shantih Shantih

ॐ पूर्णमदः पूर्णमिदं पूर्णात् पूर्णमुदच्यते।
पूर्णस्य पूर्णमादाय पूर्णमेवावशिष्यते ।

Translations: ("That is whole, this is whole, from whole comes out of whole. If Whole is subtracted from whole, still whole is left."'Whole' can be replaced as 'infinity' also. 'That and this' refers to OM.)

Shanti Mantra (शांति मंत्र)

Om Sarva Mangala Mangalye Shive Sarvartha Sadhike Sharanye
Trayambake Gauri Naaraayani Namostute

ॐ सर्वमंगलमांगल्ये शिवे सर्वार्थसाधिके ।
शरण्ये त्र्यम्बके गौरि नारायणि नमाऽस्तु ते॥

Translations: ("I salute the three-eyed Divine Mother Narayani, who brings auspiciousness and who fulfils all the desires of the devotee (both spiritual and material).)

Shanti Mantra (शांति मंत्र)

Om ! Sarvesham Svastir Bhavatu Sarvesham Shantir Bhavatu
Sarvesham Purnam Bhavatu Sarvesham Mangalam Bhavatu Om
Shantih Shantih Shantih

ॐ सर्वेषां स्वस्ति भवतु । सर्वेषां शान्तिर्भवतु ।
सर्वेषां पूर्ण भवतु । सर्वेषां मङ्गलं भवतु॥

Translations: (Om. May auspiciousness be unto all. May peace be unto all. May fullness be unto all. May prosperity be unto all.)

THINGS YOU NEED TO KNOW

(When you try yoga for the first time)

As a new student of Yoga, you deserve the best possible start. Yoga is a scientific process that activates, detoxify and strengthen every part of the body through a series of postures, Yogic Breathing, bandhas, mudras, relaxation and meditation. Each component takes care of something different in the body and yet they all work together synergistically, contributing to the success of the other. It's never too late, it's never too bad, and you're never too old or too sick to start from scratch. Yoga is friendly for beginners yet it is still challenging for advanced students of Yoga.

How does Yoga work? Hatha Yoga flushes away the waste products, the toxins from all the glands and organs of your body. It provides a natural irrigation to the body through the circulatory system with the help of the respiratory system. It brings nourishments to every cell of your body so that each one can perform its function and keep your body healthy. You sweat impurities out of the body through the skin. You learn to control your breath through Pranayama. Practicing Pranayama not only increases our supply of oxygen, but also teaches us how to utilize that oxygen properly and efficiently in all our bodily functions.

Can I do it? Yes, you can. Yoga is not difficult. In fact Yoga is easy. It's just about stretching your body, relaxing, and allowing your muscles to open up. Do not miss the warm up. The warm up is the most crucial part of the practice. It makes sure your muscles don't get

overstrained or injured. Be committed to it. Go at your own pace. It will take a little while before you can catch up with the rest of the class. Just do what you can and push yourself with a little more effort in each class. Difficult postures will come much later. It is suitable for all levels of fitness, but if you have a special medical conditions, consult your doctor first, then Yoga teacher.

Diet and Hydration: Always practice on an empty stomach. No food 2 to 3 hours before yoga class. A small quantity of simple, easily digestible food is recommended for the meal prior to class. Drink lots of water for several days before your first class if you are not in the habit of drinking water. Doctors estimate you need at least 2 liters or 8 glasses of water per day for normal body maintenance.

Perfect Postures: There's no such thing as a perfect posture, but there is such a thing as a perfect stretch. Yoga is not about competition and perfection. If your muscles are feeling stretched then you are doing perfect. Simply follow the basics as guided by a guru. Everything takes a little time. Focus on enjoying the class rather than achieving. You will end up achieving more.

Attitude: Casual & Serious. Don't be too serious. Don't be too casual: If you're too serious you miss out the real joy. If you're too casual, you miss out the real joy. Somewhere in between is good. Maintain a happy, balance medium at all times.

Mind Control: Don't let your mind wander! The mind wanders. It is the nature of the mind to do so. Focus on the posture. Focus on your breath. Leave your worries behind. Just be present in the class. Everything else will happen on its own time.

Logical Questions: Questions are good. But if you're the kind of person who needs logic for everything relax your tendencies for a while and just follow the teacher. When you start seeing the change in yourself your questions will answer themselves.

Obsessive Breathing: Don't be obsessed with right breathing initially. If you're doing the posture right, chances are that you are breathing fine. When you start Yoga don't get caught up with right methods of breathing. It will come in the way of your practices. Obsession for right breathing will prevent you from enjoying the classes. Just focus on practices and enjoy the classes.

Yoga Etiquettes: It will help you to navigate your practices. We practice yoga etiquette to show our respect for ourselves, peers and all teachers. You may take yoga etiquettes as yoga rules. These rules of good yoga will help you feel comfortable when entering an unfamiliar setting. They are based on common sense and courtesy. More importantly, it is about programming your mind right. So, be ready to lead disciplined yoga routines to experience many blessings with various benefits in your physical, mental, emotional, intellectual and spiritual body. Here are some yoga etiquettes for group classes: Arrive on time in class, remove your shoes before entering yoga hall, switch off your gadgets, respect & follow the teachers, keeping variations appropriate, come to class sober & be great role models, avoid gum, grunting & moaning. Finally, most important point to remember, is never skip savasanas.

Secret : 1

SHATKARMAS
(YOGIC CLEANSING TECHNIQUES)

Shatkarma is a compound word consisting of two components: 'shat' meaning six and 'karma' meaning art or process. The word 'Kriya' or karma is used in Hatha Yoga in a special technical sense regarding the techniques of cleansing. The Hatha Yoga Pradipika and Ghenad Sanhita are the main source books of Shatkarma Techniques. According Hatha Yoga Pradipika, if there is excess fat or phlegm in the body, six clensing kriyas should be performed first before proceeding to the practice of pranayama. (H.Y.P-2.21)

धौतिर्बस्तिस्तथा नेतिस्त्राटकं नौलिकं तथा।

कपालभातिश्रेच्तानि षट्कर्माणि प्रचक्षते

Dhautirbastistatha Netistratakam Naulikam Tatha
Kapalbhatiscaitani Satkarmani Pracaskate

(H.Y.P-2.22)

It means Shatkarmas are 6 detoxification techniques which include: Dhauti, Wasti, Neti, Nauli (Lauliki), Kapalbhati and Trataka. Regular practice of Shatkarma (cleansing of the different systems) is important to achieve maximum benefit from yoga practices. Purification of the organs will prepare your body for the higher practices of yoga. These simple techniques are highly important for healing effects as well. These processes are both preventive and curative in nature.

Shatkarma activate, detoxify and vitalize almost all of the vital systems in the body, especially the digestive, respiratory, circulatory and nervous systems. Every individual organ of importance, like the food pipe, stomach, colon, lungs, eyes and ears, receives equal attention. Purification of the different systems of the body results in pure energy flowing freely throughout the body. It increases the capacity to work, enhances thoughts patterns, digestion, emotion, sight, taste, touch for quality experiences in our daily lives.

1. NETI - NASAL CLEANSING

Jala Neti
For Jala Neti you require a special Neti pot with a specifically designed nozzle so that it fit into the nostrils. It can be made of brass or any other suitable material so that it does not contaminate water. Fill the pot with warm and slightly salted water.

Technique
- Stand firmly, legs apart, body weight evenly distributed between the feet.

- Lean forward - tilt the head to the right side and place the Pot's nozzle in the left nostril.

- Open the mouth slightly and breathe through the mouth only.

- Keep the whole body relaxed and let the water pass out through the right nostril.

- Remove the Neti Pot when you have used half of the water.

- Remain bending forward; keep the head in the centre and let the water run out of the nose.

SHATKARMAS

Cleansing Processes (Hatha Yoga Pradipika)
Dhauti
Neti
Basti
Trataka
Nauli
Kapalabhati
Vastra
Gajakarani / Kunjal

Cleansing Processes (Gherandasamhita)
Dhauti
Neti
Basti
Trataka
Nauli
Kapalabhati
Antardhauti
Dantadhauti
Hariddhaui
Mulasodhana
1. Vatasara
2. Varisara
3. Vahnisra
4. Bahiskrta
1. Dantamula
2. Jihvamula
3. Karna Dhauti-(2)
4. Kapalarandhra
1. Danda
2. Vamana
3. Vastra
Vatakrama
Vyutkrama
Sitkrama
Jala
Suska

Satkarma with the help of
Water
Air
Simple appliance
Manipulation of bodyorgan
1. Varisara
2. Vamana
3. Jalabasti
4. Vyutkrama
5. Sitkrama
1. Vatasara
2. Suska basti
3. Vatakrama
1. Dantamula
2. Danda
3. Vastra
4. Mulasodhana
5. Neti
1. Vahnisara
2. Bahiskrta
3. Jihvamula
4. Karnayugma
5. Kapalarandhra
6. Trataka
7. Nauli

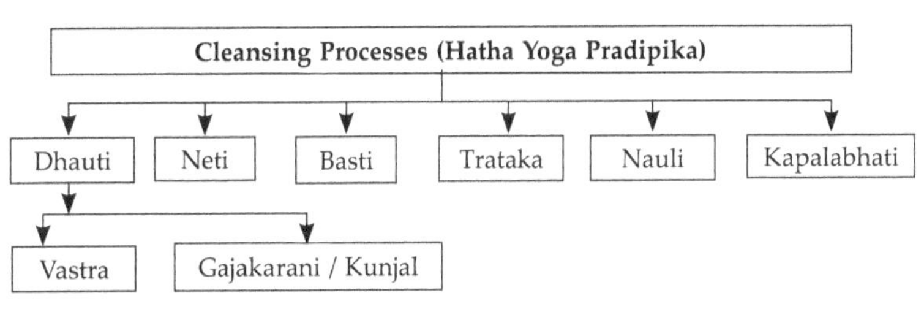

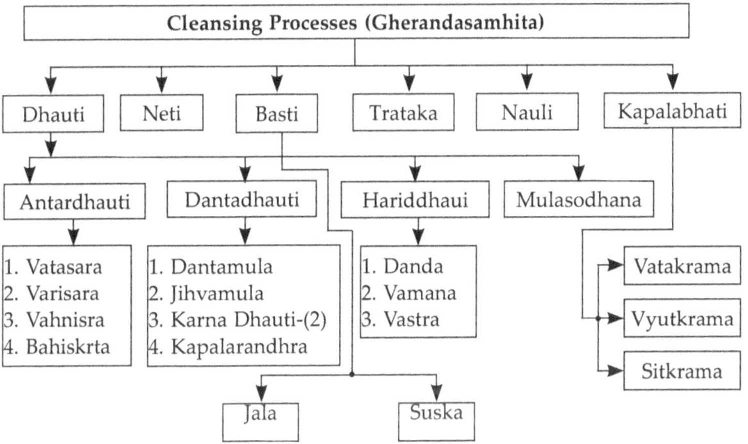

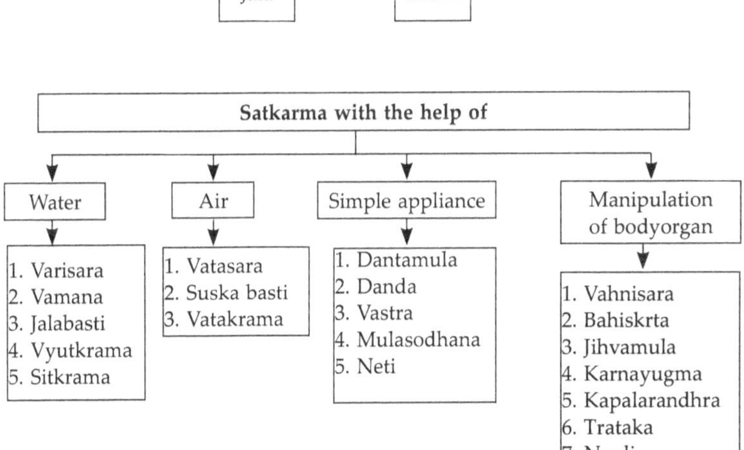

- Close the right nostril with the fingers and blow gently through the left nostril so that all the remaining water comes out.

- Practice the other side in the same way.

Note: Do not blow the nose very hard, otherwise the remaining water may be pushed into the ears, and irritation of the sinuses and mucus membrane may result. Although you can practice Neti squatting, it is better to stand. Too little salt will create pain while too much will cause a burning sensation. During practice, perform respiration through the mouth.

Neti can be practiced every day especially if you are suffering from sinusitis, colds, insensitivity to smell, nosebleed, headache and eye strain or eye infections. Those suffering from chronic haemorrhage should not attempt Neti unless under expert guidance. It is advisable to practice Bhastrika or Kapalbhati Pranayama after Jala Neti. This will dry the nose and generate heat in the nostrils.

Dugdha, Ghrita & Urine Neti

Instead of water you can use warm milk to practice dugdha Neti or warm ghee to practice ghrita Neti. (If oil is used instead of ghee, it must be unconcentrated and with no added chemicals.) These two practices are classified as variations of Jala Neti. Though urine neti is not mentioned in the Hatha yoga texts, it is particularly useful for curing inflammation of the nasal passages and sinuses as well as bleeding.

Sutra (Thread) and Rubber (Catheter) Neti

Sutra/rubber Neti performed by passing a length of thread through the nose to take out from mouth. Traditionally this was done with a bundle of cotton threads, carefully twisted and soaked in beeswax, but presently a thin rubber catheter is commonly used. The width should be about 4mm and the length 36 cm. It is good to practice Jala Neti first to make sure the nostrils are clear.

Technique

- Squat - Tilt the head slightly back.

- Very gently insert the sutra into the left nostril until it is felt at the back of the throat.

- Insert the first two fingers into the mouth and pull the sutra out through the mouth leaving a few inches of thread hanging out of the nose.

- Now hold the sutra from both sides in f r o n t of nostrils and mouth

- Slowly and gently pull the sutra backwards and forwards thirty to fifty times.

- Remove it slowly and repeat through the opposite nostril.

- Deep breathing, bhastrika or nadishodhan pranayam should be practiced upon completion.

Which nostril to start, right or left?

Neti can and should be done with, whichever nostril is flowing at the time of practice. This facilitates entry of water and forces any blockages to open. It is seen that, when Neti is performed with the nostril which is blocked, the water is not going to go in, and if it does go in it will be in drops or maybe a trickle. This will be a very time-consuming process. However, the nostril which is open provides an easier entry for the water within the nasal passage, and that water, once it enters, is able to force its way out through the other nostril much more easily.

Benefits of Neti

Neti cleanses the cranium and bestows clairvoyance. It massages the airways and strengthens the membranes. It makes them more efficient, clean, and warm, humidify and disinfect the air before it reaches the lungs, so that the air entering the lungs is in optimum condition. It also destroys all diseases which manifest above the throat. It removes accumulated mucus from the nostrils, associated passages and sinuses, allowing air to flow without obstruction. Neti also exerts a relaxing and irrigating effect upon the eyes by stimulating the tear ducts and glands. Regular practice of Neti maintains healthy secretions and drainage mechanisms of the entire ear, nose and throat areas. This helps to ward off colds and coughs, hay fever, cataract and tonsillitis. Sutra Neti stimulates the nerves and related brain functions of the eyes, tear ducts and olfactory zones. It increases mucus briefly, flushing out the toxins in glands and removes stagnation in blood stream, increases resistance to invasion by viruses. It strengthens resistance to various diseases of the ears, eyes and throat, such as myopia, tension headaches from eyes strain, certain cases of deafness.

Many people breathe through their mouths because their noses are too blocked; this leads to infections and asthma.
Poor memory, concentration and under development caused by mouth breathing in children can be improved by Neti. Neti relieves muscular tension of the face and helps maintain facial freshness and youthfulness. It releases emotional tensions and is beneficial in anxiety, depression, epilepsy and hysteria. The frontal lobes of the cerebrum, responsible for the higher mental faculties, begin to function optimally. It promotes balance between the left and right nostrils, and consequently the right and left hemispheres of the brain. This induces a state of harmony and balance throughout the central nervous

system and those systems governing respiratory, circulatory, digestive and excretory functions. At a more subtle level, Neti practices engage the different koshas and stimulate the Ajna chakra, the Midbrain Psychic centre.

Divya Drishti (Clairvoyance) and Jal Neti

Neti provides a state of mental clarity which is useful for the higher practices of yoga. It is not simply the act of pouring water through one nostril and making it come out through the other. It is not only a practice of putting a catheter through one nostril and bringing it out through the mouth. Rather, the physical practice of Neti gives birth to an internal state of Neti which is the flow of Prana Shakti in the three channels of Ida, Pingala and Sushumna. Once the flow in Ida and Pingala is balanced, then the harmony of their two flows will accentuate the flow of Sushumna. The awakening of Sushumna will, in turn, be responsible for the development of higher mental faculties, leading towards a natural tendency of a genius, intuition and creativity.

The term 'Divya Drishti' means 'Divine Vision' and has been wrongly interpreted as 'Clairvoyance'. Clairvoyance represents a state of mental achievement whereas 'Divine Vision' is an experience of an awakened personality. The practice of Neti helps in attaining the awakening of the inner personality with the regulation of Ida, Pingala and Sushumna flow, ultimately resulting in the awakening of the Chakras and Kundalini.

2. DHAUTI - INTERNAL CLEANSING

As a cleansing practice, dhauti assists the efficient movement of food throughout the digestive tract. Sluggishness in any section negatively affects the entire tract and associated organs e.g. liver, gallbladder, pancreas etc. Health of an individual depends on the effective function of the digestive system, which is habitually abused, either through ignorance or desire. The Dhautis provide methods for redress. Dhauti cleans out old bile and mucus at the same time permits release of impurities from the blood. These kriyas rebalance the natural harmony of the subtle chemistry with the help of the subconscious inner wisdom of the body. According to Ghenad Sanhita, Dhauti is divided into four categories:

Antardhauti	Hrid Dhauti	Danta Dhauti	Mulsodhan
1. Vatasara	1. Danda	1. Dantamula	Mulsodhan
2. Varisara	2. Vamana	2. Jihva Sodhana	
3. Vahnisra	3. Vastra	3. Karna Dhauti-2	
4. Bahiskrta		4. Kapalarandhra	

ANTAR DHAUTI (INTERNAL CLEANSING)

(A) Vatsara Dhauti

Vat means Vayu or Air and Sar means Essence. In this process air is used as essence to bring cleansing effects. Vatsara dhauti is performed by breathing in slowly through the mouth in kaki Mudra (contract the mouth like a beak of a crow) and then swallowing the air into the stomach while expanding the abdomen. It can be done up to ten times or until the stomach is fully expanded. Then the air should be passed through the large intestine. It will be helpful to assume an inverted posture to facilitate this better. Pashinee Mudra* is best suitable for the practice. The air should then pass out of the anus easily.

Pashinee Mudra: Come to sarvangasana. Bend your legs from knee and rest your knees on forehead or you may try to press your ears with your knees from sides.

Benefits Vatsara Dhauti

Vatsara Dhauti is essentially a sacred technique to purify the body. It destroys all diseases and increases gastric fire. The air that goes through the digestive canal improves its efficiency, removes gas, and prevents acidity and heartburn. Some air is normally taken in as one eats, it can be as much as half a litre. The stomach functions better with some oxygen. This practice removes stale air or gases.

(B) Varisara Dhauti (Shankha Prakshalan)

Varisara dhauti is more commonly known as shankhaprakshalana. In this practice you drink about sixteen glasses of warm salty water and evacuate it through the bowels. First you drink two glasses and perform a series of five specific asanas: tadasana, tiryaka tadasana, kati chakrasana, tiryaka bhujangasana and udarakarshanasana. After every two glasses the asanas should be performed until the water starts flowing out of the anus. Once clear water starts coming through, you will know that the stomach and intestines are perfectly cleansed and you can stop the practice. Thirty minutes after completing the practice, a salt-less liquid mixture of cooked rice, mung dal, and ghee has to be eaten until the stomach is completely full. There are dietary restrictions to be observed for a the minimum period of one week after the practice. It is a major cleansing process and it must be done under expert guidance.

SHANKH PRAKSHALAN
(VARISAR DHAUTI)

Digestion of food eaten is very important. There should be neither indigestion nor constipation. Excretion of stool is a very essential aspect in the protection of our health. The sequence of yoga asana that is practiced to help the practitioner in this regard is Shankh Prakshalan. In Shankh Prakshalan the whole food pipe is cleansed. Shankh Prakshalan Kriya is most important among all the Yogic cleansing kriyas. This is an activity, which must be practiced with great care.

There are four asanas to be practiced in Shankh Prakshalan. Before practicing the asanas, saline warm water is drunk so that 30 to 40 ft long canal from mouth to anus is thoroughly cleansed. We require more water to clean a zigzag tube than a straight tube. Similarly, we require more water to clean the zigzag passage in our abdomen. This entire water is pushed into the stomach through the mouth, from stomach to small intestine, from small intestine to large intestine, and from large intestine to the rectum. All the undigested particles of food and other accumulated wastes are pushed forward and conveniently let out along with the water through anus.

Before attempting Shankh Prakshalan, 5 to 6 liters of warm water either with some salt or juice of 4 to 5 limes mixed should be kept ready. Every time before attempting these asanas, one glass of salted or lime warm water is to be drunk.

Procedure of Sankh Prakshalan

First of all sit in Kagasana. Drink 2 glasses of the water you have prepared. Now, practice the sequence of asana as explained below:

1. TADASANA (MOVING VARIATION)

First Step (Basic Tadasana/The Heavenly Stretch Pose)

- Stand with your feet together.

- Interlock your fingers and turn the palms downwards.

- Inhale as you raise the arms up over your head.

- Slowly rise up on your toes, stretching and lengthening the abdominal area.

- Exhale as you slowly come down resting the hands on top of your head between the rounds.

- Repeat 10 times on consecutive breaths with no rest in between. All 10 rounds should take no more than about 30 seconds.

Benefits: The water in the stomach is pushed down along with the waste into the 20 to 25 ft long small intestine.

Second Step (Tiryaka Tadasana/ Side stretching pose)

- Stand with your feet and shoulder width apart.

- Interlock your fingers, turning the palms downwards.

- Inhale as you raise your arms up over your head.

- Exhale as you bend to the right side, then inhale as you straighten back up to the centre.

- Exhale as you bend over to the left side, then inhale as you straighten back up to the centre position.

- Repeat bending to right and then left for 10 times without any break in the breathing. All 10 rounds should take no more than 30 seconds.

Benefits: The water that is in the stomach is pushed along with the waste into the small intestine with proper pressure and pumping effect.

2. KATI CHAKRASANA
(STANDING SPINAL TWISTING)

- Stand with feet and shoulder width apart.

- Inhale as you raise your arms forward at shoulder level.

- Keep the feet flat on the floor.

- Exhale as you twist your upper body to the right side, wrapping the right arm behind the waist and the left hand onto the right shoulder.

- Turn the head fully to the right to look behind.

- Inhale back to the centre position. Exhale as you twist to the opposite side.

- Return to the centre position.

- Do 10 twists for each side, moving in the posture fast from side to side All 10 rounds should take no more than 30 seconds.

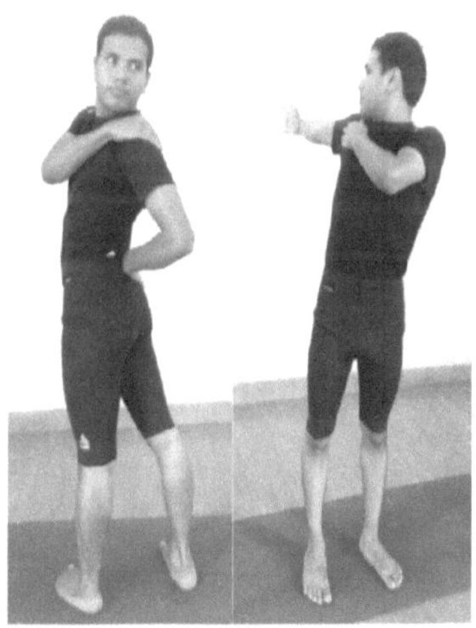

Benefits: The water with the undigested wastes that is in the small intestine is pushed further into 6 ft long large intestine.

3. TIRYAKA BHUJANGASANA (TWISTING COBRA)

- Sit in Kagasan.

- Place your palms on the ground keeping them shoulder width apart.

- Take both legs back and lay down on your chest.

- Inhaling, come to cobra pose, raising your front body.

- As you exhale, twist the upper body to the right, turning the head to look over the shoulder at the left foot.

- Inhale as you come back to the centre position.

- Exhale as you twist the body to the left, looking over the left shoulder at the right foot.

- Repeat the right and left twists 10 times without any break, on the last exhalation, coming down to the starting position. All 10 rounds should take no more than 30 seconds.

Benefits: The water that is drunk moves down with proper cleansing effect.

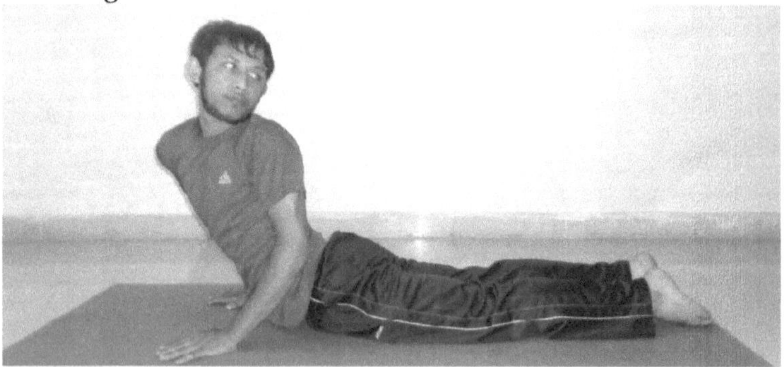

4. UDARAKARSHANASANA (ABDOMINAL MASSAGE)

- Sit in Kagasan, place hands on knees.

- Inhale at the centre position.

- Exhale as you twist the upper body and head around to the right, dropping the left knee onto the floor.

- While twisting and holding for a few moments, push the right knee over the left thigh so as to exert pressure into the lower abdomen.

- Inhale when coming back into the centre position.

- Exhale as you twist to the left side, pushing the left knee and massaging into the groin area.

- Inhale back to the centre position.

- Do 10 twists to each side without rest. All 10 rounds should take no more than 30 seconds.

Benefits: The water that has travelled for about 35 to 40 ft, with all the wastes, proceeds towards the anus.

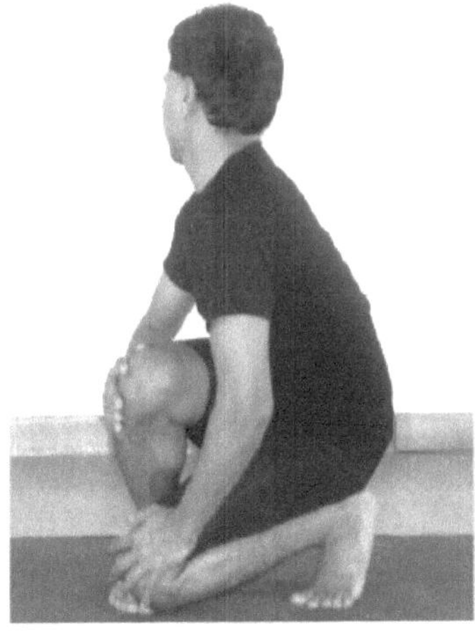

Note: The above four asanas constitute one set. Drink two glasses of salted or lime water before starting first set and from next set onward drink one glass of water each. Generally excretion starts after completing 5 or 6 sets. At the beginning, a bit of solid waste starts coming out. During these exercises, up to 4 or 5 times, the water is excreted with impurities; later entire waste comes out along with the water. After that finally almost clean water is excreted as it is. It indicates the successful completion of the cleansing process.

Rules to be followed strictly during Shankh Prakshalan:

- The above four asanas are to be practiced regularly for at least one week, before undertaking Shankh Prakshalan Kriya, so that during Prakshalan the asanas are exercised conveniently with ease.

- Three days before undertaking Shankh Prakshalan, Gaja Karni or Jala Dhauti Kriya should be practiced every morning before breakfast. This practice enables you to drink enough water during Shankh Prakshalan and there will not be any vomiting sensation.

- Except liquids, no solid thing should be eaten after 4.00 pm a day earlier of undertaking Shankh Prakshalan.

- It takes half an hour to one hour for the completion of Shankh Prakshalan and the salted or lime water cannot remain warm for so long. Therefore the water should either be warmed at intervals or hot water is added so that warmth is maintained while drinking.

- Those who don't have the feeling of excreting the motion even after having 8 – 10 glasses of water, further drinking of water should be stopped for some time and the whole body should be rolled on the floor for some time. This will accelerate the main Kriya.

- After completion of the Shankh Prakshalan some water remains in the stomach. To get it out, Jala Dhauti Kriya is done using 5 to 6 glasses of fresh warm water without any salt.

- After Jala Dhauti, Jala Neti Kriya should be done.

- Every machine is oiled when it is overhauled. Similarly after cleansing the internal parts of the body, pure ghee (melted butter) is to be consumed compulsorily. That completes the overhauling of the body.

- Before undertaking Shankh Prakshalan, pudding (Khichdi) with 100 gms of rice, 100 gms of Moong Dal (Green Gram) with a pinch of salt is cooked and kept ready. After the Shankh Prakshalan is completed, 75 grams of pure ghee (melted butter) is thoroughly mixed in the pudding and eaten. The same pudding is prepared for lunch and supper. On the whole nearly 250 gms of ghee is to be consumed on that day. Khichdi (pudding) should be eaten within 45 minutes of Shankh Prakshalan.

- The ghee produces energy in the body. Nothing should be eaten or drunk on that day except the prescribed pudding. Tea, coffee, milk, curd, buttermilk, fruits, curries, tobacco, alcohol, paan, pickles and smoking must strictly be avoided for minimum 3 days after the Kriya.

- Light food is to be taken on the second and third day along with 100 gms to 150 gms of ghee respectively.

- Bath can be taken before starting the Prakshalan process. After Shankh Prakshalan, bath should not be taken. Soon after the process, clothes are changed.

- All the parts of the body become very delicate when Shankh Prakshalan Kriya is undertaken. Therefore

24 hours rest must be given to the body and mind. Complete rest is a must; no work should be attempted during rest. One should get up only either to eat the food or to attend the calls of nature. (Physical rest on the following 2 days is much preferable.) Fans or air conditioning should be avoided.

- Persons suffering from ulcer, heart trouble and weakness; children, aged people, pregnant and those women who have their periods due within a week should not attempt Shankh Prakshalan.

- Persons with high B.P. should use lime juice instead of salt in the warm water. For the first time, Shankh Prakshalan should be undertaken strictly under the supervision of Yoga experts only.

- In case of very weak persons and adults above 55 of age, Laghoo (smaller version) Shankh Prakshalan can be done. Laghoo Shankhaprakshalana is terminated after 1 or 2 excretions.

- This process should not be undertaken on a cloudy or rainy day nor when stormy winds blow nor in very hot or very cold seasons.

- During this Kriya, stool excretes with great force, so toilet should be made available for passing the stool immediately.

- Sexual activity should be avoided a day before and 5 days after Shankh Prakshalan Kriya as the inner organs become very sensitive.

- Check List of the items required before the start of practice: 6-7 litres of warm saline (lime) water, glass, jug, Jala Neti pot, towel, napkin, soap (to wash the hands), Khichdi (with ghee) and undisturbed toilet facility with flowing water.

- Following the above rules Shankh Prakshalan Kriya can be performed once in 6 months.

Benefits of Shankh Prakshalan

There are a number of benefits if it is done according to the prescribed procedures. Internal organs including stomach, liver, kidneys, intestines are cleansed hence their diseases are brought under control. Gastric trouble, acidity, indigestion, constipation etc. are totally eradicated. The fat accumulated in the stomach and waist is reduced. This Kriya also helps in curing chronic diseases and disabilities like diabetes, asthma, eczema etc. Skin becomes brighter as the blood is purified. High blood cholesterol and high lipid levels are brought down to normal.

This is highly useful for entering into the higher Sadhana of Meditation as it recharges the body and mind. This process influences all the organs and parts of the body. Therefore, after consuming two glasses of fresh water, one should practice this set of exercises three or four times regularly every day that is considered as Laghu Shankha Prakshalana.

Laghoo Shankhaprakshalana: This is a shortened form of shankhaprakshalana. 'Laghoo' means 'short'. In this practice, only about six glasses of warm saline water are taken. After every two glasses, the same series of asanas are to be performed as in 'poorna' (complete) shankhaprakshalana. There are various other herbs and juices which can be used, such as a few drops of lemon, onion or garlic. Though not compulsory, it is recommended to practice kunjal kriya, and then jala neti immediately after completing shankha prakshalana. This gives the best possible cleansing to the entire system.

(C) Vahnisara Dhauti (Agnisar Kriya)

Vahnisara Dhauti, also known as Agnisara Kriya is a practice which involves moving the Fire Element in the body. Vahni and Agni mean Fire. Sar means Essence. This Essence of Fire is located in the navel region. On a physical level, the practice involves conscious movement of the abdominal muscles and organs which creates internal heat. The practice is very useful as a preparation for Kapalbhati and Bhastrika pranayama.

Method

- Sit in a comfortable position and take a deep breath.

- Exhale completely and apply Jalandhara bandha; drop your chin to your throat and push the abdomen in and out rapidly while holding your breath.

- Breathe in and breathe out again.

- Repeat the process to move the navel push against the spine; from 20-100 times, as per your ability, which creates internal heat.

Benefits of Agnisar Kriya

Agnisar Kriya counteracts the sedentary lifestyle which can lead to many hidden inefficiencies in all the koshas and the underperformance at all levels of the body. This practice deeply massages all the abdominal nerves, strengthens the muscles and stimulates the associated nerves, encouraging the best possible functioning of these organs. It harmonises all abdominal conditions of the bowel, liver, kidney, spleen and pancreas allowing optimum assimilation of nutrients. It promotes the correct secretions of digestive enzymes and thereby allows optimum assimilation of nutrients. It prevents and removes various digestive maladies such as constipation, indigestion, hyperacidity, hypoacidity, flatulence and sluggish liver. It reduces abdominal fat, strengthens the muscles, especially after child birth. It has a dynamic effect on the five pranas (Pancha Pranas)*, raising energy levels and remove dullness and depression.

हृदि प्राणे गुदेऽपानः समानो नाभिमण्डले।

उदानः कण्ठदेशस्थो व्यानः सर्वशरीरगः॥

**Hrdi prana gude panch samano nabhimandale
udanah kanchadesastho vyanah sarvasanragarh**

(Sivasamhita 3.7)

Note : The seat of Prana is heart, of Apana anus, of Samana the region about navel; of Udana throat; while Vyana move throughout the body.

(D) Bahiskrta Dhauti
Since it is an advanced practice, it is not required for common therapeutic purpose. So, it is not explained here.

HRID DHAUTI
The word 'hrid' means 'heart' or the chest region. Hrid Dhauti is concerned with purifying the chest region of the body.

(i) Jal Dhauti (Kunjal) or Vaman Dhauti
It is a cleansing process that helps to remove acid and other undigested foods from the stomach. It is performed on an empty stomach. There is no unpleasant taste, smell or nausea because it is done on an empty stomach. There are no dietary restrictions afterwards.

Preparation: Prepare about three litres of lukewarm water (1 tsp salt - 1 litre). Salty water for kunjal kriya inhibits excessive secretion of acid into the stomach. Clean your hands and scrub the nails thoroughly.

Method

- Relax the body and the mind. Focus on the concept of cleansing that increase the flow of Prana*.

- Squat on the ground or sit on a lawn chair.

- Begin to drink the water. Keep drinking glass after glass of the prepared water as rapidly as possible in succession, until you cannot take another drop.

- Drink one more, until the sensation of fullness reaches right up to the back of the throat. Make sure the oesophagus is filled right up to the top with water.

- Lean forward horizontally and tuck one fist under the left ribs, so that there is pressure on the stomach.

- Press the back of the tongue firmly with 2 fingers of the other hand and slide the fingers down the back of the throat. This should spark the reflex and the water should flow out.

- As the water comes out, remove the fingers. If water does not come out press the root of the tongue more firmly and consciously relax.

- Vomit all the water out.

- Keep warm afterwards. Relax with deep breath or do short yoga nidra (Savasana). Wait 30 minutes for the stomach to reline itself with mucus before eating.

Note: Five Pranas: Pran, Saman, Vyan, Udan, Apan

Benefits of Jal Dhauti (Kunjal)

This practice cleanses both the upper alimentary canal and the respiratory system. Intentionally vomiting may seem unnatural but this action of last resort to get rid of poison, or over-rich food by washing the organ regularly has a curative effect. Kunjal removes impurities that can contaminate the body causing hyperacidity, halitosis (bad breath) phlegm and sore throats. It enhances general health by permitting the best possible assimilation of nutrients. The powerful contractions during kunjal improve circulation, tone the muscles in the entire abdominal area and raise the internal body temperature.

Asthmatics patients may observe large globs of phlegm in the expelled water. The strong reflex from the pyloric valve controls mucus secretions from the bronchial tubes. Kunjal is recommended as a safe procedure even during an attack, as the forceful action of the vagus nerve (10th Cranial nerve that interfaces with parasympathetic control of heart, lungs and digestive tract) releases the spasm in the respiratory system. Even though drinking water quickly is difficult when breathing is laboured, the stomach should still be filled to bloating. Daily Kunjal is recommended for asthmatics to practice under the strict guidance of a qualified teacher. It is especially recommended for those with cold extremities.

Precautions: People with stomach ailments such as ulcer, hernia, heart problems, high blood pressure, cancers and asthma should seek guidance from a qualified Yoga Therapist before learning this technique.

(ii) Vyaghra Kriya or Baghi Kriya
Vaman is to vomit and Vyaghra means tiger. Just as a tiger regurgitates its food a couple of hours after eating; in Baghi kriya one vomits the food from the stomach three hours after eating meal by using saline water and pressing the very back of the tongue.

Method
- Drink 2-3 glass of warm saline water.
- Tickle the back of the throat/tongue with the first two

fingers to induce vomiting.

- Remove the food from the stomach properly with the help of water.

- Eat some sweets, milk or rice pudding after performing this practice.

Precaution: You should not repeat this more than once a month. Constant repetition may cause frequent unnatural vomiting by damaging the pharynx.

Benefits of Baghi Kriya

Food that is easy to digest passes quickly through stomach to the intestines, leaving the most difficult and least nutritious food for later. The remainder needs a lot of energy and activity from the digestive organs to process and eliminate for very little gain. (Hence the Tiger vomits what is left 3-4 hours after eating) Baghi clear the stomach of its contents so that one feels light and free from heaviness and laziness. It is very good for gastric, acidity, asthma and related problems.

(b) Vastra Dhauti

A cotton strip of 4 fingers wide wet cloth and 1¼ metres (Hatha Yoga Pradipika suggest to use approx. 7 mtrs.) in length is swallowed and then taken out as instructed by the guru. This is known as Vastra Dhauti. In this process of cleansing, a cloth is used for cleansing the alimentary canal. The cloth for vastra dhauti should be of finely woven cotton which is clean and new. Synthetic material should definitely not be used. The cloth must also be trimmed neatly so that no fraying takes place. It should be no wider than the tongue or it will fold as it passes down the throat and should be at least one meter.

Method

Wash, rinse and boil the cloth well and keep it in a container of warm water.

- Squat on the ground or sit on a low chair and relax the whole body.

- Gently chew an end of cloth like food (but do not cut it) so that saliva is secreted to ease its passage and then swallowed.

- Use a sip of water if there is difficulty in getting the cloth down but restrict the use of water. Sweetened milk or honey may be used instead of water if that makes it easier.

- The cloth tends to stick in the lowest point of the throat, so keep swallowing it and resist the urge to vomit. Once the cloth passes a little further down the oesophagus the problem will end.

- When two-thirds of the cloth has been swallowed, leave the remaining few inches hanging out of the mouth and stand up. Practise nauli or Agnisar Kriya.

- The cloth can be left in the stomach for five minutes but no longer.

- Five minutes is sufficient to clean the stomach; beginners may find that one minute is enough.

- Squat and gently but firmly draw the cloth out, there could be some resistance initially, take care not to pull too hard. It will be thick with mucus.

Benefits of Vastra Dhauti

According to Ayurveda, the seat of kapha dosha is in the mucus element of the chest and stomach. Vastra Dhauti helps to loosen and remove the mucus from the chest. It has a great reputation in treating asthma by creating a chain reaction in the brain and relaxing the bronchial tubes. The autonomic nervous system is toned by consciously controlling the reflex to vomit. Vastra dhauti thoroughly scrubs the walls of the stomach and stimulates peristalsis and the digestive juices. It brings both Pitta (Bile element) and Kapha doshas back into balance. It improves all conditions related to the upper gastrointestinal tract.

(c) Danda Dhauti (Cleansing the Esophagus)

Danda is the Sanskrit word for stick. The practice of Danda Dhauti is to insert a soft stick into the esophagus. This stick is usually the stem of a banana or also a lotus stem. Nowadays it is commonly practiced with rubber catheter.

Method

Always perform this technique with empty stomach. Sit in Utkatasana and drink a glass of water or two, so that the esophagus is wet. Then you take a banana stem or lotus stem or rubber catheter which is properly cleaned. Bend your head backwards and slowly insert the stem into your throat. Start with only inserting it one centimetre down the throat. On the next day, you insert it two centimetres, then four and further and further until it one day reaches your stomach. Slowly bring it back out.

If you use a catheter or lotus stem, these also work as siphon and bring the water and any bile out of your stomach. Wait till all the water comes out from the catheter.

Precaution: This Kriya should be learned and exercised only under guidance of an experienced yoga teacher. Please do not practice this Kriya if you are not experienced or do not have an expert next to you because you can seriously injure your esophagus when you do it wrong or under tension. It is not generally advised as a regular practice.

Benefits of Danda Dhauti

It will help get excess bile or mucus out of the stomach. It will remove something that was stuck in the esophagus as well. It is effective to control bad mouth odor and cleans the mucus which gives relief in swallowing.

DANTA DHAUTI

Danta Dhauti is of 5 kids: purification of the teeth, of the root of the tongue, of the two holes of the ears and of the frontal sinuses.

a) Dantamula

Rub the teeth with teeth cleansing powder or pure mud, so long as dental impurities are not removed. This teeth washing is an important practice of yoga for the yogis. It should be done daily in the morning to preserve the teeth.

b) Jihva Sodhana

Elongation of tongue destroys old age and diseases. Join together the three fingers (index, middle and ring finger), put them into the throat, rub well and clean the root of the tongue, and by washing it again expel the phlegm. Rub it with butter, squeeze it and pull it out slowly to lengthen the tongue. Do it daily with diligence before sun rising and setting for elongation of tongue.

c) Karna Dhauti-2

Clean the two holes of ears by index and ring fingers. Daily practice will help you achieve clairaudience (you will be able to hear mystical sounds).

d) Kapalarandhra

Rub on the depression in the forehead near the bridge of the nose with the thumb. It will help cure diseases arising from derangements of phlegmatic humours.

MULSODHAN

If the rectum is not purified, apan vayu does not flow freely. For the purification of rectus and large intestine, it is very useful to clean rectum using turmeric root or middle finger with water over and over again. It helps to cure constipation, indigestion, dyspepsia. It will kindle the gastric fire and increase the beauty and vigour of the body.

Benefits of Dhauti Series:

According to Hatha Yoga Pradipika, "There is no doubt that cough, asthma, diseases of the spleen, leprosy and diseases caused by excess mucus are destroyed as the effect of dhauti." The Dhauti Kriyas cleans the entire digestive and respiratory tract. It removes excess old bile, mucus and toxins. It restores the natural balance of chemical composition in body and removes the ailments caused by such imbalances. This helps to remove infectious bacteria from the mouth, nose, eyes, ears, throat, stomach, intestines and anus. As a result, reduces excess fatty tissues that give relief from flatulence, constipation, poor digestion and loss of appetite.

3. NAULI

Nauli is foremost of the Hatha Yoga practices. It kindles the digestive fire, removing indigestion, sluggish digestion and all disorders of the Tri Doshas, and brings about happiness." ("Hatha Yoga Pradipika" 2:34)

Nauli comes from the Sanskrit word Nala which means rectus abdomen or a halo. Nauli is the practice of contracting and expanding the rectus abdominal muscles. The rectus abdominis is the two long vertical muscles situated in front of the abdomen, which run from under the centre of the ribcage to the pubic bone. Though these are the muscles you manipulate in Nauli, the external oblique and transverse abdominal colon muscles are also activated.

There are three practises of Nauli viz. Madhyama Nauli, Vama Nauli and Dakshina Nauli. It requires a proficiency in Uddiyana Bandha with the ability to hold external breaths for some time. It is strongly recommended that you do not eat for at least two hours before this practice. Dynamic Nauli is also practiced as a combination of all 3 Naulis done in a dynamic way.

Madhyama Nauli

Madhyama Nauli is practiced by pulling the 2 sides of abdominal muscles together and the middle group of muscles protrude.

Steps:

- Stand with the feet shoulder-width apart.
- Bend the knees; place the palms just above the knees, thumbs on the insides of the thighs and fingers touching the outer side.
- Breathe in deeply through the nose and exhale quickly and completely.
- Hold your breath to perform uddiyana bandha.
- Start to roll the muscles to the other side, but before they reach the opposite side, hold them in the middle.
- In order to roll the muscles, slowly shift the weight on the hands which were lifted from the knee.
- Contract the rectus abdominal muscles so that they form a central arch running vertically in front of the abdomen.
- Continue as long as you can hold your breath.

Vama Nauli (Left)

When the muscles protrude on the right side, it is called Vama Nauli.

Steps of Vama Nauli (Left)

- Stand with the feet shoulder- width apart.
- Bend the knees; place the palms just above the knees, thumbs on the insides of the thighs and fingers touching the outer side.
- Breathe in deeply through the nose and exhale quickly and completely.
- Hold your breath to perform Tri Bandha.
- Release Moola bandha and lift the right hand slightly off the knee, keeping all the pressure on the left side, to isolate the rectus abdominal muscles on the left.
- Return the weight of the body to both hands with Moola Bandha.
- Release Moola, Uddiyana and Jalandhara bandhas.
- Stand erect slowly and breathe in very slowly and consciously through the nose.

Dakshina Nauli (Right)

Perform in the same way but isolate the right side. When the rectus abdominal muscles protrude on the left side, it is called Dakshina Nauli.

Steps of Dakshina Nauli (Right)

Stand with the feet shoulder-width apart.

- Bend the knees; place the palms just above the knees, thumbs on the insides of the thighs and fingers touching the outer side.

- Breathe in deeply through the nose and exhale quickly and completely.

- Hold your breath to perform Tri Bandha.

- Release Moola bandha and lift the left hand slightly off the knee, keeping all the pressure on the right side, to isolate the rectus abdominal muscles on the right.

- Return the weight of the body to both hands with Moola Bandha.

- Release Moola, Uddiyana and Jalandhara bandhas.

- Stand erect slowly and breathe in very slowly through the nose.

- Consciously follow the process of inhalation.

Dynamic Nauli - Advanced

Steps of Dynamic Nauli

- Stand with the feet shoulder-width apart.

- Bend knees placing the palms just above the knees, thumbs on the insides of the thighs and fingers touching the outer side.

- Breathe in deeply through the nose and exhale quickly and completely.

- Hold your breath to perform Tri Bandha.

- Start moving abdominal muscles in a wave-like motion from right to left 4 and left to right 4 times.

- Do it slowly with total concentration.

- Return the weight of the body to both hands with Moola Bandha.

- Release Moola, Uddiyana and Jalandhara bandhas.

- Stand erect slowly and breathe in very slowly through the nose.

- Consciously follow the process of inhalation.

Mastering the Nauli: Increase the number of motions or movement gradually. Initially, practice Nauli with the hands just above the knees and the body bent forward. Gradually, begin to control the practice, keeping the hands fixed on the legs. You can practice Nauli in Siddhasana, Vajrasana or Padmasana after perfection to practice Nauli in a more erect position.

Precaution: Anyone with a history of heart diseases, high blood pressure, hernias or ulcers as well as those after an operation should not practice Nauli Kriya. The same is true for women who are pregnant.

Benefits of Nauli

Nauli stimulates the digestive fire, thereby removing toxins, indigestion and constipation. It is an internal cleansing for excess phlegm, mucus or fat. Nauli give a deep massage and profound toning to the abdominal muscles as well as those organs. It generates heat in the body. It stimulates digestive fire and balance the endocrine functions. It balances the hormonal secretion, which helps to get rid of emotional disorders, lethargy and diabetes. Nauli has a profound effect on pranamaya and manomaya koshas, creating mental clarity and increases the storehouse of prana in Manipura chakra. It improves breathing capacity, strengthening and toning the abdominal muscles, increasing awareness of your physical centre as well as honing your sense of balance & grounding. Every part of the internal system is stimulated by this practice so it is especially helpful for digestion. According to the Gheranda Samhita, "it destroys all diseases and increases the bodily fire. Nauli can be the answer for constipation, indigestion, disorders in nervous systems, diarrhoea, acidity, flatulence, anxiety, depression, hormonal imbalances, sexual and urinary disorders, laziness, dullness, lack of energy and emotional disturbances. One can control sensual desires and strengthen one's will power with regular practice of Nauli.

4. BASTI KARMA

You should be familiar with Uddiyana bandha and Nauli to perform Basti. There are two types of Basti Karma: Jala Basti and Sushka (Air) Basti. Jala Basti is done in water while Sushka Basti is done on land with air. Nowdays, enema is commonly used as an easy replacement of Basti.

Method of Jal Basti

Stand in Utkatasana in water to the height of the navel. Perform Uddiyana bandha and Madhyama nauli sucking the water up into the anus. Hold for a few breaths. Expel the water and stool into the toilet. Repeat until the stool has been excreted. Now more water can be taken in. Madhyama nauli is repeated many times until the colon is full followed by rotational nauli. The water can be held in for ten minutes to release encrusted stool. This practice can be repeated until the water is completely free of stool. Do Bhujangasana slowly five times to release any remaining water or air. Relax in Savasana for some time.

Variation: A more approachable method that gives the same benefit is to perform Ashwini mudra while sitting in cool fresh water up to the navel.

Benefits of Jal Basti

Basti generates energy, removes heat from the body. It develops strength and control of the abdominal muscles; massages and tones the internal organs and nerves. Water Basti completely cleanse the intestines. Air Basti stimulates peristalsis. Both are good for constipation. If intending to go on a fast, it is recommended to do Basti to thoroughly cleanses the intestines permitting the greatest purification of the body. Urinary, Digestive, and Wind problems are cured by Jala Basti. The body becomes pure and looks like Kamadeva - Cupid - God of Love. Advanced Yoga practitioners use Basti to cool down the abdominal heat generated by their practices (Sadhana).

Method of Air Basti (Sushk Basti)
Sit in Paschimottanasana. Contract and release the anus (Ashwini mudra) sucking the air up.

Benefis of Sushk (air) Basti
This practice prevents abdominal problems. It stimulates digestive fire and eliminates wind problems. Sushka Basti can be done very frequently but Jala Basti not as often. It is desirable for a certain amount of stool and its associated bacteria to be present in the colon. (After cleansing, eat organic yogurt to replace lost bacteria in colon.)

5. KAPALBHATI
KAPAL means the cranium or forehead. BHATI means light or splendour. Altogether Kapalbhati means shining forehead. Kapalabhati is a detoxification technique that invigorates the entire brain and awakens the dormant centres responsible for subtle perception.

Vatakramena vyutkramena shitkramena visesatah kapalabhati tridha kuryat kapha dosha nivarana //G.S./ 1.54// HINDI RAKHNA HEI

There are three variations of Kapalabhati. Vatakrama (wind cleansing), Vyutkrama (sinus cleansing) and Shitkrama (mucus cleansing) to be practiced in three ways to cure imbalances of the kapha dosha.

Vatakrama Kapalabhati (Breathing)

Variation-I: This is similar to Kapalbhati Pranayama. Sit comfortably in a cross-legged position. Take three deep breaths through both nostrils to prepare. Inhale deeply and exhale sharply, lifting the diaphragm and contracting abdominal muscles. Let the inhalation happen passively and continue this cycle of forceful exhalation and passive inhalation at a fast pace. Do three rounds of hundred breaths each, coming back to deep inhales and exhales between each round. Keep your physical eyes closed and gaze internally toward the third eye (ajna chakra). Come back to normal breathing if you feel lightheaded at any time.

Variation-II: Vatakrama can also be done through alternate nostrils. Using the right hand in Vishnu mudra (placing index finger and middle finger at the bottom of thumb) to direct the passage of air through the left and right nostrils alternately. Follow the same process as variation I.

Variation-III: Sit in a comfortable position with the spine erect, hands on the knees. Close the eyes and relax. Inhale deeply and perform 20 rapid respirations through both nostrils, placing more emphasis on exhalation. The inhalation should be short. After the last exhalation, inhale deeply through the nose and exhale quickly through the mouth, slightly opening the lips. With external retention perform Tri- Bandha simultaneously. Using your mental power but not any other force; pull Moola Bandha gently up the spine. Maintain for as long as possible and release Moola, Uddiyana and Jalandhara Bandha in order while inhaling. Inhale slowly through the nose, totally concentrating on the process of inhalation. Practice Kapalabhati every day. Gradually, add one more round a day to 5 rounds. Adding 10 breaths to each round and gradually increase to 100 – 200 breaths in each round.

Note: It is best to practice after Neti, before or after asanas and before meditation. Do not use too much force but more awareness to avoid dizziness. Let the inhalation be spontaneous and not controlled.

Vyutkrama Kapalbhati

Vyutkrama is similar to Jala Neti and is sometimes practiced as part of Neti. VYUTKRAMA means Expelling System.

Preparation: Prepare lukewarm salty water (ratio 1 tsp: litre). Dilute salt in the water aiming for tear-taste. If the water is over salted or not salty enough you will experience irritation in the nostrils. If you have any chronic nasal diseases, you may add one or two drops of iodine.

Variation – I: Lean forward. Place the edge of the glass on the root of the nose. Make sure that the lower part of the nostrils is under water, but you can still breathe through the upper part. Sniff the water through the nostrils. Spit the water from the mouth. Practice until the glass is empty. Perform Bhastrika and Jala Neti after completing.

Variation – II: Take a bowl of warm mildly salted water, scoop some water into the palm of your hand and sniff the water through the nostrils. Let the water flow down into the mouth and then spit the water out from the mouth. Repeat several times.
Note: It is important to relax while sucking the water in and there should be absolutely no fear.

Benefits of Vyutkrama Kapalbhati

This practice has all values of Neti and Kapalabhati , but the stimulating effect is stronger; as well as it stimulates cleansing of the bronchus. This practice should be done after perfection of Neti and Kapalbhati.

Shitkrama Kapalbhati

This practice is the reverse of Vyutkrama. You take a mouthful of warm salty water, push it up through the nose and blow it out.

Preparation: Prepare lukewarm salty water (ratio 1 tsp: ½ litre).

Steps: Fill your mouth with water. Push the water up expelling it through the nose. Repeat several times. Perform Bhastrika.

Benefits of Shitkrama Kapalbhati

On a Physiological level: It strengthens the immune system and balance Kapha Dosha by removing excess phlegm from the tissues of the body. This makes the body of the practitioner beautiful and attractive as the ''God of Love, Kamadeva-Cupid. Kapalbhati induces a reversal in the flow of the nerve impulses to and from the brain bringing about stimulation and awakening of the brain centers. It also massages the brain. It transmits messages to brain cells and all the organs. It detoxifies the entire body. It cures almost all diseases caused by deposition of toxins in the body. It is excellent for asthma, migraine, arthritis, thyroids, female reproductive problems. It aids in burning fat and weight loss. It is instrumental in improving blood lipids formation and maintain healthy heart functions.

On a psycho-spiritual level: regular practice creates an electrical charge which results in an upward attraction, and pulls energy toward the brain and higher centers. Kapalabhati purifies the Manipura Chakra. It develops self-awareness and self-confidence as the ego personality is offered to the supreme-self with each exhalation, resulting in a vibrant mind, radiant halo and a balanced aura.

Awakening Chakra with Kapalbhati

According to GHERANDA SAMHITA Kapalbhati practice not only rids the body of old mucus and sinuses, but also makes one attractive and prevents the aging process from occurring by relaxing facial muscles and nerves. It rejuvenates tired cells and nerves, keeping the face young, shining and wrinkle free. On the spiritual level, these practices stimulate and open Ajna Chakra.

The correct practice of kapalbhati helps to awaken various chakras. Kapalbhati stimulates the nerves. In turn they activate the Nadis which then activate the Pranas, and the Pranas are attracted towards that region where some kind of activity is taking place in the structure of the nervous system; in the muscles and the forehead. Due to concentration during the practice, once the pranas gravitate towards those areas, where the action is taking place, the corresponding chakra in that area may feel stimulated. With proper control, that stimulation will manifest into the awakening of that particular chakra.

6. TRATAKA

According to Hatha Yoga Pradipika "Looking intently with an unwavering gaze at a small point until tears are shed, is known as Trataka." Trataka is a very simple but powerful practice. Trataka means 'to gaze steadily at a fixed point'. There are two forms of this practice. One is 'Bahiranga' or external trataka and the other is 'Antaranga' or internal trataka. In the practice of trataka an object is gazed at until its subtle form manifests in front of the closed eyes. The point of concentration is usually a symbol or object which activates the inner potential and can absorb the mind. The symbol most commonly used is a candle flame, because even after the eyes are closed, the impression remains naturally for some time, and then Antaranga Trataka can easily be performed. There are many other equally effective symbols for Trataka apart from the candle flame, such as the full moon, a star, the rising or setting sun (when it is orange, not yellow), a Chakra, the symbol OM or your own shadow. These are the most effective symbols. Trataka can also be done on a rose, a tree, a mountain, the sea, the sky, a rock, a black dot or any object of your choice that can be a positive symbol. The purpose of focusing the eyes on an external object is to arouse the internal vision and make it absolutely steady by stopping the eye movements.

Trataka is a process of concentrating the mind and curbing its unstable tendencies. The one-pointed concentration of mind is termed 'Ekagrata'. There are numerous distractions which obstruct that concentration. Association and identification through the eyes and sight are major contributing factors to this leakage. Furthermore, the eyes move constantly, either in large movements or tremors. Even when the eyes are focused on an external object the perception is always fluctuating due to these spontaneous movements. When the same object is constantly seen, the brain becomes accustomed or habituated, and soon stops registering that object. Habituation coincides with an increase of alpha waves indicating diminished visual attention to the external world. When alpha waves are produced, it indicates that a particular area of the brain has ceased functioning. When the awareness is restricted to one unchanging sense stimulus, like touch or sound, the mind is turned off. Complete absorption in a single perception induces withdrawal of contact with the external world.

Bahiranga Trataka (External)
Bahiranga Trataka is easier to practise because one simply has to gaze at an object or symbol. Practice it in a dark room which is free from drafts, insects and noise.

Procedure

Place a candle at an arm's length in front of you with the flame at the eye level. Sit in a comfortable meditative pose, preferably Siddhasana. Place the hands on the knees in gyan mudra. Relax your whole body close your eyes and prepare yourself as for any meditative practice. Make yourself quiet and be prepared to keep your body perfectly still throughout the practice. Practice kaya sthairyam for a few minutes. Open your eyes and gaze at the middle portion of the flame (ideally focus on the red tip of the wick as it does not move due to draft). Gaze as long as possible without blinking and without strain until the eyes begin to water. You will be able to increase the time (gradually with practice) to ten minutes. Remain a silent witness throughout, observing all thoughts and feelings which may arise. Close your eyes, keep them fixed on the impressions in your mind.

If the after image moves, bring it back to the centre and continue gazing until the impression disappears. Once you can stabilize the afterimage, study it and look intently at its colour. Slowly bring your attention to your body, the hall and the surrounding. Rub your palms together and place them on your eyes. Gently relax (massage) your eyes with your palms and rub them on your face with a smile. Slowly open your eyes and look around.

Antaranga Trataka

Antaranga Trataka involves clear and stable inner visualisation of an object. It is one pointed concentration focussing on an object seen within the inner spaces of the mind. The preparation is the same as Bahiranga Tratak, but a point of light or symbol is chosen.

Procedure

Prepare yourself as in the technique for Bahiranga Trataka. Keep the eyes closed and concentrate on your symbol. If you have no symbols, try to visualize a point of light, like a twinkling star, or a crescent or full moon. Try to see the object clearly and steadily in the dark space in front of the closed eyes. Practice for five to twenty minutes. This practice has to be cultivated over a long time.

Timing of Trataka: Trataka can be done at any time but is more effective when performed on an empty stomach. The most suitable time is between four and six in the morning after Asana and Pranayama practices. If you wish to delve deeper into the mind, Trataka should be done late at night before going to bed and before Japa or Meditation.

Benefits of Trataka

According to 'Hatha Yoga Pradipika' "Trataka eradicates all eye diseases, fatigue and closes the doorway of these problems." Trataka benefits not only the eyes but a whole range of physiological and mental functions. It brings positive changes in the perception by inducing a strong sense in Ajna Chakra. Trataka calms the mind, and develops concentration. It begins the journey into the deeper levels of the Mind. Tratak further develops strong will power and improves memory.

Trataka unlocks the inherent energy of the mind and channels it to the dormant areas of the unconscious. It arouses clairvoyance as well as other capacities such as telepathy, telekinesis, psychic healing etc. Trataka is therapeutic in conditions like depression, insomnia, allergy, anxiety, postural problems, poor concentration and memory. Trataka relieves eye ailments such as eye strain and headache, myopia and even early stages of cataract. The eyes become clear, bright and able to see the reality beyond appearances.

Blanking out of visual perception with awareness leads the central nervous system to function in isolation. This is known as Sushumna by Yogis. When the brain is isolated from the sense modalities and from the associated mental processes, ideas, memories etc. spiritual consciousness emerges.

MENSTRUAL CYCLES AND SHATKARMAS

There are no absolute restrictions and rules for the practices of Neti, Trataka or Kapalbhati, but it is assured that, in the practices of Dhauti and Basti, undue pressure is not created in the sensitive system of the female sadhaka at the time of the monthly cycle. Nauli, Basti and Dhauti should be done only after the monthly cycle by ladies to avoid any kind of hormonal or glandular imbalance within the body.

Secret : 2

SUKSHMA VYAYAMA

(Subtle Yoga)

Years ago, in the distant lands of the Himalayas, there lived a Yogi who possessed the secret of the fountain of youth. His name was Maharishi Karthikeyaji Maharaj, a Himalayan yogic master who was believed to have lived for over 300 years of age. The secret of his long life has remained hidden from much of the world until now. The secret of Maharishi Karthikeya's long life was an ancient form of yoga called Sukshma Vyayama, a precious collection of advanced techniques that free the body from the ravaging effects of disease and aging. This self-healing art has been practiced by those serving some of the most demanding roles of their day, including government officials, respected scientists and elite athletes. These powerful yogic practices allow the body to optimally express the blueprint of its DNA, bringing out the best version of the Practitioners. This yoga of youth and immortality first became known to people of India in the 1940s when Swami Dhirendra Brahmachari Ji, a devoted student of Maharishi Karthikeya taught and propagated it through his writing and TV Program. He taught it to India's first prime minister, Jawaharlal Nehru, who was later succeeded by his daughter, Indira Ghandi, also a devoted practitioner. In her own words, she writes, "My father attributed his fitness to a lifelong habit of beginning the day with Yoga-asanas. I myself was initiated at an early age. Later, when my father and I met Shri Dhirendra Brahmchari, we learnt his system of Sukshma

Vyayam which I found more convenient to follow as a keep-fit routine when one is rushed for time and constantly on the move.

In the practice of Sukshma Vyayama (Subtle Yoga Exercises) every body part are activated to facilitate circulation. Improvement of blood circulation helps to detoxify the body and at the same time nourish the cells with oxygen and nutrients. Yogic Breathing is included in this process as an integral part of the practice which will improve the oxygen intake. This practice is done with certain level of resistance which will increase the strength and stamina of entire system of the body. At the end, relaxation is done to activate parasympathetic nervous system which will bring Alfa wave state of brain activities that facilitates healing, maintenance and optimization of internal system which is the secret of a long, healthy and happy life.

1. MIND POWER DEVELOPING KRIYA

POSTURE: With your feet together, the body erect and the mouth closed, tilt your head back as far as possible and keep your eyes wide open.

EXERCISE: Concentrating on the crown of your head, inhale and exhale rapidly and vigorously through the nose with the bellows method. Start with 25 times to begin with.

2. MEMORY POWER DEVELOPING KRIYA
POSTURE: Keep your feet together, the body erect, mouth closed and the eyes focused on a spot 5 feet in front of the toes.

EXERCISE: Concentrate on the Brahmarandhra (crown centre), inhale and exhale vigorously through nostrils with (bellows effect). Do it 25 times to begin with.

BENEFITS: This is especially beneficial in cases of mental fatigue. There is a marked improvement in memory. This exercise is useful for all those whose work causes mental strain and nervous exhaustion.

3. INTELLECT DEVELOPING KRIYA

POSTURE: Close your eyes, keeping your feet together, back erect and chin down (chin lock).

EXERCISE: According to Yogic science, the centre of intellectual vigor is in the depression at the back of the neck (head base). Concentrate on head base with all the force you possess and start bellows breathing exercise (inhaling and exhaling with equal force). Do it 25 times to begin with.

4. EYE-SIGHT IMPROVING KRIYA

POSTURE: Stand with your feet close together. Keep your back straight.

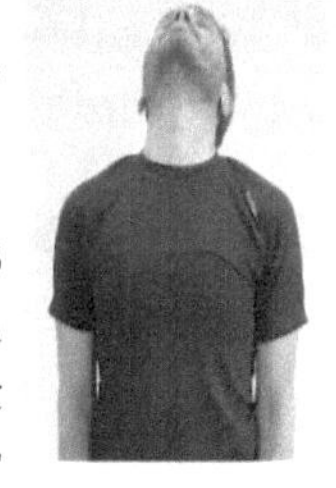

EXERCISE-A: Tilt your head back as far as possible. Concentrate with all your will on eyebrow centre without blinking. The eyes must squint in doing so. When your eyes feel tired or start watering, discontinue the exercise and resume it after a short rest. Start with five minutes in the beginning.

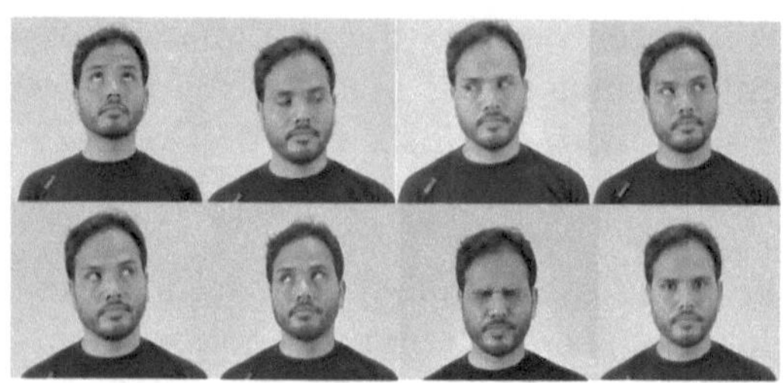

EXERCISE-B: Move your eyes up and down for 10 times each.

EXERCISE-C: Move your eyes right and left for 10 times each.

EXERCISE-D: Move your eyes right side up and left side down for 10 times each.

EXERCISE-E: Move your eyes left side up and right side down for 10 times each.

EXERCISE-F: Rotate your eyes clockwise for 10 times and anti clockwise for 10 times.

EXERCISE-G: Blink your eyes for some times and tightly close your eyes and release, tightly close and release for 10 times.

EXERCISE-H: Rub your palms together to make them warm. Cover your eyes and gently massage them. Open your eyes while blinking.

BENEFITS: This stimulates the nasociliary nerve plexus of the autonomic nervous system as well as the fibres of the nerves moving the eye-ball and internal structures of the eye. It improves the muscular power, balance and co-ordination of the various muscles that move the eye-ball. It exercises the muscle of the iris which constitutes the muscular diaphragm surrounding the pupil of the eye and is instrumental in increasing or decreasing the amount of light entering the eyes and falling on the retina. Gazing at one point also helps activating the muscles attached around the lens of the eye and whose contraction or relaxation result in changing the shape of the lens which is required for accurate focussing of the light on the retina to form a sharp image of the observed object. Thus the entire neuromuscular apparatus of the eye-ball gets toned for a better performance and endurance. This exercise has an even more important effect on training in the methods of concentration of the mind apart from having an immediate utility for the eyes.

5. CHEEKS REJUVENATING KRIYA

POSTURE: Stand straight with feet together. Join the tips of the fingers and close the nostrils with the two thumbs.

EXERCISE: Keeping the eyes open and pouting your lips (in the shape of crow's beak), suck in air vigorously through mouth with a sibilant sound and blow out your cheeks. Now close your eyes and with your chin resting against the cavity of your throat, hold your breath as long as you can. Let the neck return to the normal posture, open your eyes and exhale through the nose slowly and effortlessly. Begin with five times.

BENEFITS: This Kaki Mudra deepens aeration and oxygenation of the oral cavity. In normal breathing the mouth remains closed and fresh air does not enter it which may lead to unhindered multiplication of germs. Frequent forceful air flow on teeth and gums has beneficial effects. It can prevent and cure many oral infections. Pouting and holding the mouth in that shape for some time and puffing out the cheeks would exercise most of the muscles of the face which ordinarily are inactive except for the mild action involved in speaking or eating. The habitual inaction of these muscles makes them flabby. Kaki Mudra gives fresh bloom to cheeks. The teeth become stronger. Pyorrhoea, dental cavities and halitosis (bad breath) are cured. Sunken cheeks fill up gradually and once again look normal. Pimple, boils etc. disappear.

6. HEARING IMPROVING KRIYA

POSTURE: Stand straight with the feet close together.

EXERCISE- A: Close your mouth, plug your ears with the thumbs and close your eyes with index fingers on your eyes. Encircle your mouth with middle and ring fingers making crow beak like structure of mouth. Now suck in air, blowing out your cheeks and press your chin down (chin lock). Hold the breath as long as possible, release while opening your eyes and exhale through the nose. While holding your breath, keep the cheeks fully puffed out.

EXERCISE- B (Ear Massage): Placing index finger behind ears and other fingers in the front side of fingers gently massage for few seconds.

EXERCISE-C (Stretching): Pull your ears down for 10-20 times. Stretch your ears from center for 10-20 times. Stretch your ears up for 10-20 times.

EXERCISE-D: Put your index fingers in ears and rotate clockwise and anti-clockwise for 10-15 times each.

EXERCISE-E: Cover your ears with palms and press, hold for some time hearing the sound within and release, repeat it 5 times with pumping effect.

Benefits: The pressure inside the mouth forces air through the auditory tube which connects the mouth cavity with the middle ear. The healthy functioning of this tube is essential for equalisation of pressure inside and outside the ear as well as for the free vibrations of the ear drum. Absence of it will result in defective hearing. The Jalandhara Bandha (chin lock) which forms part of the whole process ensures stimulation of the endocrine glands as well as nervous components, both somatic (voluntary) and autonomous, situated in this region. You can purify the passage of sound by closing your ear holes, nostrils, eyes and mouth. It will help you hear the pure (inner) sound.

7. MOUTH & THROAT STRENGTHENING KRIYA

Fill the mouth with air and inflate both the cheeks together. Now deflate the cheeks without conscious exhalation. Do it 2-5 times. Repeat it by inflating and deflating left and right cheeks separately 2-5 times each. Now move the upper jaw, first left side, then right side and finally upside. Do it 2-5 times. Open the mouth and place 3 fingers together (index, middle and ring finger) inside mouth by pressing the teeth and jaws together and utter - AAA --- AAA --- AAA -- as long as possible, as per capacity. Repeat 2-5 times.

Benefits: It strengthens the muscles of face and mouth, removes wrinkles of face and cheeks, improves vocal cord, voice becomes resonant,cures teeth diseases by strengthening the teeth and strengthens throat.

8. NECK STRENGTHENING KRIYA

POSTURE: Keeping your feet together, stand erect.

EXERCISE-A: Relaxing your neck, turn your head towards your right shoulder, then towards your left shoulders. Start with 10 times in the beginning.

EXERCISE -B: Standing straight, jerk your head first forward, then backward. When it goes back it should touch the nape of your neck. When it is forward your chin should touch the sternal notch. Keep breathing normally. 10 times to begin with.

EXERCISE-C: Keep your chin in and rotate the head from left to right and then right to left alternately. Breathe normally. Try to make your ear touch your shoulder, taking particular care to avoid raising the shoulder. Five times to begin with.

EXERCISE-D: Inhale and exhale through the nose ("Bellows effect") making the veins of your neck stand out. Blow out your stomach while inhaling, draw it in while exhaling. Do it 25 times to begin with.

EXERCISE-E: Interlock your fingers and palms together. Place your palm on your neck and push your head creating opposite resistance. Hold this for 10-20 seconds and release.

EXERCISE-F: Interlock your fingers and palms together. Place your palm on your forehead and push your head creating opposite resistance. Hold this for 10-20 seconds and release.

EXERCISE-G: Interlock your fingers and palms together. Place your palm on right side of head and push your head creating opposite resistance. Hold this for 10-20 seconds and release.

EXERCISE-H: Interlock your fingers and palms together. Place your palm on left side of head and push your head creating opposite resistance. Hold this for 10-20 seconds and release.

EXERCISE-I: Interlock your fingers and palms together. Place your palm on top of the head and push your head down creating opposite resistance. Hold this for 10-20 seconds and release.

EXERCISE-J: Interlock your fingers and palms together. Place your palm on the chin and push your head up creating opposite resistance. Hold this for 10-20 seconds and release.

EXERCISE-K: Place your right hand on lower back pushing it up possible with palm facing outward. Place your left hand on cervical pushing it down possible with palm facing inward and pat for 20 times. Interchange your hands position and repeat the same.

Benefits: These exercises strengthen the neck and beautify it. Diseases peculiar to the throat, such as tonsillitis, laryngitis, pharyngitis etc. can be checked. The voice becomes resonant and speech defects such as lisping and stammering are completely removed. With perseverance, this exercise, in conjunction with a couple of others, yields marvellous results in cases of dumbness. Singers will derive great benefit from it. This series of neck exercises will improve the alignment of cervical joints. It will help cure neck pain and prevent cervical spondylitis. It will help prevent frozen shoulders and stiff neck.

9. SHOULDER STRENGTHENING KRIYAS

POSTURE: Feet close together, your back straight, your fingers clenched into fists with the thumbs tucked in.

EXERCISE: With your mouth pouting and forming the shape of a crow's beak, suck in air, blowing out your cheeks and hold your breath with your chin resting on the sternal notch. While keeping your back straight, move the shoulders vigorously and stiffly up and down, in a pumping motion. The arms should be kept rigidly straight at the side. Assume the normal posture and straightening your neck, open your eyes and exhale gradually through the nose. Repeat the process five times to begin with. The bones, blood vessels, the muscles and the nerves in the shoulder are toned up.

10. WRISTS STRENGTHENING KRIYAS

POSTURE: Stand with feet close together, with the body straight. Stretch out your two arms straight in front of you at shoulder level, keeping them parallel to the ground.

EXERCISE-A: With loosely clenched fists, let your wrists move the fists up and down with force. While bringing your fist up and down, try to touch the forearm. The arms should be kept as stiff as possible. Five times to begin with.

EXERCISE -B: Raise the arms, bent at the elbow, sideways to shoulder level. The wrists should be moved up and down as in exercise `A'. While doing so, the fists should try to touch the forearm. Five times to begin with.

11. FINGERS STRENGTHENING KRIYA

POSTURE: Stand with the feet close together and the body erect. Throw out your arms in front, keeping them parallel to the ground at shoulder level.

EXERCISE `A': Let your fingers form the shape of the hood of a cobra, taking particular care to stiffen the entire length of the arms from the shoulder-joints to finger-tips. The exercise will not be effective if enough force is not put into it to make the arms tremble. Five minutes to begin with.

**EXERCISE `B':** Posture the same as for `A'. Repeat the exercise `A', with the arms bent at the elbows. The fingers should be spread in the shape of a cobra's hood. Hold for 5 minutes to begin with.

12. ARMS STRENGTHENING KRIYA

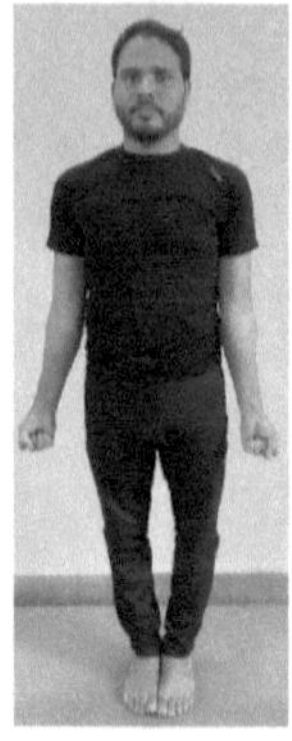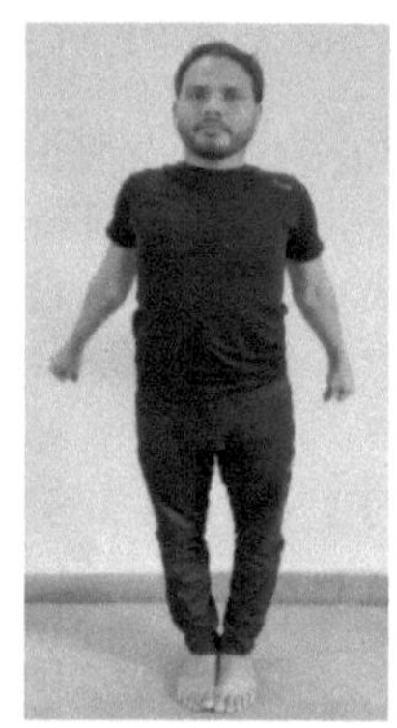

POSTURE: Keep the feet together, body erect, the hands clenched into fists with the thumbs tucked in.

EXERCISE -A: Inhaling through the nose and holding your breath, swing your right arm clockwise in a circle as many times as you can. When you cannot hold your breath any longer stop with your arm bent at the elbow and breathe out forcefully while thrusting your arm forward at shoulder level. Repeat it anti-clockwise.

EXERCISE-B: Now repeat the exercise with the left arm clockwise and anti-clockwise equally.

EXERCISE -C': With both hands clenched into fists, rotate your both hands in full upward circle clockwise, and exhale with a hissing sound. Repeat it anti-clockwise.

Benefits: This set of exercise tones up the nerves. The entire length of the arm becomes stronger.

13. CHEST STRENGTHENING KRIYA

POSTURE: Stand with the feet together, body erect. Arms by your side, palms turned backwards with the fingers together.

EXERCISE- A: Swing back your arms, describing a semi-circle. While doing this, inhale through the nose and lean back as far as possible and remain in that position as long as you can. Exhale slowly while reverting to the original position. Repeat 5 times to begin with.

Benefits: This exercise is helpful in many chest diseases. The chest expands and becomes strong. Tuberculosis, asthma and chronic bronchitis can be effectively tackled with the help of this exercise. Persons suffering from weakness of the heart will benefit by its tonic effect if they do this exercise for five minutes every morning.

EXERCISE- B: While inhaling though the nose, bend backward from the waist as far as you can go. At the same time raise your arms behind you as high as you can. Maintain this posture as long as you can, exhale slowly while resuming your original position. Begin with 5 times.

Benefits: In addition to the benefits of previous position, this one gives vitality and strength to the chest and back.

The arms are also strengthened. Thin persons will find their protruding bones covered with healthy flesh. Regular practice of this exercise will keep the back straight.

14. ABDOMINAL MUSCLES STRENGTHENING KRIYA

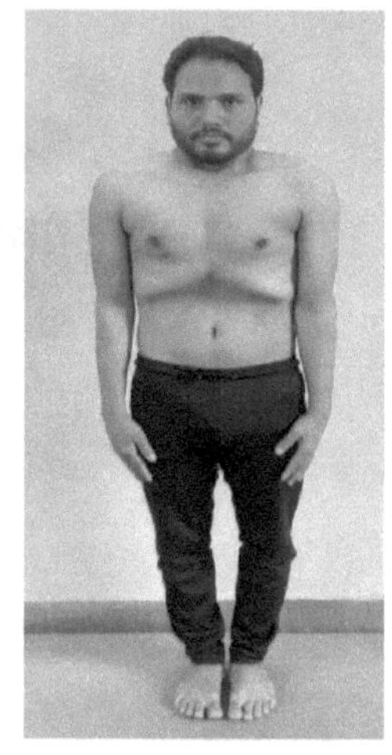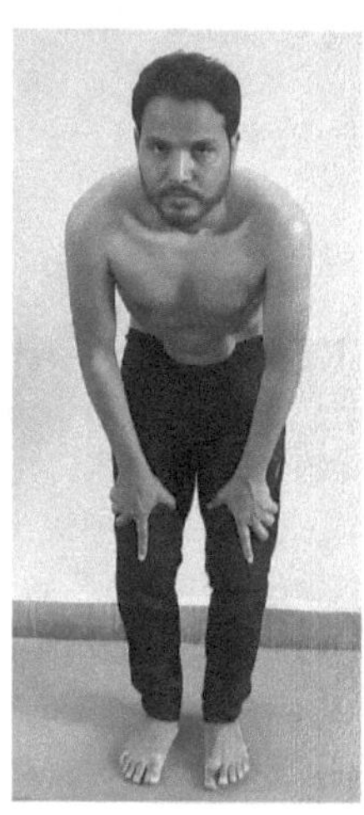

POSTURE: With the feet together, stand erect.

EXERCISE-1: Inhale through the nose slowly. While doing so, distend your abdomen as much as you can. After holding the breath in this posture, release it slowly and gradually, while drawing in the abdomen as much as you can, till it becomes hollow. This exercise is also known as 'Uddiyanabandha'. Practise this exercise repeatedly. Five times to begin with.

EXERCISE-2: Raise your neck an inch above the normal. Breathing quickly and deeply through the nose (Bellows effect) distend your abdomen, and while exhaling, contract it. 25 times to begin with. Particular care must be taken to distend and contract the abdomen to the fullest extent; the inhaling and exhaling should be rhythmic.

EXERCISE-3: With your feet together, stand erect and tilt your chin down. Breathe in and out quickly (Bellows effect) while distending and contracting the stomach. 25 times to begin with.

EXERCISE-4: Look at a spot four to five feet forward from your toes. Inhale and exhale sharply (bellow effect) distending and contracting your abdomen. 25 times to begin with.

EXERCISE -5: Pouting your lips suck in air and at the same time lower your chin to touch the sternal notch. This exercise is also called Jalandharabandha. While holding the breath, close your eyes and puff out the cheeks. Exhale gradually through the nose so that there is no sound at all in doing so. If you have held your breath for a considerable time, take particular care not to blow out violently. That would be harmful. Begin with 5 times.

EXERCISE-6: Bend the upper part of your body forward at an angle of 60 degrees and place your hands on your hips with the fingers at the back, thumbs front. Inhale and exhale sharply through the nose (Bellows effect) taking care at the same time to distend and contract your abdomen. 25 times to begin with.

POSTURE-7: Bend the upper part of your body forward at an angle of 90 degrees and place your hands on your hips with the fingers at the back, thumbs front. Inhale and exhale sharply (Bellows effect). While inhaling, the abdomen must distend; while exhaling it must contract. 25 times to begin with.

EXERCISE-8: Breathe out through the nose and hold it, distend and contract your abdomen in rapid succession. After you have held your breath to the fullest limit of your endurance, breathe in slowly. Then breathe out and distend and contract your abdomen again. Care should be taken to see that while you are busy exercising your abdomen, breathing remains suspended. Five times to begin with.

POSTURE: With feet two feet apart, place your hands on your knees and bend forward from the waist to form an angle of 90 degrees.

EXERCISE-9: Exhale completely. Then contract your abdomen to the fullest extent. This is called complete Uddiyana. This done, stiffen the arms and allow the Nauli to stand out. Try to rotate it right and left, describing a circle. Begin with 5 times clockwise and anti-clockwise.

15. BACK STRENGTHENING KRIYA

PSOTURE-1: With your feet together, back straight, clench your right hand to form a fist with the thumb tucked in. Hold it behind your back, place your left hand on the right wrist, keeping them both in contact with the back.

EXERCISE -1: Breathe deeply through the nose while bending backward as far as you can. Maintain this posture for a few moments. Then, while exhaling, bend forward and try to touch your knees with your head. Repeat this five times to begin with. Change your hand position and repeat it equal times.

EXERCISE-2: Keep your legs stretched apart as far as possible, arms on hips, keeping the fingers to the rear, and the thumbs in front. Inhaling, bend back from the waist as far as you can go. Maintain this posture for some time. Then, while bending forward to touch the ground with your head, exhale gradually. Repeat it five times to begin with.

EXERCISE-3: Stand erect with your feet together. Inhaling, bend back with a jerk as far as you can. While exhaling, bend forward with a jerk trying to touch your knees with your head. Take care that during this exercise your hands do not touch your thighs or your knees.

EXERCISE-4: With your feet together, stand erect with your arms stretched out sideways. With your arms spread out, bend the trunk to your left as far as you can and return slowly to the normal position. Then bend towards your right. While doing this exercise, particular care should be taken to see that your arms do not move up or down and that the trunk does not bend forward or backward. At the same time while bending to right or left you must stretch so that the hand touches the calf. Begin with 5 times.

Repeat the exercise with your feet two feet apart. Five times to begin with.

EXERCISE-5: Stand with your feet two feet apart with hands forward at shoulder level. While inhaling quickly, swing the trunk and the outstretched arms to describe a semi-circle to the right and exhale. Repeat the process, this time exhaling with the trunk turned to the left. Repeat it 10 times to begin with.

Benefits: The five exercises for the back make it supple and symmetrical. Regular practice removes all minor deformities of the back. Men and women under twenty-five can add to their height, while those between twenty-five and thirty will also find themselves taller than when they started. It is a boon for short people. These exercises are especially good for strengthening the back. Artists, actors and actresses will find them of great help. A short course of this exercise will add several inches to the chest and take away many more from a flabby back, while regular practice will make the body symmetrical and strong.

16. THIGHS STRENGTHENING KRIYA

POSTURE: Stand erect with your feet together.

EXERCISE A: Inhale through the nose and at the same time throw up your arms while jumping up with your feet together and coming down on your toes with feet apart. While exhaling, lower your arms, while jumping up and coming down on your toes with your feet together. Care should be taken to see that when coming down your arms do not touch thighs, nor should your legs bend at the knees. 25 times to begin with.

EXERCISE B: Stand erect with your feet together. In this exercise, exhale when the arms are thrown up and inhale when bringing them down. 25 times to begin with.

EXERCISE C: Keep your feet together and stand erect. Exhaling through the nose, bend your knees gradually, with your arms parallel to the ground in front. Stop when your thighs are parallel to the ground and try to maintain this position as long as you can. Take care to prevent the heels or the toes from rising above the ground. The knees must be together. Then begin to rise gradually, while inhaling. If in the beginning you find it difficult to hold your breath while doing this exercise, you can breathe normally, until, with sufficient practice, you can hold your breath.

EXERCISE D: Shifting your weight on the toes and keeping your feet together raise your heels up, body erect and arms spread on sideways. Breathing in and spreading your knees apart bend your knees but without sitting on your heels. While in this position, hold your breath as long as you can. While rising, exhale slowly. You can breathe normally to begin with if it is difficult to hold your breath. Start with 5 times to begin with. These exercises strengthen the thighs and improves shape. Thin limbs acquire healthy flesh, while flabby ones get rid of the superfluous flesh. Within a very short time, benefits of a lasting nature are noticed.

17. KNEES STRENGTHENING KRIYA

POSTURE: With the feet together stand erect.

EXERCISE: Raise your foot forward with a jerk of the knee and then raise it backward and repeat while keeping the upper part of your body in the same erect position. After doing this exercise with one leg, repeat it with the other. When taking your leg back, the heel must touch the buttock. Ten times to begin with. This exercise is good for rheumatic condition of the knees as it improves the circulation of blood in the region. It is particularly efficacious for football players.

18. YOGIC SQUATS FOR STRENGTHENING THE CALVES

POSTURE: With your feet together, stand erect, your hands clenched into fists, neck relaxed.

EXERCISE: While inhaling through the nose, squat with your arms held out in front of you, keeping them parallel to the ground. Your feet should remain on the ground, with your knees closed. Go down as

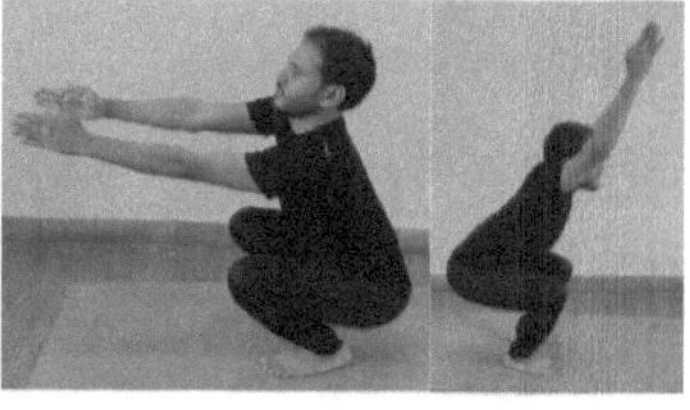

far as you can. Hold your breath while holding the posture. Stand up while exhaling.

19. ANKLES & FEET STRENGTHENING KRIYA

POSTURE: With the feet together, stand erect.

EXERCISE: Lift your right leg forward and hold it about 9 inches off the ground. Rotate your foot clockwise 10 times and repeat it anti-clockwise with the ankle. Repeat with the other foot. This exercise relieves rheumatism of the ankles and strengthens the toes and the feet.

20. SOLES AND TOES STRENGTHENING KRIYA

POSTURE: Stand on your toes, body erect and relaxed.

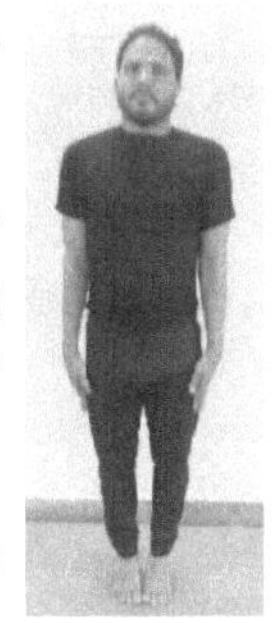

EXERCISE `A': Throwing the weight of your body on the toes, raise and lower you body in a spring like motion. The heels and toes should be together throughout. 25 times to begin with.

EXERCISE `B': Balancing on the toes, jump up as high as you can and come down on the toes. During this kriya the toes should be used to maximum effect. Care should also be taken to maintain the original position of contact between the heels and the toes, and to bring them down on the spot from which you jumped. 25 times to begin with. These exercises give the calves strength and symmetry and rheumatic conditions are cured. The calves become firm and the soles of the feet strong.

EXERCISE C: Stand with the feet together, body erect and relaxed, and your arms spread out. Keeping heels together, shift the entire weight of the body on the tips of your toes. Try to maintain your balance in this position as long as you can. Three minutes to begin with.

Benefits: This exercise strengthens the feet and the toes and their joints. Deformed toes improve in appearance. Those interested in running will derive much benefit from this exercise. It is specially recommended to inhabitants of hilly area. This exercise makes the toes elastic.

21. WALKING IN A STRAIGHT LINE

EXERCISE: Place your right foot in front of left foot so that the right heel touches the toes of the left foot. Walk fifty steps ahead with the heel of one foot touching the toes of the other, taking care to see that the entire distance is covered in a straight line. Then walk backward, in the same manner and in a straight line. The eyes must look in front and not at the feet.

Benefits: This exercise increases the power of concentration and improves the balance of the body. It is of special benefit to acrobats and to persons in the army or the police force. Regular practice of this exercise makes it possible to walk on a thin rope.

SAVASANA (Corpse Pose): After completing all these exercises, you must assume the `corpse pose' (Savasana). This is nothing but giving your body complete rest while lying down. It makes the blood flow through the body in an even course and the fatigued limbs are refreshed. Maintain this posture till your breathing and your heart-beat are normal once again.

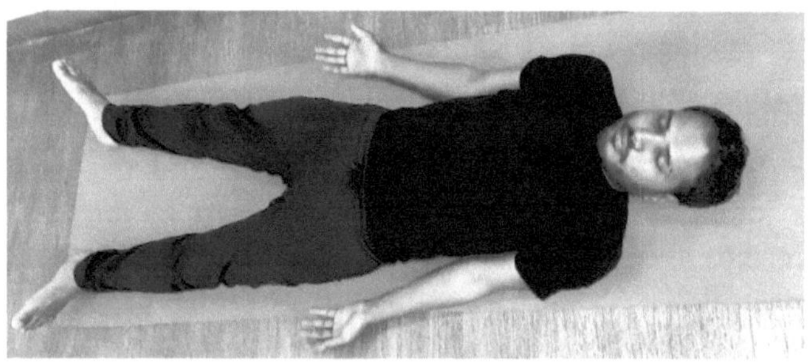

✧✧✧

Secret : 3

ASANA (POSTURE)

Asana is a Sanskrit word that means sitting down or to sit down. It is a body position, intended primarily to restore and maintain a practitioner's well- being, improve the body's flexibility and vitality as well as to promote the ability to remain in seated position for extended period.

In the context of Yoga practice, asana refers to two things.

1. The place where a practitioner; yogi (male) yogini (female) sits.
2. Position in which a yoga practitioner sits.

स्थिरम् सुखम आसनम्।

'Sthirasukhamaasanam—P.Y.S. 2.46

In the Yoga sutras, sage Patanjali suggests that asana is "to be seated in a position that is firm but relaxed. Modern usage of asana has come to include variations from lying on the back and standing on the head, to a variety of other positions. In the Yoga sutras, Patanjali mentions the execution of an Asana as the third of the eight limbs of Classical Yoga or Raja Yoga.

According to Gherand Samhita, there are supposed to be 84 lakhs of asanas. Asanas can be divided into different categories:

On the basis of position: Standing, Sitting and Lying.

On the basis of movement: Static and moving

Here are a few selected and more therapeutic postures:-

SUKHASANA (EASY POSE)

The Easy Posture or Sukhasana is a relaxation pose intended for Meditation. It promotes inner calm and straightens the spine, opens the hips and relieves tiredness. As the name suggests, this pose is very easy to do.

Procedure

- Sit down on the floor or on a Yoga Mat.
- Cross your legs, placing your feet below your knees.
- Place your hand in selected Mudra. Keep your head and body straight.

Note: Beginners can try doing this pose with a thick cushion for added comfort.

VAJRASANA (Thunderbolt Pose)

This asana is good for meditation. One can sit comfortably for a prolonged period in this Asana.

Procedure

- Keep both your legs straight while sitting on the floor or a mat.
- Fold the left leg from the knee and place the toe on the floor.
- Fold the right leg in the knee and place the toe on the floor and join the two toes.
- Sit on the pit formed by the parted heels. Place the palms on the knees.

- Keep the spine, neck and head, upright.
- Don't have any pressure on the hands.
- Continue smooth breathing, while holding the posture.

Releasing: Remove the palms from the knees and bring them to the sides. Take out the left leg and straighten it. Take out the right leg and straighten it.

Duration: After a little practice, this Asana can be maintained for a long time. In the daily routine it should be done for 5 minutes to experience good results. With more practice it can be done for 1 hour.

Benefits: This asana stabilise the mind along with body. It suitable for Pranayama. The special folds of the legs control the blood circulation in legs and supply more blood to the abdominal region. This will improve digestion, absorption and assimilation of the food. This is the reason, it is suggested to practice even after taking food.

Precaution: Any one having stiff knee joints and whose movements have become difficult should practice this Asana with a lot of care. Such persons should practice this Asana after getting their knee joints free and relaxed. Arthritis patients should avoid this Asana.

SIDDHASANA

Siddhasana is one of the most popular meditative postures. Siddha in Sanskrit refers to those hidden powers within the body that enable individual to attain spiritual growth. It helps to achieve perfection in meditation. Siddhasana is useful to learn as it is very much appropriate seating position for some of the Pranayamas and the Mudras.

Procedure

- Keep both your legs straight in a sitting position.
- Bend your right leg and place your right heel close to the perineum.
- Bend your left leg and place your left heel just above your right heel pressing into the opposite calf, thigh, or groin.
- If you use this position regularly, make sure you alternate the leg so that you develop flexibility evenly in both legs and hips.

Benefits: Siddhasana directs the energy upward from the lower psychic centers through the spinal cord. It stimulates the brain and calms the entire nervous system. It redirects blood circulation to the lower spinal cord and abdomen. It tones the lumbar region of spine, pelvis and abdominal organs. It balances the reproductive systems and blood pressure. It stabilizes the sexual energy. It is beneficial for those suffering from wet dreams.

PADMASANA (LOTUS POSE)

Padma means Lotus in Sanskrit. Position of the legs look like blooming lotus in this asana. So, it is called Lotus pose. This Asana has been given great importance in the Yogashastra as it is best suited for Pranayam, Concentration and Meditation. This is the only Asana which erects spinal cord from the lower back without extra effect.

Procedure

- Spread both legs and keep them at a distance of 1 to 1.5 feet.
- Bend your left leg and place it on the right thigh.

- Bend your right leg and place it on the left thigh.
- Keep the wrists of both hands on the respective knees and do Gyan Mudra (Join the tips of thumbs and index finger).
- Slightly bend your hands from the elbows.
- Keep your chin slightly down, face forward and backbone erect and sightly straight.
- Stabilize your body. There should not be any strain on any of the muscles.
- Continue normal breathing.

Releasing: Bring the hands beside the waist. Straighten the right leg. Straighten the left leg.

Duration: Start practicing Pranayama and Meditation in this asana for 10 minutes. After more practice you can increase this period to 1 hour. Sitting for a longer time in this asana alone can make you experience the pleasure of this asana.

Benefits: The backbone is kept erect in this asana, which greatly improves its functions. Gyana Mudra further helps in stabilizing the pulse rate. Consequently strain on muscles is reduced, which in turn reduces strain on the heart. It reduces breathing rates; as a result, one can achieve greater concentration of the mind.

KUKKUTASANA (COCK POSE)

In Sanskrit, Kukkuta means a Rooster. When the Asana is demonstrated it resembles a Rooster.

Procedure
- Sit in Padmasana.
- Put both arms between the calves to the elbows.
- Place the palms on the ground, with fingers pointing outwards.
- Balance the body and raise the entire body on the arms.

- Look upwards.

Variations: Urdhva Kukkutasana (Upward Cock Pose) & Parsva Kukkutasana (Sideways Cock Pose).

Benefits: It improves the digestive system and increases your appetite. It cures constipation and destroys worms in the stomach. It helps cure obesity by burning excess fat. The muscles of the chest and arms become stronger with this asana.

GARBHASANA (FETUS POSE)

The Sanskrit word Garbha means fetus. During the performance of this asana, the body takes on the shape of a fetus. Therefore, this Asana is called Garbhasan.

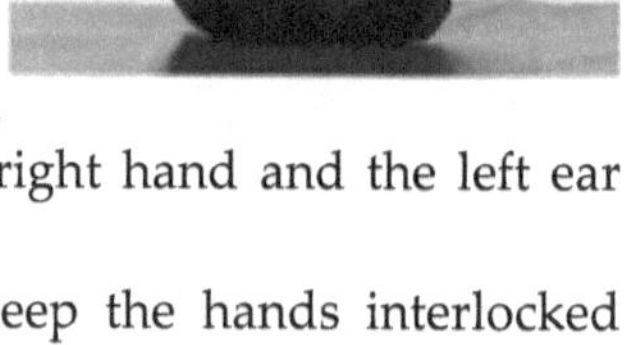

Procedure

- Take posture as in Kukkutasana.
- Bringing out the elbows, catch the right ear with the right hand and the left ear with the left hand.
- As an alternative position keep the hands interlocked behind the neck.
- Initially maintain this position for some time. Gradually increase the duration.

Benefits: It helps cure obesity by reducing fat, makes the muscles supple and strong. This asana reduces the speed of inhalation and exhalation giving complete relaxation to the body. The thighs, buttocks, calf-muscles and neck become strong and healthy. It is beneficial in cases of Hernias and painful Menstruation. The appetite and digestive power gets better increase. You will get clear motions. Many intestinal diseases are removed. Hands and legs will become stronger.

SIMHASANA (LION POSE)

Simha means Lion in Sanskrit. One assumes the pose of a seated lion in this asana; hence the name Simhasana is given to this pose. In this majestic sitting pose the entire body and facial expressions are modified to  invoke a great regal force in the practitioner.

Procedure

- Sit in Vajrasana.
- Open your knees out with back upright and palms resting in between the thighs.
- Inhale deeply and then exhale with your mouth opened wide, tongue extending out.
- Look up to a point between your eyebrows.
- Slightly bend your arms spreading and extending your fingers out.
- Hold this position while inhaling and exhaling for two to five times. Alternately, you can create roaring sound like Lion while exhaling.
- Feel the breath in the back of your throat.
- Exhale as you return to the starting position.

Benefits: Simhasana helps to remove double chin (a flat, thin, rectangular-shaped muscle on the front of the throat). It makes face and arms supple. It relieves tension in the chest and face. It can relieve a sore throat and other respiratory ailments. It helps to control the Thyroid and Parathyroid related complications. It increases courage and confidence. It can cure fear, anxiety and depression related problems. According to traditional texts, Simhasana helps to cure diseases and facilitates the three major Bandhas (Mula, Jalandhara, Uddiyana).

DANDASANA (Staff Pose)

Danda means staff or rod. Your spinal cord is the "staff or "rod in this pose. Dandasana is the starting posture for seated poses much like Tadasana is the starting posture for standing  poses. In this pose, your ear is above the shoulder which is above the side of your mid-hip.

Procedure

- Sit on the floor with your legs stretched out in front.
- Reach back with hands and move your buttock flesh backwards and out to the sides to adjust the angle of your pelvis.
- Place your palms on the floor next to the hips with your fingers facing forward.
- Press down through your hands to extend your spine.
- Stretch your body up with an erect spine, open chest and widen shoulders.
- Pull your abdomen in.

- Get as much length as you can between the pelvis and ribs by extending the spine upwards.
- The extended spine should be perpendicular to the floor.
- Retain the normal spinal curves. The lower back should be slightly concave.
- Extend the legs forward with energy from the heels and pull your toes in.
- Bring the knee caps toward the torso and up the leg using the quadriceps muscles.
- Your heels may come off the floor when your legs are straight and active.
- Press your thighs into the floor.
- Raise both hands up while inhaling.
- Hold for 30-60-90-180 secs depending upon your ability and capacity
- Bring your hands down while exhaling.

Beginner's Tips: It is helpful to do the pose with the back against the wall. This will allow you to feel the arching of the lower back and the verticality of the spine. As a way to learn alignment, sit on the floor against the wall. Your lower back (sacrum) and your shoulders will touch the wall. The wall should help you achieve a normal lumbar spinal curve with an erect and extended spine. Keep weight on the front of the sit bones throughout.

Benefits: This pose strengthens the back and legs. Your hamstrings are stretched and strengthened. It assists your sitting posture throughout the day especially if you routinely spend time sitting at a desk. Your back will feel better if you take time to practice this posture daily. It relieves bloating in the abdomen due to gas, and helps those with gastric problems. The waistline is trimmed and the kidneys are toned.

GOMUKHASANA (COW-FACE POSE)

Gomukhasana derives its name from Sanskrit where Go means cow and Mukha means face. The word Go also means light thus Gomukh refers to the light in or of the head or lightness of the head.

Procedure

- Sit on the floor with your legs stretch out in front.
- Place your palms on the floor next to the hips with your fingers facing forward.
- Bend your left leg and cross it over your right leg placing your left foot on the ground.
- Bend your right leg placing your heel close to perineum and thigh on the ground.
- Make sure your left knee is just above your right knee.
- Sit upright with extended spine.
- Bring feet in as close to your hips as you can.

Arm Position

- Inhaling raise your left hand up.
- Exhaling drop it back pointing your elbow upward and palm down on your back.
- Inhaling take your right hand on your lower back, palm facing back.
- Hook both hands together.
- Keep your head upright.
- Stay in this pose for about 1 minute.
- Release the arms, uncross the legs.
- Repeat twice with both sides.

Benefits: Gomukhasana is beneficial in relieving pain in hip and lower extremities. It makes the spine straight and improves body posture. It is very useful in arthritis and dry piles. This asana also assists in respiratory problems as it automatically provides exercise for the lungs.

Precautions: People suffering from bleeding piles should avoid this asana.

ARDHA MATSYENDRASANA (HALF SPINAL TWIST)

Ardha-Matsyendrasana, the half spinal twist is a very important classic postures of Hatha Yoga. There are many benefits to this posture, but the most important is that the entire length of the spine receives a lateral twist in both directions left and right. The chest is open and the spine is erect. One side of the abdomen is compressed and the other side is stretched.

Procedure
- Keep your both legs straight in sitting position.
- Bend the left leg and place the left foot on the ground crossing over the right knee.
- Bend the right leg and fold it so that it rests on the ground with the right heel near the left buttock.
- Bring the right hand over the left knee and grab the big toe of the left foot.
- Inhale and while exhaling twist the trunk of the body as much as possible.
- Turning the neck to gaze over the left shoulder.
- Encircle the waist with the left hand with keeping palm facing outwards.
- Continue to maintain the asana with focus on chest breathing.

- Hold this asana for 30 seconds and gradually take it up to 2 minutes.
- Advanced practitioner should hold it up to 5 minutes on each side.

Releasing

- Inhale and while exhaling turn your head forward.
- Release the hands and place them beside the body.
- Straighten the right leg then left leg and return to sitting position.
- Practice the same on the opposite side.

Precautions: Should be avoided during pregnancy and menstruation. Care should be taken for those with peptic ulcer or hernia. Those with mild slipped disc and spinal problems can benefit but in severe cases it should be avoided.

Benefits: This asana is very good for the spine, hips, abdomen, chest and arms. Increases the elasticity of the spine, tones the spinal nerves and improves functioning of the spinal

Variations &
Modified Aasana

cord. This asana is therapeutic for Constipation, Anorexia, Cervical Spondylitis, Urinary tract disorders, Indigestion and Menstrual disorders. Relieves back pain and stiffness from between the vertebrae. Useful for slipped disc. Massages the abdominal organs and increases the digestive enzymes making it useful in for loss of appetite and constipation. It is very useful for diabetes, as it improves the efficiency of the pancreas and liver. Regulates the secretion of bile and adrenaline. Relieves tension that may have built up in the back from forward and back bending asanas. Opens the chest and increases the oxygen supply to the lungs. Loosens the hip joints, relieving stiffness. Releases tension in the arms, shoulders, upper back and neck. Increases purification of the blood as well as the internal organs.

Benefits for Women: Increases the different circulation to the pelvic region that provides fresh blood, nutrients and oxygen, improving the health of the reproductive organs as well as the urinary system. Useful for preventing urinary tract and pelvic disorders as well as UTI related problems. Beneficial for menstrual disorders.

JANUSIRSASANA (Head to Knee Pose)

The name comes from the Sanskrit words janu meaning Knee, Sirsha meaning head, and asana meaning posture.

Procedure

- Sit in Dandasana with your spine straight upward.
- Bend your right leg opening it out to the side and pressing your knee down to the ground.
- Press your right heel into the left inner thigh as close to your groin as possible.
- Now, inhaling raise both arms up alongside your ears, fingers pointing upwards.

- Bend forward from your hips while exhaling, keeping the spine extended.
- Take hold of your left foot with both hands, keeping your head and neck in line with the rest of your spine, or move into the full position with head to knee.
- Remain for 30-60 seconds in this pose.
- Repeat it with the other leg.

Benefits: Janu Sirsasana is excellent for the digestive organs as they are exercised and toned with this asana. It improves the efficiency of all the abdominal organs including liver, pancreas, kidneys, spleen etc. This Asana is good for nervous system and brain. It calms the mind and helps relieve mild depression, anxiety, fatigue, migraines and headaches. People suffering from high blood pressure, diabetes, insomnia and sinusitis get relief with the practices of this asana. It helps to relieve the symptoms of menopause and also menstrual discomfort.

Precaution: If you have back pain do it only under supervision of expert. You need to work on stretching and not on bending down.

MARICHYASANA (Sage Twist)

Marichi literally means a ray of light. Historically, Marichi was the Son of Brahma and Chief of the Maruts (also called Vayu or wind-gods). He is one of the seven sages (Rishis) or Lords of Creation (Prajapatis), who intuitively see and determine the divine law of the universe (Dharma). Marichi is the great-grandfather of Manu (man, thinking, intelligent), the Vedic Adam and the Father of Humanity.

Procedure

- Sit in Dandasana (Staff Pose) with the legs stretched out straight in front.
- Keep the spine upright.
- Bend the right knee and place the sole of the foot on the floor.
- Pull the heel as close to the right sitting bone as possible.
- Keep the left leg strong and straight.
- Press the left thigh firmly into the floor.
- Keep the spine straight (unrounded) throughout the pose.
- Bending slightly forward, place the left upper arm on the

outside of the right knee with the palm facing inward.

- Bend the left elbow and bring the left hand toward the back.
- Wrap the right arm behind the back and try to hold the two hands together.
- If the hands don't reach each other, you may use a strap with the two hands and try to bridge the gap between the two hands.
- Look over the right shoulder.
- Make sure your left leg and right foot are firmly grounded.
- Continue lengthening the spine with each inhalation, and twist a little more with each exhalation.
- Hold the pose for about 10 to 30 breaths.
- Then release and repeat on the other side.

Variations

Precautions: Practice this asana only with the supervision of an experienced teacher, if you have serious back or spinal injury, high or low blood pressure, migraine, diarrhea, headache and insomnia.

Benefits: This asana is very good for abdominal organs and chest organs. It strengthens legs and improves spinal health. It helps to cure and prevent diabetes, asthma, hernia etc.

Advanced Variations

PASCHIMOTTANASANA

The front side of the body is called east side, while the back side is called the west side. In this Asana complete back side, i.e., the west side, right from the heels to the head gets stretched and therefore, it is called Paschimottanasana.

Procedure

- Sit in Dandasana and raise both your hands up while inhaling.
- Exhaling go forward keeping your spine straight while expanding your lungs and contracting your abdominal muscles.
- Hold the big toes of both feet with both hands.
- Pull your toes inside and stretch your calves (hamstring) muscles.
- While keeping your knee caps tight, stretch hamstring muscles.
- Keep the heels, calves and thighs on the floor, keeping the spine straight.
- Rest your forehead on the knees and continue smooth breathing. Do not raise the knees in order to get the forehead on to the knees.

- Try to rest the elbows on the floor.
- Hold for 30-60-180 seconds.
- Inhaling raise your head up and hands up to come to dandasana.

Benefits: This posture stretch entire west side. Organs from this region get purified and their functioning is greatly improved. At the same time, the muscles of the front side also contracts and this massages the lungs, intestines and other internal organs which help to improve their functions. This Asana activates the Kundalini lying dormant in our lower spinal region. This asana increases the blood circulation in face and head to bring glow in face and nourishes the brain. It is very good posture to control anger and aggression. It will help the mind to internalize by reducing sensory input and to achieve peace of mind.

Precaution: This Asana is useful for troubles in the spine but maintaining proper alignment is very important. So, do it only under strict supervision of yoga guru if you have back pain.

PURVOTTANASANA (Upward Plank Pose)

Front Part (east) of the body get stretched in this asana that's why this asana is called Purvottanasana.

Procedure

- Sit in Dandasana (Staff Pose) with your hands several inches behind your hips and your fingers pointing forward.
- Bend your knees and place your feet on the floor, big toes turned inward, heels at least a foot away from your buttocks.
- Exhaling, press your inner feet and hands down against the floor to lift your hips until you come into a reverse

tabletop position.

- Keep your torso and thighs approximately parallel to the floor; shins and arms approximately perpendicular.
- Straighten your legs one at a time without losing the height of your hips.
- Lift your hips still higher without hardening your buttocks. Press your shoulder blades against your back (torso) to support the lift of your chest.
- Without compressing the back of your neck, slowly drop your head back.
- Hold for 30 seconds, then sit back down in Dandasana while exhaling.

Benefits: It strengthens the arms, wrists and legs. It gives great stretches to the shoulders, chest, and front ankles. It helps to remove fatigue.

Precautions: Avoid if you have wrist injury. Support the head on a wall or chair seat if you have neck injury,

MANDUKASANA (Frog Pose)

The shape of this formation resembles a frog that's why this asana is called Mandukasana. In Sanskrit - Frog is called Manduk.

Procedure

- Sit in Vajrasana keeping the both heels opened out.
- Sit with waist and back straight placing the buttocks on the two heels.
- Now, separate the knees as far apart as possible. This is

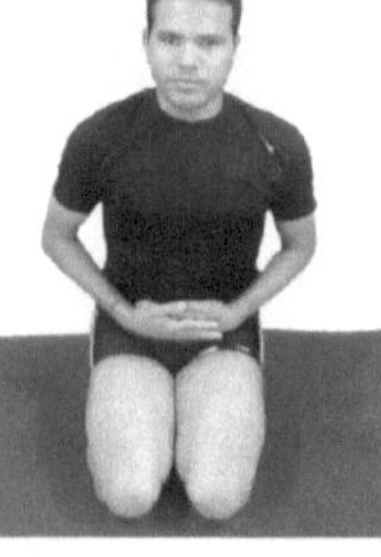

  Manduk sitting.
- Now, for Mandukasana bring both the knees in the front touching each other.
- Place your right palm on navel centre and keep your left palm upon it.
- Inhale deeply and exhaling go forward with pressure on your abdomen. Let the forehead touch the ground. Hold for 30 seconds.
- Inhaling come up and interchange your hand.
- Exhaling go forward and hold for 30 second.
- Come up while inhaling. Repeat 5 sets of it.

Variation-I

- Make fists of your hands and keep them on the belly on both the sides of the navel.
- Exhaling lower the body in front.
- Hold this position for 30 seconds.
- Inhaling come up in first position and relax.
- Repeat 5 times.

Other Variations: There are many other variations of mandukasana. Here are some images.

Precaution: Not for people who are suffering from peptic or duodenal ulcer, severe back pain, cardiac problems and patients who have undergone abdominal surgery.

Benefits: Mandukasana improves functions of all organs. This asana stimulates the digestive system. It is advised for the treatment of constipation, diabetes and digestive disorders. It is good for hernia patient. This asana is effective in reducing the weight of thighs, hips and the abdomen. This asana strengthens the lower body. This asana increases sexual ability. It removes the defects of the reproductive system of women and men.

CHAKRASANA (Wheel Pose)

The name comes from the Sanskrit words Chakra meaning wheel and Asana meaning posture.

Procedure

- Lie down on your back (in supine position).
- Pull in your legs and place your feet on the mat.
- Maintain the hip distance between your feet.

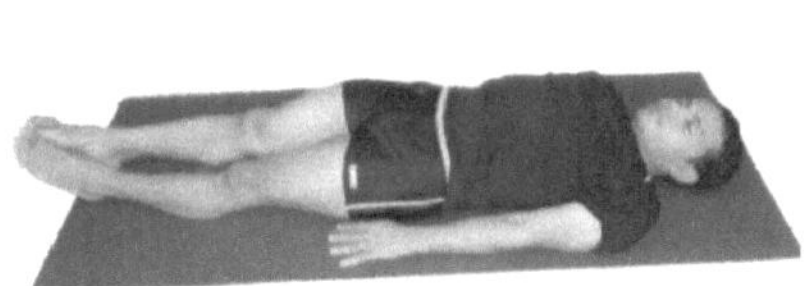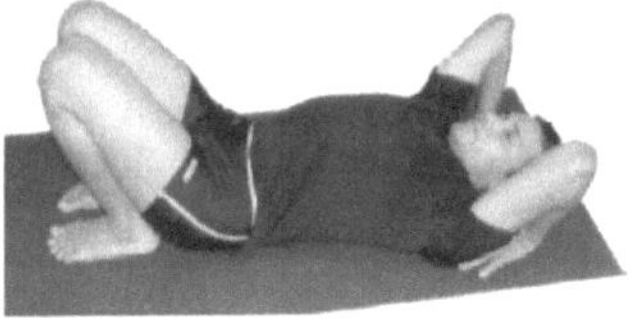

- Move your hands towards your head and spread your palms on the floor beside your head, fingers pointed inside.
- Inhale and while exhaling lift your hips, with your head still on the Yoga Mat.
- Keep your feet and knees parallel as you push yourself up until you stand on the ground with the crown of your head.
- Inhaling, stand on your feet and stretch out your arms lifting your head as well.
- Let your head fall backwards with good stretch on throat.
- Try to achieve bending through entire back and not just through a few vertebrae.
- Look at the floor. Try bending the upper back further and further with every exhalation.
- Keep the knees together, stretch the legs without tightening the buttocks and relax the shoulders.
- Hold this position from 30-60-90-180 seconds.
- Exhaling, gently get back without jerk.
- Repeat this twice.

Variations: Eka Pada Urdhva Dhanurasana (One-Legged Upward Facing Bow) & Eka Hasta Urdhva Dhanurasana (One-Handed Upward Facing Bow) etc.

Benefits: The more you practice this asana, the more flexible your back becomes. The more flexible your back, the less strength you will need to do it. This Asana strengthens your legs, arms and wrists. It makes your back, and spinal column supple and flexible. In this asana the front part of the body is stretched and the back side of the body is bent. This asana has therapeutic values in numerous health problems i.e. Asthma, Bronchitis, as well as poor spinal alignment etc.

PAWANMUKTASANA (Wind Releasing Pose)

The Sanskrit word Pawana means air or wind and Mukta means freedom or release. The wind relieving posture so named because it assists in releasing trapped digestive gas from the stomach and intestines. Beginner may start with Ardha Pawanmuktasana.

Procedure

- Lie down on your back with you leg straight and hand parallel on both side of body.
- Exhale and while inhaling slowly raise your right leg up to 90 degree angle.
- Exhaling bend your leg at the knees.
- Inhaling hold your knee with both hands.
- Exhaling pull your knee to your chest.
- Inhale and exhale again to raise your head to place your chin on the knees. Do not strain your neck. It is better not to raise your head if there is neck pain.
- Continue to maintain the asana, breathing normally witnessing abdominal effect.

- In this position the right thigh is pressed against the abdomen.
- Point the toes forward.
- Hold this position for 30-60-180 seconds.

Releasing

- Inhaling bring your head down on the mat, raise your folded leg up by releasing your hands, place your hands on the mat parallel to the body.
- Exhaling bring your leg down.
- Repeat this asana with other leg and both leg together as well.

Benefits: This Asana releases the compression in the lower back. It activates, massages and enhances the powers of the Manipura Chakra. It tones up the muscles of thighs, abdomen and all the abdomen organs. It gives great stretches in the neck and back. The abdominal muscles are contracted and internal organs are compressed which increases the blood circulation that stimulates the nerves, increasing the efficiency of the internal organs. The pressure on the abdomen releases any trapped gases in the large intestine. Blood circulation is increased to all the internal organs. Digestive system is improved. It is helpful in flatulence, constipation, menstrual disorders, sterility and impotence. It is especially beneficial for women as it massages the pelvic muscles and reproductive organs that help to control menstrual disorders. It reduces fats in the abdominal area, thighs and buttocks.

Precautions: This asana must be avoided if there is recent abdominal surgery. Anyone suffering from piles should avoid this asana. Pregnant women should not practice this asana. If there is any pain, stiffness or injury in the neck, cervical spondylitis, the head should remain on the floor.

MARKATASANA (Spinal Twisting Asana)

Markata means monkey. This asana resembles a monkey. This is the reason the name of the asana is Markatasana. Secondly monkeys have very flexible spine and they have great reflexes. With this practice you are supposed to achieve those qualities.

Procedure

- Lie down straight on your back and spread the hands parallel to the shoulder level, with palms facing up.
- Inhaling raise your left leg up at 90 degrees.
- Exhaling drop it down to the right turning your head to the left.
- Hold for 30 seconds, while pulling abdominal muscle in and hip muscle tight.
- Inhaling, raise your left leg up and while exhaling drop it straight down on the ground.
- Repeat it with the other leg and you can do it with both legs together as well.
- Repeat this 5 times

Variation (One leg folded)

- Lie down straight on your back and spread the hands parallel to the shoulder level, with palms facing up.

- Inhaling raise your left leg up at 90 degrees.
- Exhaling drop it down and place your left foot on your right thigh.
- Inhale and while exhaling drop your left knee to the right side turning your head to the left.
- Hold for 30 seconds while pulling abdominal muscle in and hip muscle tight.
- Inhaling, raise your left leg up and while exhaling drop it straight down on the ground.
- Repeat it with the other leg. This becomes one set.
- Repeat it for 3-5 sets.

Variation (both legs folded-feet separate)

- Lie down straight on your back with toes and heels joined together.
- Bend your knees placing your heels close to buttocks and feet resting on the ground.
- Inhaling raise your left leg up at 90 degrees.
- Exhaling drop it down and place your left foot on your right thigh.
- Inhale and while exhaling drop your left knee to the right side turning your head to the left.
- Hold for 30 seconds while pulling abdominal muscle in and hip muscle tight.
- Inhaling, raise your left leg up and while exhaling drop it down on the ground keeping your knee folded.
- Repeat it with the other leg. This becomes one set.
- Repeat it for 3-5 sets.

Variation (both legs folded-feet together)

- Lie down straight on your back with toes and heels joined together.

- Bend your knees placing your heels close to buttocks and feet resting on the ground.
- Interlock your fingers; place your palm below your head with elbow resting on the ground.
- Inhale and while exhaling, drop your knees and legs to the right and turn your head to the left.
- Your left knee will rest on your right knee and left ankle will rest on right ankle.
- Try to touch the floor with your right knee.
- Look to the left as far as possible.
- Remain in this position for 30 seconds.
- Now exhale and inhaling come back to the starting position.
- Repeat it other side. This becomes one set.
- Repeat it 5 to 10 sets.

Note: You can do it with folded legs keeping them separate and touching opposite heel with opposite knee.

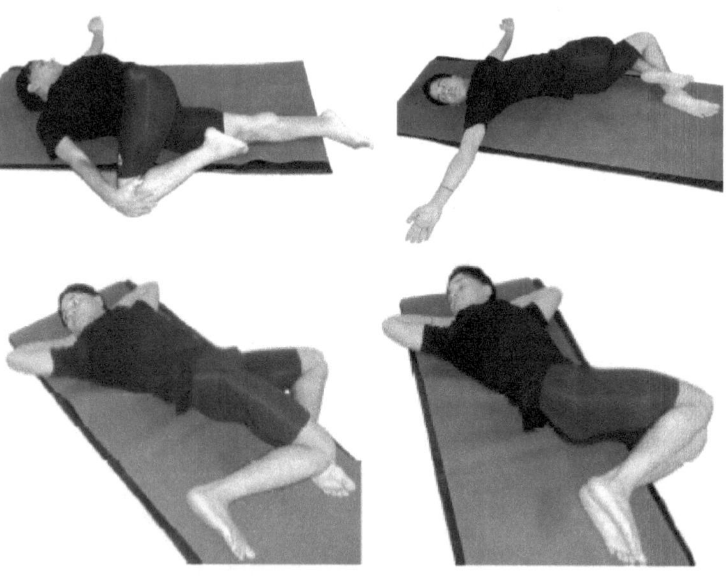

Variation (both legs interlocked)

- Lie down on your back with legs straight.
- Bend your knees placing your heels close to buttocks.
- Interlock your fingers; place your palm below your head with elbow resting on the ground.
- Interlock your legs placing your left knee up.
- Inhale and while exhaling, drop your knees and legs to the right and turn your head to the left.
- Try to touch the floor with your left knee.
- Look to the left as far as possible.
- Remain in this position for 30 seconds.
- Now exhale and while inhaling come back to the starting position.
- Repeat it other side. This becomes one set.
- Repeat it 5 to 10 sets.

SETU BANDH ASANA (Bridge Pose)

In Sanskrit Setu means Bridge; Bandha means energy-binder that directs subtle energy flow. Thus literally, Setu Bandha means a bridge that flows the energy into body.

Procedure

- Lie down on your back with legs straight.
- Bend your knees placing your heels close to buttocks.
- Keep your feet at pelvic width gap and parallel to each other.
- Rest your arms on your sides with palms facing down.
- Inhale deeply and while exhaling press down on your

feet and start by pressing your navel toward the ground as you begin to raise your hips upward.

- Gradually allow the middle and upper sections of your spine also to rise.
- Raise your spine off the ground until the thighs are about parallel to the floor.
- Hold this position for 5-10 breaths for the static version.
- While inhaling drop your hips down.

Dynamic Variation

- Alternatively, move on with the dynamic version.
- Inhale as you move up to the bridge position.
- Exhale as you return to the starting position.
- Repeat moving in and out of the Bridge while inhaling and exhaling.

Other Variations

- Hold your ankle with your hand before lifting your hips up.
- Support your back with your palms while resting elbows on the ground to lift your hips.
- Inhaling raise your one leg while supporting your back with hand and placing elbows on the ground. Hold for 30-60 seconds. Exhaling drop your raised leg down. Inhaling raise your other leg up and hold for 30-60 seconds. Do it for 2 sets.

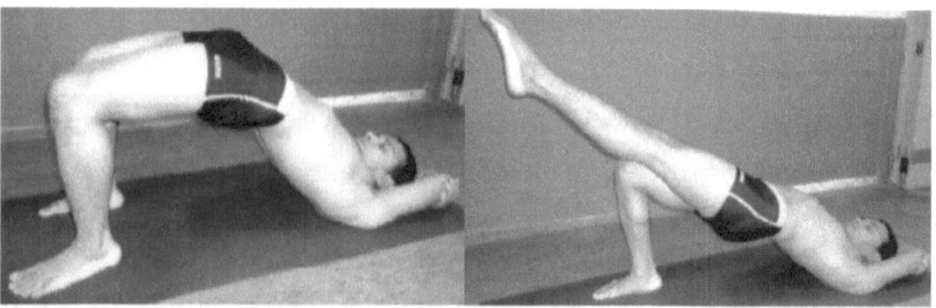

- While supporting your back with elbow, walk ahead with your feet to keep your legs straight possible. Touch the ground with your toes. Inhaling, slowly bring your feet back and exhaling drop hips down.

Precautions: If you have neck injuries or other problems do this asana with care. Don't move your neck from side to side and prevent your spine from any jerk.

Benefits: This asana calms the brain and rejuvenates tired legs. It is healthy for body and mind. It stretches the chest, neck and spine. It stimulates abdominal organs, lungs and thyroid. It improves digestion, reduces anxiety, fatigue, backache, headache and insomnia. It is a good asana for women as it helps to relieve the symptoms of menopausal and menstrual discomfort. It is a therapeutic posture for Asthma, High Blood Pressure, Osteoporosis and Sinusitis. It helps to alleviate Stress and mild Depression.

UTTANPADASANA (Leg Raised Pose)

The name comes from the Sanskrit words uttana meaning intense stretch or straight or stretched and pada meaning leg or foot and asana meaning posture or seat.

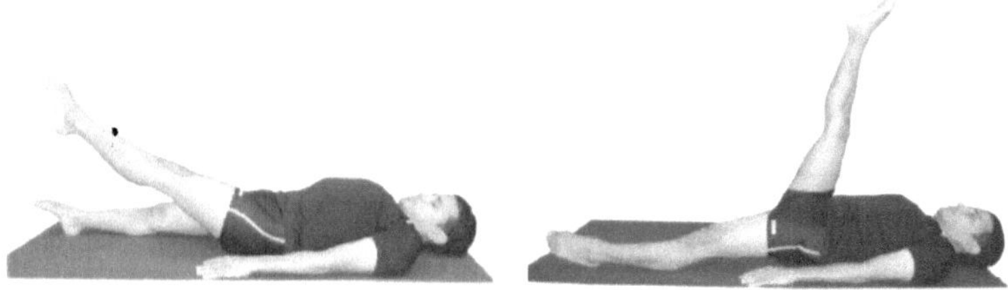

Procedure

Variation (Single Leg Lifting)
- Lie down on your back (in supine position).
- Keep your legs together, arms touching the sides and

palms down.
- Exhale and inhaling raise your right leg up at 30 degrees.
- Hold this position for 30-60-90-180 seconds.
- Exhaling slowly drop your leg straight down.
- Repeat the same at 60 degrees, then at 90 degrees.
- Do the same with other leg as well.

Variation (Both Legs Lifting)
- Lie down on your back (in supine position).
- Keep your legs together, arms touching the sides and palms down.
- Exhale and while inhaling raise your both legs up at 30 degrees.
- Hold this position for 30-60-90-180 Seconds.
- Exhaling drop your legs straight down very slowly.
- Repeat the same at 60 degrees, then at 90 degrees.

Note: While raising your legs up, keep them straight with knees tight and toes pointing forward. Keep the back & buttocks on the ground. Head straight and eyesight fixed on the raised toes. Alternately, if your back and abs muscles are strong enough you can place your hands below your head or straight up.

Precaution: One should avoid movements of legs with jerks or speed. The movements should be controlled otherwise this asana can strain the back muscles. If you have back pain, recent surgery of back or abdomen, do not lift both legs together. You may do it with single leg only. It is suggested not to do during pregnancy. You can practice it with one leg during menstrual cycle but avoid it if you have mild or severe pain and cramps.

Benefits: It is a good cure for obesity; wind related digestive disorders and diabetes. In this asana, thigh muscles and stomach muscles are strengthen. The active positive effects reaches the inner organs of the small intestines, enzyme producing glands and other organs and helps to increases body capacity. The vertical position of the legs help to improve blood circulation.

VIPARITA KARANI (Half Sarvangasana)

Hatha Yoga Pradipika, an important book on Yoga accepts this as Mudra rather than Asana. But since this position very much resembles an asana, here we have treated it as an asana. It is as an inverted position, hence it is called Viparita Karani (Inverted Position).

Procedure

- Lie down on your back keeping your legs straight.
- Exhale and while inhaling raise both legs upward and stop when they make 90 degree with the floor.
- Exhaling raise the waist and push the legs backward over the head.
- Inhaling support the waist with both hands placing your arms up and elbows on the floor.
- Rest your shoulders on the ground.
- Head straight and eyesight fixed on the raised toes.
- Do not move the neck while in the position.
- Initially, if it is difficult to maintain this asana keeping the legs straight, bend the legs slightly while maintaining your balance.
- Continue normal breathing.
- Hold this asana for 2 to 3 minutes after sufficient practice to get the desired results.

Note: After supporting your back with your hands, straighten the legs and stretch the toes upwards.

Releasing

- Inhale and while exhaling slightly lower the legs towards head.
- Maintaining the balance of the body bring your hands down.
- Place the waist on the ground keeping legs straight while inhaling as in the Uttanpadasana.
- Exhaling, bring legs back to the normal position without jerk using your core strength.

Benefits: Most of the times we remain either in standing or sitting position. Quite opposite position is taken in this asana. This helps improve blood circulation. You can get certain benefits of Sirsasana (upside down). This asana is great for balancing hormonal secretions. Good for mind and emotions. It controls emotional swings and improves perceptions.

Precaution: This asana should not be performed by people who are suffering from heart trouble and high blood pressure problems. It can only be practiced under expert guidance.

SARVANGASANA
(Supported Shoulder Stand Pose)

Sarvangasana refers to Shoulderstand asana. There are many variations of the Shoulderstand asana. The most common to be taught is Supported Shoulderstand (Salamba Sarvangasana). The name in the case of Salamba Sarvangasana (Supported Shoulderstand) comes from the Sanskrit words Salamba meaning supported , Sarva meaning all, Anga meaning body part, and Asana meaning posture, thus Salamba Sarvangasana literally translates to  supported-all-limbs-pose. So this Asana is considered the asana for all the organs. It is nicknamed Queen or Mother of all the Asanas.

Procedure
- Lie down flat on your back.
- Inhaling contract the abdomen and slowly raise both the legs up to 90 degrees angle from the floor.
- While exhaling raise the waist and the hips from the floor and take the legs backwards over the head.
- Inhaling raise your back and legs up into a vertical position in a 90 degrees position keeping the body from

the feet to the shoulders in a straight line.
- Support your upper back with your hand.
- Place your arms up to the elbows on the floor, keeping them shoulder width apart.
- Push your chest forward and the chin down forming a tie in throat which is called Jalandhara Bandha.
- Don't move the neck; don't overstrain in the chin lock position.
- All the pressure is on the neck, shoulders and the back of the head.
- Do not tense the legs or point the feet as this contracts the legs and prevents drainage of blood.
- Fix the eyesight on the toes while maintaining the asana with normal breathing.
- Hold this position starting from 20 seconds to 1-3-5 minutes after sufficient practice.
- Continue abdominal breathing while holding this posture be aware of the effects coming on neck, throat, shoulders and abdominal region.

Releasing
- Inhale and while exhaling bend the waist and lower the legs over the head.
- Release your hands from the upper back and drop them down keeping them straight.
- While inhaling, slowly lower the back vertebrae by vertebrae to the floor.
- Keep the legs at a 90 degrees angle from the floor.
- While exhaling, slowly lower both legs back to the supine position.

Benefits: The Jalandhara Bandha improves the function of the thyroid, parathyroid and pituitary glands. Due to the increase oxygen and blood flow. It improves the functions of all of the endocrine glands regulated by the pituitary gland. This results in improved functioning of all other systems of the body and reduction of emotional and mental stress. Stagnant blood from the lower regions of the body i.e. legs and abdomen is drained to the heart that improves the supply of fresh blood to these parts. Blood supply to the head area i.e. brain, eyes, ears, nose and throat is improved that improves their functioning. All of the pelvic and abdominal areas, ear, throat and nose ailments are improved. It improves lungs capacities assist in treatment of asthama. Toxins in the respiratory system is drained, which benefits health of the respiratory system. It prevents and cures varicose veins. It detoxifies the body with improved efficiency of the organs which leads to youthfulness and anti-aging effects. It normalizes body weight due to its effect on the thyroid gland. It balances the circulatory, digestive, reproductive and nervous systems due to the effect this asana has on the hormonal system, particularly the thyroid. It helps to manage stress, remove psychological disturbances and tranquilize the mind. The increased blood flow in the head region helps to cure and prevent headaches but it should not be practice at the time of headaches. The nerves passing through the neck are toned with increased flexibility.

It boosts immune system as it stimulates the thymus gland. It balances the parathyroid glands which ensure regeneration and normal development of the bones. It releases gravitational pressure from the anal muscles which helps with hemorrhoids. The digestive system is greatly improved due to the increase in blood circulation and drainage of stagnant blood. It removes digestive disorder, constipation and other chronic and natural gastrointestinal disorders. The Pranic flow is harmonized that increases energy level which has a positive effect on all the systems of the body. It acts as a powerful blood tonic and purifier. It tones the nerves. It will save your doctor's bills if you practice it daily. It is useful in gonorrhoea and other diseases of bladder and ovaries. It removes sterility and womb diseases. Sarvangasana awakens Kundalini. Sarvangasana has almost all the benefits of Shirshasana but is safer and easier to perform.

Special Benefits For Women: It is beneficial for the reproductive systems. Fresh blood flows to the pelvic region as the stagnant blood is flushed out from the organs that increases efficiency of the reproductive organs. It strengthens the uterine ligaments as the gravity on the ligaments in Sarvangasana is in the opposite direction. It improves the functioning of the ovaries. It helps to balance all moods and calms the mind. It helps to regulate menstrual cycles. It helps to minimize the negative manifestation of menopause.

Precautions And Contraindications: It should not be performed by people suffering from heart conditions or brain diseases. This asana should be avoided during menstruation and pregnancy. This asana should be avoided if suffering from very enlarge thyroid, enlarge spleen or liver as well as cervical spondylitis, slipped disc, headache and weak blood vessels in the eyes.

HALASANA (Plough Pose)

The name comes from the Sanskrit words Hala meaning plough and Asana meaning posture. In this asana the body takes the shape similar to a plough; as a plough makes the hard ground soft, in this asana, the veins are stretched which reduces stiffness in the body.

Procedure
- Lie down on your back keeping your legs straight.
- Exhale and while inhaling raise both legs upward to 90 degrees.

- Exhaling raise the waist, hips and push the legs backward over the head.
- Support your back with your hands while resting your elbows on the ground.
- Exhale once again and push the legs further back. Try to touch the ground with toes.
- Keep the toes stretched.
- Keep the knees straight or else the expected pressure on the organs is not achieved.
- In this position head, shoulders, toes and arms should rest on the ground.
- The chin pressed in Jalandhar Bandha. Continue normal breathing.

- Make sure you do not move your neck while holding the posture.
- Hold this position for 30-60-180 seconds after sufficient practice to get the desired results.

Variations

- You can extend the toes backwards so that top of the feett rests on the ground.
- Drop your hands straight down keeping them parallel to each other.
- Interlock your fingers and keep both your hands on the ground.
- Bring your hands up to hold your toes with your hands.

Releasing

- Exhale and while inhaling, lift the toes keeping the legs straight in knees.
- Exhale and while inhaling, slowly keep your back on the ground to take the Uttanpadasana position.
- Exhaling, bring legs back to the normal position without jerk.

Precaution

Avoid jerks or swift movements as it might cause injury to the backbone. Hence the movements should be controlled at every stage of this asana. People suffering from spleen and liver discomforts should do this asana under supervision of a Yoga Guru.

Benefits: All the muscles from toes to waist are stretched aiding in the functions of the veins. This Asana tones the spinal nerves, the muscles of the back, the vertebral bones and the sympathetic nervous system that runs along the vertebral column on both sides. This Asana fulfils and amplifies Sarvangasana. A large quantity of blood is poured into the spinal roots of the nerves, spinal cord, sympathetic ganglia, sympathetic nerves and muscles of the back. Hence, they get nourished. The vertebral column becomes very soft and elastic. This Asana prevents the early ossification of the vertebral bones. Ossification is quick degeneration of the bones. Old age manifests quickly on account of early ossification. Anyone who practices Halasana can never be lazy, rather becomes very lively, agile and full of energy. The muscles of the back are alternatively contracted, relaxed and then stretched. Various sorts of muscular rheumatism are cured by this asana. The abdominal, the rectal and thigh muscles are also toned and nourished. This asana cures obesity, habitual or chronic constipation, gastric, dyspepsia, congestion and enlargement of the liver and spleen. It helps to cure hormonal imbalances.

MATSYASANA (Fish Pose)

In this asana, the shape of the body appears similar to fish in the water. Secondly, you can float in water quite easily if you adopt this position in water. The fish pose is counter stretching pose for the Plough pose. Traditionally this pose is performed with Padmasana but to make it more easy for beginners the straight legs variations are commonly practiced.

Procedure

- Lie on your back with your legs straight.
- Inhaling lift your pelvis slightly off the floor, and slide your hands (palms down) below your buttocks.
- Then rest your buttocks on the backs of your hands.
- Be sure to tuck your forearms and elbows up close to the sides of your torso.

- Inhaling press your forearms and elbows firmly against the floor to lift your upper torso & head.
- Exhaling release your head back onto the floor. Depending on how high you arch your back and lift your chest, either the back of your head or the crown will rest on the floor.
- Point your toes out and create proper stretching.
- Hold there for 15 to 30 seconds with smooth breathing.
- Focus on your Belly, Chest, Spine, Shoulders and Neck regions with awareness and feel the effects happening in these areas.
- Inhaling lift your head up again and look at your toes.
- Exhaling lower your torso and head to the floor.
- Draw your thighs up into your belly and squeeze.

Other Variations

- Lift your straight legs up to 30, 45, 60 degrees position and hold.
- Lift your legs to 30 degrees angle and take your hands

above your head with 30 degrees position.

- Lift your legs to 30 degrees angle and lift your hands straight up above your chest with a 45 degrees position.

Classic Matsyasana

- Lie on your back with your legs straight and hand parallel to your body.
- Bend your left leg to place it on right thigh.
- Bend your right leg and place it on left thigh to form Padmasana.
- Inhaling press your forearms and elbows firmly against the floor to lift your upper torso along with head.
- Exhaling release your head back onto the floor. Depending on how high you arch your back and lift your chest, either the back of your head or its crown will rest on the floor.
- Lift your knees up and hold your right big toe with left hand and left big toe with right hand.
- Drop your knees down to touch the ground with both knees.
- Hold in this position for 30-60-180 seconds with smooth breathing.
- Inhale deeply to lift your head up and while exhaling drop your torso down on the ground.
- Inhale once again and while exhaling release your legs to make them straight.

Note: You can do it in Half-Padmasana if you are not able to do a Full Padmasana.

Precaution: The weight over the head should be taken out slowly. The support of the hands should be removed only when the head is completely ready to bear the weight. Also while releasing the position, one should avoid jerks and speedy movements. Maintain the asana until it is bearable and pleasant. If you have high or low blood pressure, migraine, insomnia, serious lower-back or neck injury then practice only under supervision of Yoga Guru.

Benefits: According to traditional text, Matsyasana is the "Destroyer Of All Diseases. Jalandhara Bandha in Sarvangasana pressurizes the thyroids and pituitary glands but in Matsyasana these glands are stretched. These opposite processes help improve circulation in these glands for optimum functions. This asana is therapeutic for constipation, respiratory ailments, mild backache, fatigue, anxiety and menstrual pain. It stretches the deep hip flexors and the intercostals muscles between the ribs that help to improve the strength of the muscles. It stretches and stimulates the muscles of the belly, front of the neck and throat to improve efficiency of the organs from that region.

SUPTA VAJRASANA
(Supine Thunderbolt Pose)

You should lie down on the ground while assuming Vajrasana. This is the reason it is called Supta Vajrasana.

Procedure

- Sit in Vajrasana. Breathe normally.
- Place your palms on the floor beside the buttocks.
- Inhale and while exhaling bend the elbows and slowly lean the body back until the elbows rest on the floor.
- Inhale and while exhaling lower the head backward until the top of the head touches the floor.
- Place the palms on the thighs.
- Close the eyes and relax the body.
- Breathe deeply and slowly while holding the posture for 30- 60-180 seconds.
- Maintain your awareness on the lower back, abdomen and breath.

Releasing

- With the support of elbows lift your body up to Vajrasana.
- Alternately you can rest your elbows on the ground and open your legs one by one coming to Savasana. (you can try this if you do not have any knee pain.)

Note: You can take your hands above your head and hold opposite elbow with opposite hand.

Precaution: Avoid this Asana during an asthma attack, with acute pain in the lumbar spine or knees. Also avoid after any knee or abdominal surgery. Avoid this asana in case of severe slip discs and vertigo etc.

Benefits: This asana massages the abdominal organs alleviating digestive ailments and constipation. It tones the spinal nerves, makes the back flexible and realigns rounded shoulders. The ribcage is stretched and fully expanded, which helps to fill the lungs to maximum capacity that brings more oxygen into the systems. The nerves in the neck, thyroids, parathyroid and adrenal glands are specifically stimulated. This asana stretches the back muscles and separates the individual vertebrae from each other, releasing pressure on the discs. This posture helps to relieve back ache and nerves compression that helps the discs to resume their correct position, and beneficial for slip discs. It improves spinal alignment. It enhances personality with courage and confidence. It loosens up the legs and strengthens them in preparation for sitting in meditation asanas. It tones the pelvic muscles and the sciatic nerves. It is beneficial for women who have an underdeveloped pelvis. It helps to alleviate disorders of both the male and female reproductive organs. Regular practice of this asana relieves constipation. It enhances creativity and intelligence as it increases circulation in the brain.

NAUKASANA & VIPRIT NAUKASANA
(Boat Pose)

At the time of Naukasana, the shape of the body resembles a boat, so it is called Naukasana.

Procedure

- Lie on your back with your feet together and arms beside your body.

- Take a deep breath in and as you exhale, lift your chest and feet off the ground, stretching your arms towards your feet.
- Your eyes, fingers and toes should be in a line.
- Feel the pressure in your navel area as the abdominal muscles contract.
- Keep breathing deeply while maintaining the pose.
- As you exhale, come back to the ground slowly and relax.

Variations: You can stretch your hand back or interlock your fingers and place your hands on the back of your head.

Procedure (Viparit Naukasana)

- Lie on your stomach with your feet together and arms stretched forward.
- Take a deep breath in and as you exhale, lift your chest and feet off the ground, stretching your arms forwards.
- Your head, fingers and toes should be in a line.
- Shift you body weight on navel centre and feel the strengthening effect in the whole body.
- Keep breathing deeply, while maintaining the pose.
- As you exhale, come back to the ground slowly and relax.

Viparit Naukasana is especially beneficial for back and lungs. It maintains muscular activity from the feet to the head. It removes disorders of the spine and sluggishness. It improves the functions of the lungs.

Precaution: Do not practice this pose if you are suffering from severe headache or have suffered from some chronic diseases or spinal disorders in the recent past. Women should avoid doing boat pose (Naukasana) during pregnancy and during the first two days of the menstrual cycle.

Benefits: It strengthens the lower back and abdominal muscles. It helps to tone legs. thighs and arm muscles. It is useful for people with hernia. It is beneficial for intestines, pancreas, gallbladder, spleen, liver, kidneys, thyroids and prostate gland. It relieves stress.

SHASHANKASANA (Rabbit Pose)

Shashank is made of two words, Shash meaning hare and Ank meaning lap. The Shashankasana looks similar to a sitting hare, from which it derives its name.

Procedure

- Sit in Vajrasana with hands on the thighs. The upper body is straight and relaxed.
- Inhaling raise both arms above the head.
- Exhaling keep the back straight and bend forward from the hips, until arms and forehead touch the floor. The buttocks remain on the heels.
- Remain in this position with normal breathing for a while.
- Relax the whole body, especially the shoulders, neck and back.
- Inhaling keep the back straight and raise your hands first and head and the upper body.
- Exhaling return to the starting position. Repeat this 3 times.

Variations

- To relax more, you can bring both hands back while touching the ground with both elbows, palms facing up and hands parallel to your body. This posture is normally called Child Pose.
- To increase intensity, you can hold your heels with both

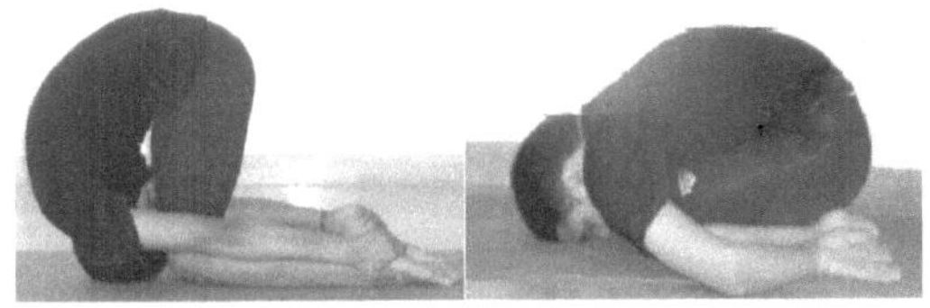

your hands and touch your knees with your forehead. Lift your hips up and push it forward. This is considered as Hare Pose.

Precaution: Do not practice hare pose (variation III), when you are suffering from diarrhea as it may worsen. Do it under supervision if you have knee pain. Pregnant women should practice under the supervision of an experienced Yoga teacher with modification of leg position (open leg position).

Benefits: The Shashankasana is a relaxation pose. It is practiced to normalize the circulation after the head stand or some intensive back side bending asana to give a counter stretch to the spine. The whole spine and muscles of the back get relaxed in this position and the breath gets deepen. Performing the Shashankasana gently stretches the hips, thighs and ankles. It strengthens the abdomen, rib cage, back and arms. It provides stretch to the back part of the body, in the gluteus, arms, back, neck and shoulders. It helps in the extension of the neck, arms and spine at the same time flexes the knees and hips muscles. This posture helps in regulating the adrenal glands. The stomach, spleen and liver are also stimulated, thus assist in their functions. It is beneficial to the reproductive organs. Practicing this pose helps to improve circulation of blood to scalp, face, eyes, brain and therefore nourish them. It gives a healthy glow to the face. It also helps relieve stress and fatigue bringing calmness in the brain. It improves concentration. Anxiety and depression are relieved due to its calming effect. It is beneficial in calming the nerves and providing a feeling of tranquility.

BHUJANGASANA (Cobra Pose)

Sanskrit meaning of Bhujanga is snake. This asana resembles a serpent with its hood raised. So, some people call it sarpaasana (Cobra Pose). Bhujanga asana is made of two word Bhuja + Anga, where Bhuja means arms and Anga means organs. This asana strengthen arms and shoulders (Bhujanga) so it is called Bhujangasana. The modified posture resembles an upward facing dog; hence it is called Urdhva Mukha Svanasana.

Procedure

- Lie on your stomach with your toes flat on the floor and forehead resting on the ground.
- Keep your legs together with your heels and toes together.
- Place your palms below shoulders, keeping your elbows parallel and close to your torso.
- Taking a deep breath in, slowly lift your head, chest and abdomen while keeping your navel on the floor.
- Stretch your throat facing up.
- Roll your shoulders back and down so that your shoulder blade comes closer.
- Keep your shoulders relaxed, even if it means bending your elbows.

- Make sure there is equal pressure on both the palms.
- Keep breathing with awareness, as you curve your spine vertebrae by vertebrae.
- If you do not have any back problems, you can, straighten your arms by arching your back as much as possible; tilt your head back and look up.
- Witness the effects on back, abdomen, chest, lungs, arms and shoulder.
- With regular practice, you will be able to deepen the stretch by straightening the elbows.
- You can lift your hips and thighs if the back is not flexible enough.
- Continue your deep breathing while holding your breath for 30-60-180 seconds.
- Repeat 3 to 5 times. Number of repetitions can be increased with practice.
- Breathing out, gently bring your abdomen, chest and head down to the floor.

Variations

- You can lift both palms in the air.
- Keep your legs separate with toes pointed out. Inhaling lift your front body from head, chest, navel and the knees by shifting your weight on your hands and feet.
- Curl your toes and lift your whole body on your hands and toes while inhaling.
- Once you achieve Bhujangasana keeping your arms straight, bend your knees up. Drop your head back to rest your head on your sole. This is called Purna Bhujangasana. Inhaling lift your head up. Exhaling drop your feet down then drop your chest, chin and head down on the ground.

Precautions: Practice Bhujangasana under supervision only if you have Back injury, Carpal Tunnel Syndrome or Severe

Headache. Do not overdo the stretch or overstrain. Avoid practicing Bhujangasana if you are pregnant, have fractured ribs or wrists. Do not practice it if you have recently undergone surgeries for your spine, brain, abdomen, heart and lungs etc.

Benefits: Traditional texts said that Bhujangasana increases body heat, destroys disease and awakens Kundalini. It strengthens the whole spine as well as entire back muscles. By arching the spine, blood circulation is increased in that region, toning the nerves along the spinal column which improves communication between the brain and the rest of the body. It stretches chest, lungs, shoulders, and abdomen; firms the buttocks and tightens the abdomen. The pressure on the abdomen is beneficial to the abdominal organs and in particular the digestive organs. It stimulates appetite, relieves flatulence and constipation. It improves flexibility of the upper and middle back. Expands the chest and improves the functioning of lungs, heart, liver, pancreas, spleen and kidney. Tones the kidneys which help in blood purification, removing any stagnant toxic blood and improving the health of the entire body. Strengthens the adrenal glands which are responsible for secretions of adrenaline, cortisol and stress hormones. It improves functioning of the thyroid gland, which is responsible for metabolic activities. It reduces fatigue and stress. It is useful for people with respiratory disorders such as asthma and bronchitis. (Do not practice this asana during the attack though). It relieves spinal pain, soothes sciatica, combat slipped or herniated disk as well as arthritis in that region. In normal day-to-day life we do a lot of forward bending but not much backward bending, therefore it is good to practice for a healthy back and to give general balances to the body.

Benefits for Women: Tones the ovaries and the uterus and helps to alleviate gynecological disorders such as leucorrhea (irregular vaginal discharge due to an imbalance in estrogen), dysmenorrhea (painful menstruation) and amenorrhea (absent menstruation). It is helpful for conception. It gives relief from menstrual disorder.

SHALABHASANA (Locust Pose)

When this pose is demonstrated, it resembles a locust or grasshopper or spider. Hence the name of this asana is Salabha-asana or Locust pose. Some people call it spider pose or superman pose as well.

Procedure

Variation-I (Single Leg Lifting)
- Lie on your belly with your arms along the sides of your torso, palms up, forehead resting on the floor.
- Turn your big toes toward each other to inwardly rotate your thighs.
- Firm your buttocks so your coccyx presses toward your pubis.
- Tight your legs, first through the heels to lengthen the back legs, then through the bases of the big toes.
- Inhaling raise one leg at a time into the air.
- Make sure that the legs are straight in knees.
- Do not lift your head.
- Hold for 30-60-180 seconds.
- Exhaling bring your lifted leg down.
- Repeat with the other leg.

Variation-II (Both Legs Lifting)
- Now place your chin on the ground and while inhaling raise both legs up as much as possible.
- Hold for 30-60-120-180 seconds.
- Exhaling bring it down.

Other Variations

1. Take both your hands forward and raise both your legs up.
2. Advanced practitioner can place the feet on head as well.
3. Take both your hands back and raise both hands and legs up in the air. This is called Superman pose.
4. Raise your right leg and support it with your left leg folding from your knee.

Precaution: People suffering from back problems, TB in intestines, Ulcer in stomach and Hernias should consult Yoga expert before practicing this asana. Jerks, heavy lifting and unbearable strains should be avoided. Person with headache, serious back injury and neck injuries should keep their head in a neutral position by looking down at the floor.

Benefits: It serves as a counter-pose to Paschimottanasana, Halasana and Sarvangasana which bend the spine forwards. It increases the intra-abdominal pressure as a result of this, the abdominal organs become more active and efficient. It tones up the muscles of the thighs and legs. It moves down the accumulated faecal matter of the stomach to ascending colon of large intestine, from ascending colon to transverse colon from transverse colon to descending colon and from there to the rectum. It cures indigestion and relieves constipation. It tones the abdominal viscera (organs) viz., liver, pancreas, kidneys etc. It removes several diseases of the stomach and bowels. It cures sluggishness of liver and hunchback. It strengthens the muscles of the spine, buttocks, back of the arms, shoulders and chest. It improves posture, and relieve stress. It is very good asana for slip discs and sciatica problems. It strengthen upper spine and relieve tennis elbow. It is beneficial for varicose veins in the legs. It helps to get rid of fatigue, flatulence and lower-back pains.

MAKARASANA (Relaxation)

In Sanskrit language Makara means Crocodile that is why this asana is known as Crocodile Pose as well.

Procedure

- First of all, lie down on stomach resting your chin on the floor.
- Now stretch out both your legs together at pelvic width distance.
- Place both legs comfortably apart and allow them to rest on the floor.
- Keep both hands on their respective sides.
- Now support your chin with palms, resting the elbows

- on the floor.
- While inhaling, bend your leg and while exhaling make it straight alternately towards hips to touch it with heels.
- Repeat it for 10-20 times each.
- Alternately bend and straighten both legs together for 20 times.

Variations

- Stretch both hands forward. Bend your right hand from elbow to place it on left shoulder. Fold left hand over right hand to put it on right shoulder. Rest your head in between. Keep your legs wide open with heel facing inside and toes outside.
- Stretch both hands forward. Bend your right hand from elbow to place it below your head. Resting elbow on right side on the ground. Bend your left hand to place your left palm above right palm. Now rest your head upon palms (alternatively, you can make fist of both hands resting one upon another). Rest your forehead upon it.

Precautions: People suffering from heart problems and high blood pressure should practice under supervision. In this asana the whole body is relaxed. As the body is relaxed, one is inclined to sleep which one should strictly avoid.

Benefits: The muscles that are put under severe strain demand relaxation and rest. Makarasana promptly and efficiently ensures complete relaxation and perfect rest to these muscles. Relaxed muscles need less blood and oxygen supply. Consequently, the heart beats and the breathing also slow down. Now, as the whole basic operation turns slow, the body become restful. It helps to ease breathing problems and disorders related to the urogenital system. It is beneficial for asthma patients. It helps to eliminate problems related to sciatica, slip disc and cervical spondylitis. It helps to reduce knee pain.

DHANURASANA (Bow Pose)

The name comes from the Sanskrit words Dhanura meaning Bow and Asana meaning posture. When this Asana is performed, it resembles the appearance of a bow (Dhanus). The stretched arms and forelegs form the string of the bow. It is a combination of Bhujangasana and Shalabhasana with the addition of holding the ankles with the hands. Bhujangasana, Salabhasana and Dhanurasana form a valuable combination to practice.

Procedure

Prep.- I

- Lie down on stomach resting your forehead on the ground.
- Bend both legs from the knees and keep them 6 to 8 inches apart.
- Catch both legs firmly near the ankles.
- Exhale and while inhaling pull the legs upward allowing the body to be stretched in a curve.
- Hold for 30 seconds and exhaling drop your legs on the ground.

Prep.- II

- Lie down on stomach resting your forehead on the ground.

- Bend both the legs at the knees and keep them 6 to 8 inches apart.
- Catch both the legs firmly near the ankles.
- Exhale and while inhaling raise your head up resting knees on the ground.
- Stay in this position for 30 seconds.
- Inhale and while exhaling drop your head on the ground.

Variation I

- Lie down on stomach resting your forehead on the ground.
- Bend both legs from the knees and keep them 6 to 8 inches apart.

- Catch both legs firmly near the ankles.
- Now exhale and while inhaling raise your legs as well as front body up as much as you can with no strain in your back.
- After taking the final position, try to raise the thighs up from the ground along with shoulders and chest.
- Push the neck backwards as much as possible.
- Hold there for 30-60-120-180 seconds.

Releasing

- Inhale and exhaling bring the knees, chin and shoulders slowly on the ground.
- Leave the ankles and bring the hands beside the body.
- Straighten the bent legs and bring them as in the prone position.

Note: After practicing it for a few days you can increase the repetitions, once you are able to do 5 repetitions easily then reduce repetitions and increase the holding time.

Advanced Variation : In advanced variations, you can raise your body up to maximum level by taking your hands from front and you may touch your forehead with your feet.

Precaution: People suffering from back problems, TB in intestine, ulcer in stomach and hernia should consult Yoga expert before practicing this asana. Jerks and unbearable strains should be avoided.

Benefits: Dhanurasana is a combination of both Bhujangasana and Shalabhasana and can deliver benefits from both of these asanas. It is a blessing for people who suffer from gastro-intestinal diseases. This is useful in chronic constipation, dyspepsia and sluggishness of liver. It removes hunchback, rheumatism of legs, knee-joints and hands. It reduces the fat, improves digestion, increases peristalsis movement, invigorates the appetite. It relieves congestion of blood in the abdominal region and tones them up. It helps to keep the spine elastic. It prevents premature ossification of bones. It improves blood circulations and strengthens the arms and shoulder. It is very good for lungs and improves breathing patterns. He, who does Halasana, Mayurasana and Dhanurasana can never become lazy. He is full of energy, vigour and vitality.

AKARNA DHANURASANA (Archer Pose)

In translation from Sanskrit, Karna means ear and the prefix A means towards or near. Dhanu means bow and asana means pose. The literal translation of the name is towards the ear bow pose. A better, non literal translation is the Archer Pose, as the position resembles an archer about to release an arrow.

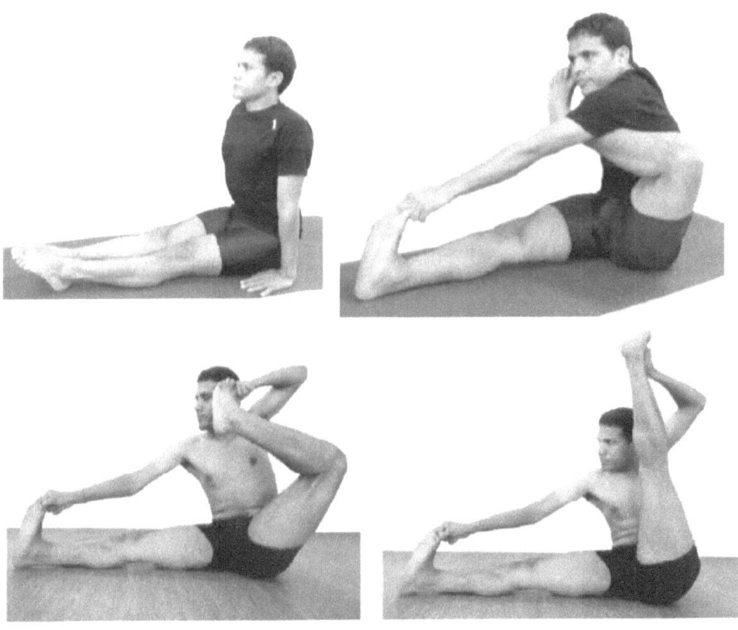

Procedure

Variation I

- Sit in Dandasana - Sit straight with leg straight forward out and spine straight upright.
- Grabs hold of each big toe between the thumb and index finger.
- Exhale, keeping the right leg in full contact with the floor, pull the left foot up towards the left ear, bending the knee.
- Hold the position up to 30 seconds. Breathe normally.
- Exhaling straighten the left leg to a vertical position and hold it for 30 seconds.
- Inhale and exhaling bring it down.
- Gently place it on the floor. Repeat it with the leg.

Variation II

- Sit in Dandasana (Sit straight with leg straight forward and spine straight).
- Grabs hold of big toe with opposite hand between the thumb and index finger.
- Exhales, keeping the right leg in full contact with the floor pull the left foot up towards the right ear, bending the knee.
- Hold the position up to 30 seconds. Breathe normally.
- Inhale and while exhaling drop it down.

Precautions: Avoid during pregnancy and menstruations. Consult yoga guru before trying this asana if you have shoulder injury, lumbar disk problems and hamstring injury.

Benefits: Akarna Dhanurasana stretches arms, legs and back that increases hip mobility. It strengthens arms, shoulders, chest, thighs, buttocks and calves. Your nerves are stimulated and refreshed. It gives beautiful shape to your legs. It is beneficial for the abdominal organs as it contracts and releases the muscles and moves the whole abdominal area and improves its core strength. It improves digestion and relieves constipation. It helps to relieve and prevent pain in lower abdomen and large intestine. For women, it helps to regulate irregular menstruations. This asana is especially good for working people who sit long hours and use hands viz. writing, drawing, typing and sewing etc. Last but not the least, it opens your chest and gives extra space for the lungs to inhale maximum oxygen. It increases oxygen supply that helps to improve energy level.

RAJAKAPOTASANA (King Pigeon Pose)

Stage-I

- Begin on all four limbs, with your knees directly below your hips.
- Place your hands slightly ahead of your shoulders.
- Slide your right knee forward to the back of your right wrist.
- Angle your right shin under your torso.
- Bring your right foot to the front of your left knee.
- Rest the outside of your right shin on the floor.
- Slowly slide your left leg back, straightening the knee and descending the front of the thigh to the floor.
- Rotate slightly inwardly, so its midline presses against the floor.
- Lower the outside of your right buttock to the floor.
- Position the right heel just in front of the left hip.
- The right knee, can angle slightly to the right, outside the line of the hip.
- Rest both your palms on the ground
- Arch your back and look forward.

- Hold this position for 10 breaths.
- Exhaling release the pose and repeat it on other side.

Stage-II

- After assuming first position, bend your left leg.
- Take your left hand back.
- Hold your left foot with your hand and place it near elbow.
- Holding your toes on elbow, bring your left hand forward and hold with right hand.
- While inhaling raise your right elbow up above your head while holding left hand.
- Look forward and hold the position.
- Hold this position for 10 breaths.
- Exhaling release the pose and repeat it on other side.

Classic Rajakapotasana

- After assuming first position, bend your left leg.
- Take your left hand back.
- Hold your left foot with your hand and place it near elbow.
- While Inhaling raise your right hand up.
- Look at your right palm and hold the position.
- Hold this position for 10 breaths.
- Exhaling release the pose and repeat it other side.

Purna Rajakapotasana

- After assuming first position, bend your left leg.
- Look left and hold your toes with your left hand.
- Inhaling raise your right elbow up while arching your back.
- Inhale once again and take your right hand up.
- Exhale bend your right elbow, drop hand and hold left

big toe.

- Arching your back bring your left foot to your upper head.
- Hold the position for 15 deep breaths.
- Exhaling release the posture and repeat other side.

Other Variations: There are many variations of Rajkapot Asan. Some of them are given here.

Precautions: If you have ankle and knee injury, tight hips or thighs do it only under supervision of experience trainer.

Benefits: Rajkapot asan stretches and strengthens the thighs, groins, abdomen, chest, shoulders and neck. It stimulates the abdominal organs. It opens the shoulders and chest. It is therapeutic for urinary disorders. It Stretches, strengthens and tones spinal column. It Strengthens the lumber joints, hip joints and groin muscles. It Stimulates metabolic and reproductive glands and organs. It increases vitality.

HANUMANASANA

The name comes from the Sanskrit words Hanuman (a divine entity in Hinduism who resembles a monkey) and asana (posture), and commemorates the giant leap made by Hanuman to reach island of Lanka from southern mainland of India. The Yogi pushes one leg forward and one leg backwards until they are in the splits position. Once the yogi has moved the legs into position, there are several variations of arm and upper body position.

Procedure

- Kneel on the floor.
- Bring the right leg straight in front with the heel on the floor.
- Exhaling lean your torso forward, pressing your fingertips to the floor.
- Slowly slide your left knee back straightening the knee.
- Descend the right thigh toward the floor.
- Stop straightening the back knee just before you reach the limit of your stretch.
- Push the right heel away from your torso.
- Gradually turn the leg inward as it straightens to pull the kneecap.
- As the front leg straightens, resume pressing the left knee back.
- Carefully descend the front of the left thigh and the back

of the right leg (and the base of the pelvis) to the floor.

- Make sure the back leg extends straight out of the hip (and isn't angled out to the side).
- Make sure the center of the back kneecap is pressing directly on the floor.
- Keep the front leg active by extending through the heel and lifting the ball of the foot toward the ceiling.
- Bring the hands into Anjali Mudra (Salutation Seal).
- Alternately, stretch the arms straight up toward the ceiling.
- Hold this posture taking 30 deep breaths.

Releasing

- Press your hands to the floor.
- Turn the front leg out slightly.
- Slowly return the front heel and the back knee to their starting positions.
- Repeat it with other leg.

Beginners: Place a blanket under the front heel to help you slide forward. Use a block under each hand to support yourself if you cannot straighten the back leg completely. Press the back foot actively into the floor and lift the shoulder blades firmly into your back to increase the length of the torso and spine.

Advanced Variations

Variations I : After achieving the classic Hanumanasana, bend forward over the front leg and hold the foot with your hands. Hold this position for 10 to 15 breaths, then come up while inhaling.

Variations II : Bend your back leg from the knee. Hold it with your same side hand with other side hand on the floor or use both hand to hold the toes of the back leg. Try to touch the head on the sole.

Variations III : Bend your back leg from the knee. Hold the toe with your same side hand. Take your other hand forward to hold the toes of the straight leg.

Precautions: Avoid, if you have groin or hamstring injuries.

Benefits: This asana is of utmost spiritual significance. It requires significant physical flexibility. It stretches the hamstrings and groin. It stimulates the abdominal organs. It is very therapeutic for Sciatica pain, help to prevent slip disk. It is very healthy for the thighs, hamstring, abdomen, groins, chest, shoulders and vertebral column as it strengthens them, improves flexibility, blood circulation and helps to prevent all type of problems in these areas.

YOGA MUDRASANA (Psychic Union Pose)

Yoga Mudrasana is considered ideal yoga asana for awakening the higher senses. This asana has been used for centuries by yogic sages to go deep within their own internal landscapes and to commune with the divine. There are both beginner and advanced versions of this posture. Its full expression requires extreme flexibility in almost every limb of the body especially

the hips, knees, ankles, entire spine, shoulders and wrists. It is also called the 'seal' because one closes off the energy that normally escapes through one's hands and feet by making a complete seal or circuit. It is done in Padmasana, which is a difficult asana for many beginner students. If Padmasana is difficult, one can do it in Vajrasana as well.

Procedure for beginner

- Sit in Padmasana (if it is not possible you can sit in Vajrasana or Ardha Padmasana or Sukhasana).
- Inhale and take both hands back, interlock fingers.
- Keep both hands straight with palm facing out.
- While exhaling, bend forward from the waist resting the forehead on the floor.
- Hold this position with smooth breathing for 30-60 seconds.
- Inhaling raise your head up while pushing your body

forward.
- Exhale and while inhaling be straight from the waist.

For advanced practitioner
- Sit in Padmasana.
- Hold your big toe of right foot with right hand and left big toe with your left hand from back side.
- Inhale and exhaling bend forward from the waist and rest the forehead (alternatively you can place your chin on the ground, while stretching your throat) on the floor.
- Continue smooth breathing. Hold for one minute; after long practice you can hold this posture for 5 minutes.
- Inhaling raise your head up while stretching your body forward.
- Exhale and inhaling be straight from the waist.

Precaution: Bending process should be slow and stretch your spine while going down. Practitioners with back problems should practice this Asana only under supervision of a Yoga Guru.

Benefits: As the belly gets folded in this Asana, there comes tremendous pressure on intestines, liver, spleen and certain glands, this pressure improves their functioning and removes complaints regarding digestive system. It is helpful to cure constipation. This Asana is useful awaken the Kundalini shakti, with prolonged practice as it energizes the Manipura Chakra. This is where we develop personal power and learn to stand up for yourself without being overly aggressive. It helps to have a healthy self esteem by balancing the Chakras. It intensifies the peristaltic activity and pushes down the accumulated waste matter in the colon and there by relieves constipation and increases digestive power. It helps to control diabetes, improve metabolic rates and aids nutrients absorption.

USHTRASANA (Camel Pose)

The name comes from the Sanskrit words Ustra meaning camel and Asana meaning posture. In this asana the practitioner's body resembles a camel. Ustrasana is the Queen of backbends. This classic pose is strong, elegant and inspiring.

Procedure

Variation-I (For Beginners)

- Sit in Vajrasana.
- Keep hips width distance between the knees.
- Place the palms on the ground just behind your body, fingers facing forward.
- Firm the core area by contracting the naval.
- Inhaling, raise your hips up with the support of your hands and knees.

- Once you reach up, drop your head back while exhaling.
- Hold for 15-30 breaths.
- Inhaling bring your face forward.
- Exhaling drop your hips down to come to Vajrasana.

Variation-II (Baby Camel Pose)-For Beginners

- Sit in Vajrasana.
- Keep hips width distance between the knees.
- Raise your hips up, making the thighs straight so that the weight of the body rests on the knees and toes.
- Firm and ground the legs, pulling the quadriceps upwards.
- Firm the core area by contracting the naval.
- Place the palms (fingers face down) on the lower back.
- With the legs and tummy strong, inhale and begin to move the upper body up and back.
- Roll the shoulder blades towards one another, lifting through the heart and collar bones.
- Draw the tail bone down.
- Keep the thighs and core strong.
- Hold for 15-30 breaths.
- Using the legs and core strength come up evenly. (Do not twist out of the pose).

Full Camel Pose (For Regular Practitioners)

- Sit in Vajrasana.
- Keep hips width distance between the knees.
- Inhaling, raise your hips making the thighs straight so that the weight of the body rests on the knees and toes.
- Firm and ground the legs, pulling the quadriceps upwards.
- Firm the core area by contracting the naval.

- Roll your right hand to hold your right heel and roll your left hand to hold your left heel.
- Contract your tailbone and lift your ribcage up.
- Exhaling allow your head to go down with stretching on your throat.
- Hold this position for 15-30 breaths.
- Continue deep breaths while holding this pose.
- Witness the effects taking place in your body.

- Exhale and inhale to roll your right hand up to bring it on your right thigh while exhaling.
- Inhale and roll your left hand to place it on your left thigh.

Other Variations: There are other variations as well. Some of the variations given directly below.

Note: Ustrasana increases the pulse rate considerably. So keep your breaths deep and slow. A deeper stretch can be achieved by separating the knees slightly wider.

Benefits: This asana helps to open and activate the heart centre. It stimulates abdominal organs. It helps to rectify slouching with regular practices by improving spinal alignment. The lumbar vertebrae are massaged and they obtain flexibility. It improves core strength. It increases spinal, hip and shoulder flexibility. It is good for improving overall stamina. It tones the nerves and muscles attached to entire spine as well as muscles of face, neck, trunk and thighs. If you are an asthmatic patient, take a sigh of relief since Ushtrasana (Camel Pose) can help you activate your respiratory system. It improves the flexibility of diaphragm that helps in expansion of lungs to maximum capacity. The activation of lungs will help people suffering from respiratory problems, bronchitis and asthma. Extension of spine makes them more flexible, particularly the lumbar region. Flexibility of spine helps to prevent accidental injuries with improved bodily movements.

Precautions: Practicing Ustrasana can make many beginners feel distinctly ill, with lightheadedness or nausea being quite common after-effects. However, this does usually improve with practice. Before trying Camel pose, ensure that you are warmed up and take some preparatory back bends. Avoid this asana if you have severe lower back pain or an enlarged thyroid. People with neck or lower back injury should not practice this asana. High and low blood pressure patients should do it under supervision only. Do not practice at the time of severe headache or migraine.

MAYURASANA (Peacock Pose)

The name comes from the Sanskrit word Mayura meaning Peacock and Asana meaning posture. When this Asana is exhibited, it resembles a peacock which has spread out the bundle of feathers at its back. You are supposed to raise your body like a horizontal stick holding the floor with both palms while supporting the body with elbows.

Procedure

- Sit in Vajrasana.
- Spread your knees to about one feet distance.
- Place your palm on the ground with fingers backside.
- Place the elbows together so that they touch the navel.
- Inhaling, shift your weight on your elbow and stretch the legs backwards.
- The thighs, knees, ankles and toes should touch each other.

- Exhale and try to raise your body on elbow keeping the whole body parallel to the ground.
- Maintain this position initially for a few seconds and later increase the duration up to 5 minutes.
- Inhale and exhaling drop your knees down on the ground and come to starting position.

Variations: Padma Mayurasana (Lotus Peacock Pose). Pincha Mayurasana (Feathered Peacock Pose), Uttana Padma Mayurasana (Intense Stretch Lotus Peacock Pose)

Precautions: Mayurasana is a very important balancing pose but it demands good physical strength. Losing balance in asana may cause injuries. So, do it with caution. It is not recommended for those suffering from cervical spondylitis or spinal injury, elbow injury or wrist pain.

Benefits: This Asana can give you maximum physical exercises in minimal time. It destroys the effects of unwholesome food. It increases the digestive power. It digests even toxic poisons and destroys its side effects. It cures dyspepsia and diseases of stomach like chronic gastritis and reduces spleen and liver enlargement by increasing the intra-abdominal massage. It helps to cure all ailments related with phlegm, gout and bile. The lungs and whole abdominal organs are properly toned and stimulated by the increase of intra-abdominal pressure. Sluggishness of liver disappears. It regulates the bowels, removes constipation (ordinary, chronic and habitual) and awakens Kundalini. It gives wonderful appetite, removes all diseases caused by an excess of wind, bile or phlegm. It cures diabetes and hemorrhoids. It strengthens the muscles of the arms. It makes the entire body shapely, beautiful and keeps it energetic.

BHUNAMANASANA (Earth Worship Pose)

The name comes from the Sanskrit words Bhu meaning Bhumi or earth and Naman means Salutation.

Procedure

- Sit in Dandasana.
- Lean the torso back slightly on your hands.
- Open your legs wide, slightly lifting them.
- Press the hands against the floor.
- Lift the buttocks forward, widening the legs.
- Rotate the thighs inwardly.
- Pressing the inner thighs against the floor keep your knee caps tight.
- Place your palms in front with your thigh bones pressed on the floor.
- Exhaling walk your hands forward between your legs.
- Maintain the spine straight moving from the hip joints.
- Inhale and exhaling place your forehead on the floor and arms extended forward.
- Inhale and exhaling place the chin on the floor and extend the arms to hold your toes.
- Hold this position for 30-60-180 seconds.
- Deeply inhale and exhaling take both your hands forward again.

- Inhaling slowly walk back with your hands to straight up position.
- Place both your hands below knees to support your hamstring muscles on its respective side.
- Slightly lift your knees up and fold your legs to place
- your feet together and relax.

Precaution: People with back pains should do it only under supervision.

Benefits: Good for opening the hip and for improving the flexibility of thigh muscles. It stretches the spine, hamstrings and calves muscles. It keeps your thigh, legs, waist, kidney, stomach and other abdominal organs disease free. It stabilizes the semen. It helps to prevent sciatica as it improves flexibility. This removes constipation and dyspepsia (indigestion, upset stomach). It calms the mind.

BADDHA KONASANA OR BHADRASANA (Butterfly)

"Titali means 'butterfly' in Sanskrit. In this pose the legs are spread out the way a butterfly opens its wings in flight. This is a simple exercise that can easily be performed even with minimum instructions. Targeting primarily the legs, it is the perfect antidote to relax and stretch the muscles of the legs especially after a long day of work or after an intensive work out.

Procedure

- Sit on the floor with your legs stretched in front.
- Keep your head, neck and spine erect.
- Bend your knees and place the soles of your feet together.
- Grab your feet with your hand.
- Pull them as close to the groin as possible so that you feel the stretch.
- Make sure your spine is straight (up right) position.
- Now, start moving your knees up and down (inhaling up & exhaling down).
- Move your knees maximum up and maximum down possible.
- Close your eyes and continue flapping the knees as long as possible.
- Alternately, you can place your palms on your respective thighs.
- Take a deep breath to pull it up and exhaling press your knees down.

Variation-I: Supta Baddha Konasana (The Reclined Butterfly

Pose): As the name suggests. It is a variation of the standard Purna Titli Asana that is performed while lying down flat

on your back instead of while sitting up. This supine pose provides a deeper sense of relaxation and is a good stretch for not only the thighs but also the back and chest. This pose is very effective when you are tired and want to stretch your back and legs at the same time.

Variation-II: Baddha Konasana (Bound Angle Pose): It is another popular variation of the Butterfly pose. Where the Butterfly Pose is a mixture of static and dynamic stretching. It involves mostly static stretching and allows you to further deepen the stretch experienced by the Butterfly Pose.

To perform this pose, clasp the soles of your feet and concentrate on trying to open them as if you are opening the pages of a book. At the same time, bend forward while keeping your back rounded so that the weight of your elbows allows the thighs to further open up.

Note: Beginners can use cushions to support the knees and Hunchbackers should use cushions below the pelvis. Do not lean in front or back while doing this posture.

Benefits: The Butterfly pose is good for the spine and lower back as well as your hip joints. It relaxes your inner thigh. This pose is known for its stress relief. It helps to overcome fatigue. It soothes your legs. It strengthens the muscles of the hips and legs. It makes the hamstrings more flexible. It is especially beneficial for those who run, walk or cycle for long distances or have a job that requires them to constantly be on their feet. It also helps to open up the hips, thighs and improves flexibility. It stimulates and activates the energy of the Swadhisthana Chakra. It is very beneficial for urogenital systems and increases sexual energy. It is good for menstruation, cure

Therapeutic Applications : This is an excellent posture for women during menstruation as it helps to relieve some of the discomfort and pain associated with menstruating. This posture is also supposed to be very beneficial for women after menopause. The Butterfly Pose helps to open up the hips and genital areas and is very good for pregnant women to practice in third trimester. Regular practice of this posture can help in easing the pain associated with natural childbirth. Regular practice of this posture is beneficial to the kidneys, bladder, prostate gland and ovaries.

YOGANIDRASANA

Yoganidrasana is one of the advanced pose. Even though it takes a lot of effort to get into this pose, you should feel comfortable and stay calm. The ancient yogis fell asleep in this pose to attain the state of inner stillness and calm leading to Pratyahara.

Procedure

- Lie down on your back.
- Fold your right leg. Pull up and place it on the back of your head.
- Pull your left leg and place it upon right in your back of your head.
- Interlock your feet.
- Place your hand in front of your chest in Namaskar Mudra.
- Alternately, Wrap your upper limbs around your torso and hug in.
- Breathe smoothly through your nose.
- Inhale and exhaling drop your left leg with hand support.
- Inhale and while exhaling drop your right leg.

Precautions: Open hips and loosen hamstrings are essential to practice this pose safely. If your hip rotators and hamstrings are tight but your knee joints and sacroiliac (Joint of Sacrum and iliac bone of junction of spine and pelvis) are flexible; you'll unknowingly recruit those joints to compensate for the lack of flexibility in your muscles, which can lead to injury. Stop doing Yoganidrasana if you feel any knee, lower back or neck pain.

Benefits: As you draw your awareness inward, like a tortoise retreating into its shell, your breath slows, your muscles relax and you feel yourself completely letting go. The sights and sounds around you feel far away but at the same time you feel connected to the universe. It may be a state you've never felt before but once you do, you'll want to return to it. Good for Reproductive systems.

TADASANA OR URDHVA VRIKSHASANA
(Palm Tree Pose)

Tada meaning Palm Tree and Asana meaning posture. A tree is always in a standing position, remains stable and grows upward. The similar process is involved in this asana and hence it is called Urdhva Vrikshasana as well.

Procedure

Variation- I (Samasthiti)

- Stand straight keeping your feet together.(variations: 1. we can keep the feet apart with the heels and big toes in one line pointing straight forward 2. Heels together and toes outside).

- Keep your feet grounded involving metatarsals and each individual toe.
- Balance your weight on your heels and toes of both legs. Keep the left and right hips in level with each other.
- Keep your Knee Cap Tight.
- Keep your hips, buttocks and upper thigh muscles contracted (pulled upwards).
- Broaden your chest.
- Roll your shoulders back, and drop your shoulder blades pulled down. The shoulders may be lifted slightly, then brought back and down to achieve this.
- Retain 3 bandhas (root lock, abdominal lock and chin lock).
- The gaze is toward the tip of the nose.

Variation- II (Urdhva Tadasana)

- Stand straight in Samasthiti.
- Bring both hands forward and interlock your fingers.
- Inhaling take both arms up above the head.
- Lift the heels and stand on the toes pulling the whole body upward.
- The whole-body (right from the heels to the fingers of the hands) is stretched upward.
- Push the hands upward as much as possible.
- The more the body is kept stretched, the more it is good for balance.
- Keeping the legs stable, stretch the body upward.
- Continue smooth breathing witnessing the effects in the entire body.
- Hold this position for 15-30-60 seconds.
- Inhale and exhaling drop your heels slowly down and come back to samasthiti.
- Repeat this for 3-5 times.

Benefits: This asana strengthens the abdomen and legs. It may help relieve sciatica, reduce back, belly pain and flat feet. Improves the strength of deeper feet muscles which support the feet. Increases awareness and improves muscle strength as well as flexibility. Helps to prevent muscle injury. In this asana all the muscles are stretched in each direction keeping them relaxed at the same time. This helps to remove all strains. The muscles are rested and relaxed, even the earlier strains caused by other asanas are removed. It is good for kids to increase height.

VRIKSHASANA (Tree Pose)

The name comes from the Sanskrit words vriksha meaning tree. In this asana weight is shifted to one leg.

Procedure

- Stand straight with arms by the side of your body and feet joined together.
- Lift your right leg and fold it at the knee.
- Holding the ankle with right hand, pull the leg up.
- Rest your right foot on the upper part of the left inner thigh with toes pointing down.
- Make sure that your left leg is straight.
- Balance your body properly on your left leg.
- Once you are well balanced, take a deep breath in, grace-fully raise your arms to place palm in front of your chest in Namaskar Mudra.

- Inhale slowly and gradually raise both your hands up above your head.
- Stretch your hands and body further up to the maximum.
- Look straight ahead in front at a distant object.
- A steady gaze and controlled breaths helps maintain a steady balance.
- Ensure that your spine is straight.
- Relaxing your body more and more with each exhalation hold it for 30 seconds 3 minutes.
- Exhaling, gently bring down your hands from the sides.
- Gently release the right leg.
- Stand straight as you did at the beginning of the posture.
- Repeat this pose with other side as well.

Precautions: Raising the arms above the head for long may involve risks for persons with High Blood pressure. The arms can be held at chest height in Anjali Mudra (Namaskar) for those at risk. Avoid doing this posture if you are suffering from migraine attack and insomnia.

Benefits: This elegant pose is not as easy as it looks but over a period of time, it builds tremendous inner and outer strength. It gives a great feeling of accomplishment as you learn to balance on one leg for long. It is a powerful pose which increase balance, coordination and concentration. It improves the range of motion in the hips. It Tones the muscles of the legs, back and chest. This helps to alleviate the pains of rheumatism. It strengthens the entire legs including ankles, leg muscles and ligaments up to the buttocks. It gives relief in some cases of sciatica. It strengthens the bone of the hips and legs. It improves stability in the legs. It improves the neuromuscular coordination. This pose helps to achieve a state of rejuvenation and invigorates you. It brings balance and equilibrium to your mind.

GARUDASANA (EAGLE POSE)

The name comes from the Sanskrit words Garuda meaning Eagle and asana meaning posture. It is just another tough yoga pose to execute since it requires a great deal of balancing. This is mainly about balancing that can bring improvement on your physical and mental health.

Procedure

- Stand straight with feet together and arms on the sides at shoulder level.
- Open your palms. Cross your left arm below your right arm.
- Raise your right arm with your hand stretching towards the ceiling.
- Bring your palms together (as close as possible), depending on your flexibility.
- Your fingers should be pointing upwards.
- Maintain the position of your arms.
- Slightly bend your knees without going over your toes.
- Inhale and while exhaling lift your right leg, cross it to your left thigh as you curve your right foot around your left calf.
- Hold it for 30-60 seconds.
- Inhale and while exhaling return to Tadasana.
- Repeat for the same length of time with the arms and legs reversed.

Variations: Beginners can slightly lean forward to make it easy. This can be done in sitting position (by crossing legs).

Precautions: Avoid in case of Arthritis and Knee injuries.

Benefits: It helps in strengthening your legs and improving major joints of your body. This gives you enhance concentration and balance. It is good for ankles, calves, thighs, hips and shoulders etc. It helps to cure asthma, backache and sciatica.

UTKATASANA (Chair Pose)

The name comes from the Sanskrit words Utkata meaning powerful, fierce, intense or heavy and asana meaning posture. This is also called chair pose because the posture resemble a chair. This posture seems easy but looks can be deceiving. This pose will challenge beginners and advanced students alike.

Procedure

- Stand in Samasthiti.
- Keep your hands parallel to the body.
- Maintain pelvic width gap between your feet.
- Inhaling raise your hands forward.
- Keep the arms parallel and palms facing down.
- Face forward to focus on strength.
- Exhaling bend your knees.
- Take the thighs as parallel to the floor as possible.
- Move your upper body forward at 45 degrees.

- Keep the inner thighs parallel to each other.
- Firm your shoulder blades against the back.
- Take your tailbone down toward the floor and in toward your pubis to keep the lower back long.
- Stay for 30-60 seconds.
- Exhale and inhaling come up, straightening your knees and lifting strongly through the arms.
- Exhale and release your arms to your sides.
- Repeat this pose twice.

Variations: As you bend your knees, lift your hands up, keeping your palms facing each other. Exhaling release the posture.

Precautions: Do it under strict supervision of yoga guru if you have knee pain, lower back pain, headache, insomnia and low blood pressure.

Benefits: In this asana, focus is placed on the legs and pelvis to stabilize and ground this asana. There is a dynamic balance between the upper and lower body that helps to develop determination capacity. A strong and straight lower back is the foundation for every position. It is important to place your lower back right to build strength in it. Utkatasana helps you to achieve that. It reduces flat feet. It strengthens the ankles, thighs, calves, glute muscles and spine. More importantly, it improves the range of motions in the ankles. It stretches shoulders, chest and creates space in these areas. It adds more space in the chest so that your breath becomes deeper, which aids for greater oxygen intake. While doing this asana, your heart rate increases but after relaxation it comes to normal. Breathing becomes deep and regular. It stimulates the abdominal organs, diaphragm and heart muscles. If you are looking for increase balance, strength, and stability, you must do it correctly and regularly.

NATARAJASANA (Lord of the Dance Pose)

The name comes from the Sanskrit words nata meaning dancer, raja meaning king, and asana meaning posture. Nataraja is one of the names given to the Hindu God Shiva in his form as the Cosmic Dancer. This is a balancing asana that strengthens the legs. It is a full body stretch which engages the shoulders, chest and abdomen. It strengthens the thigh calf muscles, knees and ankles, hips and spine. It develops concentration and grace. This aesthetic, stretching and balancing asana is used in Indian classical dances.

Procedure

- Stand in Samasthiti.
- Inhaling shift your weight to your right foot and bend your left leg back pulling your left heel toward buttock.
- Tight the right knee cap to keep the leg straight and strong.
- Take your left hand back and grasp the outside of your left ankle.
- Actively lift your pubis toward your navel and press your tailbone toward the floor to avoid compression in your lower back.
- Begin to lift your left foot up away from the floor.
- Extend the left thigh behind and parallel to the floor.
- Stretch your right arm forward, in front of your torso. Balance can be difficult initially for beginners. You can place your free hand against a wall to help you stay stable if required.
- Keep the head up and eyes fixed forward on a point of concentration.
- Hold this position with 20 to 30 deep breaths.

- Exhaling release the grasp on the left foot and place it onto the floor.
- Repeat it other side.

Variation-I *(holding back leg with both hand.)*

- Sweep your right hand behind your back and take hold of the inner left foot. Then sweep the left hand back and hold the outside of the left foot. This variation will challenge your balance even more. Then raise the thigh. It will increase the lift of your chest and the stretch of your shoulders more.

Variation-II

- Stand straight in Samasthiti.
- Bend your left leg from the knee.
- Lift your heel up towards you buttock.
- Turn your left arm actively outward (so the palm faces away from the side of the torso).
- Bend the elbow, and grip the outside of the left foot. (You can also grab the big toe with the first two fingers and the thumb.) The fingers will cross the top of the foot; the thumb will press against the sole.
- Inhaling lift the left leg up and bring the thigh parallel

to the floor. As you do this, rotate the left shoulder in such a way that the bent elbow swings around and up, so that it points toward the ceiling. It requires extreme flexibility to externally rotate and flex the shoulder joint in this way.

- Lift the right arm straight up.
- Hold for 20 to 30 deep breaths.
- While exhaling, release the pose.
- Repeat on the other side.

Variation-III

- You can do it by holding the lifted leg's foot with both hands to increase the resistance and balance.

Precautions: Do not attempt this asana if you have low blood pressure. Beginners should practice under supervision to make it effective.

Benefits : The Nataraj asana is a great position to develop concentration, steadiness, strength and balance. The anatomical focus on thighs, knees, ankles, abdomen, pelvis, groins, chest, shoulders, spine, kidneys and lungs makes it one of the most useful stamina building asanas. It stretches the shoulders, chest, thighs, groins and abdomen. It strengthens the legs and ankles. It helps to open up the upper chest and shoulder areas, release tension in the lower back and hips. It increases the flexibility of the spine.

PADAHASTASANA (The Feet and Hands Pose)

The name of this asana come from Sanskrit word Pada and Hast which means leg and hand respectively. This can be said Standing Paschimottanasana, as the technique is the same. In this position hands are extended down to the paw of the legs. This is one of the most important asana in Hatha Yoga.

There are three variations that includes holding your big toes with the yogi grip or placing your palms underneath the heel of your foot or depending upon your flexibility or simply grasping your calves or ankles.

Procedure

- Stand in Samasthiti keeping your heels close and toes apart.
- As you inhale raise your hands above your head and arms next to your ears.
- While exhaling, bend forward with back flat to touch your toes with your hands.
- Keep your legs straight and feel the stretching in your hamstrings.
- If you have neck pain or back pain, keep your head up face forwards, with stretching effect in throat.
- If you don't have neck/back pain, bend down to touch your nose to your knees.
- Slowly bend further so that your belly touches your thighs.
- While exhaling slowly pull your abdominal muscle up.
- Grasp your big toes with the yogi grip or place your hands underneath your feet and straighten your knees.

- Breathe deeply while pushing the crown of your head towards the floor.
- Hold this position for 30-60-180 seconds.
- Exhale deeply and release your hands.
- Inhaling push your hands forward and come up using your abdominal muscle.
- Repeat this pose for 2-5 times.

Precautions: This asana is not advisable for people who have spinal problems. Perform this asana with comfort. Do not use brute force by pulling your feet with too much physical strength. When you pull too hard, the body stiffens, your thinking and breathing becomes affected and worst, you take the risk of injuring yourself.

Benefits: There are manifold benefits of this Asana. You will feel greatly invigorated after practice. It makes the body lighter by dispelling Tamas (Inactivity). Adiposity disappears. Any shortening of the legs owing to fracture of the leg or thigh-bones is rectified. You will get slight lengthening of the leg by practice of this Asana. The Sushumna Nadi is purified and strengthened. It is good for liver, kidney and spinal health. It cures digestive disorders and abdominal problems. This asana greatly increases blood circulation to the head. Continuous practice of this asana helps to tone the abdominal muscle and other body parts. It releases swelling and gastric problems. It improves flexibility of your spine and strengthens your legs. The benefits of Paschimottanasana are also derived from this Asana..

KATI CHAKRASANA
(The Waist Rotating Pose)

The name of the asana comes from two Sanskrit words 'Kati' means waist and 'Chakra' means wheel.

Procedure

Variation I

- Stand straight with feet shoulder distance.
- Inhale to outstretch your arms in front of the chest

keeping them parallel to the ground and palms facing each other.

- Tightly hold your abdominal and hips muscles.
- Exhaling take both hands towards the left as far as possible.
- Hold the position for 15 seconds with deep breathing.
- Do it slowly without any jerk.
- Make sure you are twisting the body only above pelvic.
- Keep left hand straight and right arm bent from elbow.
- Gaze at the outstretched left thumb.
- Inhaling come back to the normal position.
- Exhaling repeat the practice to the right side as well.
- Repeat this 5-10 times on each side.

Variation II: Inhaling raise both hands forward and spread them at shoulder level. Exhaling, place your right palm on left shoulder and stretch left hand to touch right part of waist from back to side. Inhale and while exhaling twist your neck towards left and try to look behind. Repeated other side.

Variation - III: You can twist with both hands spreading on both side at shoulder level.

Precaution: Patients with severe back pain should avoid this asana. Those with injured knees and spine must practice it with great care. Those having severe cervical pain should not twist the neck while performing this asana.

Benefits: This asana is a very simple but powerful asana, especially for the waist. It removes fat around the waist and hence it trims the waist line. It makes the shoulders, neck, stomach and thighs strong. It increases flexibility and strengthens the spine. It helps to corrects spinal disorders. It stimulates the central nervous system and make it healthier.

It is beneficial for stomach disorders such as indigestion, constipation, gastric and intestinal problems. It activates and massages the internal organs and beneficial for diabetic patients. It helps to improve Thyroid health. It provides relief to Asthmatic patients.

TRIKONASANA (Triangle Pose)

The name of this asana comes from the Sanskrit words trikona meaning triangle. In this asana the position of the body becomes like a triangle (trikon); hence, it is called Trikonasana. Variations include Utthita Trikonasana (extended triangle

pose), Baddha Trikonasana (bound triangle pose), Baddha Parivrtta Trikonasana (bound revolved triangle pose) Parivrtta Trikonasana (revolved triangle pose) and Supta Trikonasana (reclining triangle pose).

Procedure

Variation-I

- Stand in Straight position with feet together.
- Lift the left leg and place it at a maximum distance towards the left.
- Inhaling, turn the toes of the left leg towards the left.
- Turn the right foot forward.
- Exhale and while inhaling, raise your arms parallel to the floor spreading out to the sides.
- Keep your shoulder blades closer to each other and palms down.
- Keep the heels in line with the hips.
- Inhale and exhaling extend the trunk to the left as far as possible and drop the left arm so that it reaches to shin or on a block or on the floor to the front of the left foot, with the palm down.
- Touch the ground with fingers tip. If it is not possible, place the palm on the ground. If placing palm is not possible you can hold your ankle or shin with palm.
- Extend the right arm vertically.
- Gently twist the spine and trunk upwards to the right, using the extended arms as a lever.
- Keep the spine parallel to the ground if possible.
- Turn your head up to gaze at the right thumb, slightly intensifying the spinal twist.
- Hold this position for 30-60-180 seconds.
- Inhaling come up to the hand spreading position.
- Repeat to the right side as well.

Variation- II

- Stand in Straight position with feet together.
- Lift the left leg and place it at a maximum distance towards the left.
- Inhaling, turn the toe of the left foot towards the left side.
- Turn the right foot forward.
- Exhale and while inhaling, raise your arms parallel to the floor spreading out to the sides.
- Keep your shoulder blades closer to each other and palms down.
- Keep the heels in line with the hips.
- Inhale and exhaling bend your left leg keeping left thigh parallel to the ground.
- Rap your left leg with your left hand and drop your right hand from back to hold one hand with other.
- Gently twist the spine and trunk upwards to the right.
- Keep the spine parallel to the ground as possible.
- Turn your head up slightly intensifying the spinal twist.
- Hold this position for 30-60-180 seconds.
- Inhaling keep your left leg straight while holding one hand with other.
- Hold this position for 30-60-180 seconds.
- Inhale and while exhaling drop your left hand down.
- Inhaling come up to the starting position.
- Repeat to the right side as well.

Other Variations: Beginners can do it with heel or the back of torso against a wall to make it easier. You can stretch the top arm over the back of the top ear, parallel to the wall instead of stretching towards the ceiling. Straighten your knees and wrap your right arm over your back and place it on the left thigh. You can hold your big toe of your front leg with your front side hand.

Precaution: Those prone to vertigo or high blood pressure should turn their heads to look down at the floor in the final position. Those with cervical spondylosis and neck problems should continue looking straight ahead and keep both sides of the neck long and even. Those with a cardiac condition should practice against a wall and do not raise the arm, but rest it along the hip. Those with excessive stress-related headaches, migraine, eye strain, diarrhea, low blood pressure, psoriasis, varicose veins, serious back problems, depression or extreme fatigue should practice only under the supervision of a Yoga expert.

Benefits: Practice of this asana improves flexibility of the spine. It corrects alignment of the shoulders and assists treatment of neck sprains. Reduces stiffness in the neck, shoulders and knees. It stretches and strengthens the hips, groins, thighs, hamstrings, knees, calves, ankles, shoulders, chest and spine. It is good for the people with flat feet. It corrects the effects of a sedentary lifestyle or faulty posture. It tones the spinal nerves as well as ligaments of the arms and legs. It helps in osteoporosis and sciatica pain. It stimulates abdominal organs that improve the appetite, digestion and circulation. It relieves gastritis problem, indigestion, acidity and flatulence. This posture stimulates the nervous system and alleviates nervous depression. It strengthens the pelvic area, tones the reproductive organs and helps to cure infertility. It helps to relieve the symptoms of menopause. It is great for backaches. It is useful for curve back pains especially through second trimester of pregnancy. It helps to relieve stress and anxiety.

VIRABHADRASANA (Warrior Pose)

Virabhadra asana (fierce warrior pose) is named after a warrior created by Lord Shiva according to Hindu mythology. As a yoga practitioner it should be considered the posture of a spiritual warrior, who bravely battle with the universal enemy, self-ignorance (avidya), the ultimate source of all our sufferings and become victorious in all challenges, with

greater physical, mental, emotional and spiritual health. There are three variations of this asana Virabhadrasana I. Virabhadrasana II, Virabhadrasana III.

Virabhadrasana - I

- Stand in Straight position with feet together.
- Move your legs as far apart as you can while maintaining stability.
- Keep your heels in line with each other.
- Turn your right foot 90 degrees to the right and left foot about 45 degrees to the right.
- Rotate your torso to the right.
- Bend your right knee.
- Keep your left leg straight possible.
- Right heel on the ground will allow you to go down easily and left heel up will help to bend your back from the spine.
- Make sure that the right knee is directly above your foot and it is pointed forward.
- Make sure it is not falling in or out to either side.

- Inhaling, raise both hands- palms facing each-other and fingers outstretched.
- Hold for 30-60-180 seconds.
- Return to the starting position.
- Repeat to the other side.

Benefits: This is a powerful standing pose which provides numerous benefits such as improved stamina. It strengthens legs, opens up hips joint, chest; stretches the arms and legs. It develops concentration, balance and groundedness of the body and improves circulation and respiration. It provides strength to the ankles, legs, shoulders and muscles of the back. It tones and strengthens the abdomen. It Improves balance. It energizes and revitalizes the entire body.

Precautions: This asana should not be practiced if you have recent or chronic injury to the hips, knees, back or shoulders. Do it under supervision if you have high blood pressure, heart problems, and neck problems.

Virabhadrasana -II

- Stand in a straight position with feet together.
- Move your legs as far apart as you can while maintaining stability.
- Keep both heels firmly rooted on the ground in line with each other.
- Turn your right foot 90 degrees to the right and left foot about 45 degrees to the right.
- Rotate your torso to the right.
- Bend your right knee.
- Inhaling raise your arms to the sides at shoulder level with palms facing down and fingers straight.
- Inhaling extend your spine and head upward as you turn your head to the right to look over your right hand.

- Hold for three breaths.
- Exhaling bend your right knee so that it is positioned over your right heel, forming a 90-degrees angle.
- Keep shoulders and arms in a straight line.
- Hold for 30 breathes.
- Return to the starting position.
- Repeat to the other side.

Precautions: Do it under supervision if you have high blood pressure, heart problem, neck pain and shoulder problems.

Benefits: Like warrior pose I, this pose also strengthens and stretches the legs, ankles, chest, lungs and shoulders. It also stimulates abdominal organs. It increases therapeutic effects in carpal tunnel syndrome, flat feet, infertility, osteoporosis, and sciatica pain. It increases stamina. It provides strength to lower torso and improves balance. It enhances flexibility on both sides of the body. It expands the chest, encourages deeper breathing and improves coordination and concentration.

Virabhadrasana- III (Balancing Superman)

- Bring the hands onto your hips from Warrior Pose-I.
- Bring your weight forward into your front foot as you gently kick up your back leg.
- Bring the torso forward until it is parallel to the floor.
- Keep the neck relaxed, as if it's the natural extension of the spine.
- Keep you back leg in line with your body.
- Flex the raised foot and keep the muscles of the raised leg actively engaged.
- Bring the arms back along your sides.
- Hold this position for 30-60-90 seconds.
- Repeat on the other side.

Precautions: Not suggested for those with high blood pressure.

Benefits: It is good for thighs, hamstrings, calves, ankles, hips, shoulders and spine. It strengthens ankles, calves, thighs, groins, abdomen, chest, lungs, shoulders, back and neck. It stretches the chest, lungs, shoulders, neck, belly, groins along with that it tones the abdomen. It improves balance and bodily posture. It increases focus and concentration.

Other variations: You can try even advanced variations by bringing the outstretched arms in front or into a reverse Namaste.

PARVATASANA

(Mountain Pose or Downward Facing Dog)

The name of the pose varies in different school of yoga. This posture resemble a mountain or downward facing dog. So, some practitioners call it the mountain pose and some call it Adhomukh Svanasan as well. It is a very important asana and is part of Surya Namaskar as well.

Procedure

- Position your body on the floor with your hands and knees on the ground.
- Set your knees directly below your hips and your hands slightly forward of your shoulders.
- Curl your toes in and spread your fingers out on the ground.
- Exhaling raise your knees and hips upward.
- Push your palms down and press your heels down toward the floor.
- Evenly distribute your weight between your hands and feet.
- Firm your shoulder blades against your back then widen them and draw them toward the tailbone.
- Keep the head between the upper arms or push it down to touch the ground with your upper head.
- Hold for 30-60-180 seconds.
- Then bend your knees to the floor with an exhalation and rest in child's pose.

Variations: To challenge yourself in this position, inhale and raise your right leg to the line of your torso and hold for 30 seconds, keeping the hips in level and pressing through the heel. Release with an exhalation and repeat on the left for the same length of time. Secondly hold your right leg calf/shin bone with your left hand from front side.

Precaution: Practice with supervision if you are suffering from high blood pressure or a heart condition. It should not be attempted if the wrists are injured or pain sensitive.

Benefits: It provides an overall body stretch and thus builds strength throughout the body. It stretches and strengthens the shoulders, hamstrings, calves, arms, and legs. It relieves symptoms of menopause and menstrual discomfort It aids in preventing osteoporosis.

It relieves headache, insomnia, back pain and fatigue. It calms the mind, lifts the spirits and help to reduce fatigue. It relieves stress and mild depression. The blood flow to the brain increases, which improves the efficiency of brain. It also strengthens the immune system and improves digestion. It is best known for rejuvenating the body. It is excellent for high blood pressure, asthma, flat feet, sciatica, sinusitis, lumbar, cervical pains and slip discs.

BAKASANA (Crane Pose)

The two names for this asana come from the Sanskrit words Baka (Crane) and Asana meaning Posture. In all variations, Crane is an arm balancing asana in which hands are planted on the floor, shins rest upon upper arms and feet lift up. It looks a lot harder but it is one of the easiest balancing asana. You can achieve this, once you develop a certain level of upper arm strength.

Procedure

- Start in Mountain Pose with your feet together.
- Sit down low enough (Malasana) and place your hands firmly on the floor, keeping them shoulder distance apart.
- Bend your elbows and rest your knees on armpits.
- Inhaling lift your hips high, engaging core muscles.
- Make sure your gaze is slightly forward of your hands.
- Begin to shift your weight towards your hands lifting your feet off the ground. Stay there and straighten your elbows for the full expression of the pose.
- Hold this pose for 10-30 breaths then lower your feet to the floor and you may do Standing Forward Bend (Uttanasana) as a reverse pose.

Modifications (Easy Variations)

- If you are new to this pose, build strength and prepare for the pose by lifting one foot off the ground at a time, then alternating feet.
- If you are having trouble getting your hips high enough, try the pose with your feet elevated on a block.
- Let your toes touch each other to make it easier.

Advanced Variations

- Parsva Bakasana (Side Crane Pose) in which one thigh rests on the opposite upper arm and the other leg is stacked on top of the first.
- Eka Pada Bakasana/Kakasana (One-Legged Crane/Crow Pose respectively) in which one leg remains in Bakasana while the other extends straight back.
- Padma Bakasana, in which you assume Bakasana position in Padmasana.
- If you are an advanced Practitioner you can drop down from a headstand.
- Once you achieve smooth flow, exhale and thrust your legs up and out back behind, not so much with force but more with lightness as if you are floating up and back. Your feet land behind you and you come into full plank Utthit Chaturanga Asana and continue any sequence you may desire.

Precautions: Do not practice this pose if you have chronic and current wrist pain or carpal tunnel syndrome. Do not try if you are pregnant.

Benefits: Bakasana increases both physical and mental balance, concentration and tranquillity. It strengthens the shoulders, arms, wrists and hands as well as the organs of the abdomen. It strengthens and tones the core muscles, improves a sense of balance. It prepares the body and mind for more difficult arm postures.

VRISCHIKASANA (Scorpion Pose)

Vrischikasana is an inverted backbend pose designed to enhance the strength and flexibility of the practitioner. It is one of the most difficult poses to master. It should only be attempted by advanced practitioners. The pose focuses on arms, solders, back, hips, abdomen and legs. It is effective in toning the whole body.

Procedure

- Begin in the Dolphin Pose (It is similar to the Parvatasana Downward Facing Dog Pose but instead of your body weight being borne by hands and feet; the weight is borne by forearms and feet).

- Maintain shoulder width gap between elbows.

- Keep your forearms parallel and spread the fingers facing forward.

- Inhaling lift your right leg into the air as high as you can. (You are now in the Tri Pada Adho Mukha Svanasana or the Three Legged Downward Facing Dog Pose).

- Slowly push the raised leg backwards, and lift your other leg off the floor as well.

- Balance your entire body weight on your palms, forearms and elbows.
- Center yourself as you strive for balance.
- Arch your back and try to bring your feet as close to your head as possible by bending your knees.
- Concentrate on stabilizing your core muscles in order to maintain your balance.
- Keep your head facing forward with eyes focused on an imaginary point on the floor in front of you.
- Hold this posture for 30 breaths.
- Exhale and slowly come back to the starting position.

Beginner's Tip : You can start practicing perform Scorpion Pose next to a wall, chair, or other support. When you swing your legs up into the air, you can support your legs against the wall. Once you are sure of your balance, slowly bend your knees until you come into the Scorpion Pose.

Preparatory Poses: There are a number of preparatory poses for the Scorpion Pose to get your body ready for demand placed upon it by the Vrischikasana. Some of the poses that will help you to prepare your body for the rigors of Scorpion Pose includes Shirshasana (Headstand), Pincha Mayurasana (Feathered Peacock), Urdhva Dhanurasana (Wheel), Sarvanga Asana (Shoulderstand) and Cobra Pose (Bhujangasana).

Precautions: Since this is an advanced pose, it is recommended that if you have any back injury avoid it. Do not perform this pose if you are suffering from any hip or back problems. Avoid this if you have any history of heart disease, high blood pressure or vertigo problem. Do not attempt this pose until your Yoga trainer or Guru tells you that you are ready for it.

Benefits : The Vrischikasana is a great way to strengthen your torso, back and get rid of stubborn fat from these areas. It energizes, strengthens and harmonized the whole body especially forearm muscles, triceps and shoulder muscles. It helps to build stamina and endurance. This asana stretches the abdomen, hips and thighs. This is an excellent posture for improving flexibility of the spine. It increases blood supply to all parts of the body including the brain. It activates Ajna Chakra and provides balance to all the Chakras. It improves your sense of harmony and tranquility in your mind. Since it takes a long time to master this asana, you will develop self-confidence with continuous practice.

This inverted posture allows blood to rush to the brain cells that improves memory and concentration. It stimulates the hair follicles in the scalp and can be helpful to prevent hair loss. It also helps to release stress that accumulates in the shoulders and the spine. When performed properly under the guidance of guru. It may also be used to treat back problems such as slipped discs and complaints of the upper back. It is especially recommended for Vata disorders as it brings balance and stability.

SIRSASANA (Head Stand)

The name comes from the Sanskrit words Shirsha meaning Head and Asana meaning Posture. Sirsasana is considered as the King of Asana because it is one of the most beneficial Yoga Asana. Since it is considered as one of the advanced asanas, it is highly recommended to practice under supervision of guru. In the Supported Headstand (Salamba Sirsasana), the body is completely inverted and held upright supported by the forearms, while the crown of the head rests lightly on the floor.

Procedure

- Come to your hands and knees with the wrists underneath the shoulders and knees underneath your hips.
- Bring your elbows to the floor holding your arms of one hand with the other hand.
- Interlace your fingers and take it forward so that your palm faces slightly up.
- Place the hair base (upper part of the forehead) on palm.
- Lift your knees and hips up.
- Move your feet in towards head until hips are over the shoulders.
- Raise your one leg up and hold for 30 seconds.
- Drop the raised leg and raise your other leg.
- Hold for 30 seconds.
- Press down your forearm strongly to prevent all your weight coming into your neck and head.
- Once you have a certain level of balance, you can try head stand by raising both legs up.
- Stand perpendicular on your head and try to place your hips, chest and legs in a safe way that your upper back does not form into a bump and your neck is not sunken. Focus on a point in front of you. Breathe in and out quietly and try to get completely still and experience the effects in a meditative calm.
- Hold for 30-60 breaths and with practice you can hold as well as possible for you.
- Exhaling bring your legs down and relax in Balasana (Child Pose).

Preparation : You may do Ardha Sirsasana (Dolphin pose) to increase arms and shoulder strength. Proceed to do Ardha Sirsasana. Interlock your fingers while resting your elbow on the ground. Curl your toes and lift your body up on your toes and elbow. Move your body forward to plank and move back to mountain with elbow stand. Practice 2 sets of 30 -30 movement from front to back. You may hold elbow plank as well. It will strengthen arms and shoulders which is essential for headstand.

Partnering: A partner can assist you with your alignment in this pose. Have your partner stand to one side and look at the major alignment along the side of your body viz. the outer ankle, the center of the hip, the center of the shoulder and the ear hole etc. These points should all be in one line (perpendicular to the floor).

Variations: Beginners should start with Eka Pada Sirsasana.

Advanced Variations
- Bring both legs up at the same time keeping them straight. Interlock your legs to make Peacock position.
- Lower down the same way, holding the pose with the legs spread at 90 degrees.
- Interlock the legs into a Lotus position.
- Release your interlaced fingers and bring the forearms flat on the floor. Lift your head off the floor coming into forearm stand.
- Rest your palm on both sides of your head and assume Sirsasana.
- Place both your hands forward in headstand.

Precautions: The neck is very sensitive and incorrect alignment can cause injuries when you are aligned incorrectly in the Headstand, you can easily get injured. Practice this asana slowly under supervision of guru until you develop comfort and able to go up and down smoothly. Beginners tend to take too much weight on the neck and head. This is potentially dangerous and harmful to your neck and head. So, be careful about it.

Benefits: In Head Stand, you build power and structure in both neck and upper back, while you train your arm muscles and bring better coordination. Likewise, standing with your body upside down in good alignment also has a calming effect on your mental faculties.

The practice of Sirsasana increases the flow of blood to the brain that improve memory and other functions of the cerebrum. It helps to move stored fluids into the body for oxygenation, filtration and elimination of metabolic wastes. It stimulates the pituitary and pineal glands. It strengthens the arms, legs, lungs and spine. It tones the abdominal organs. It improves digestion. It can relieve the symptoms of menopause. This is very useful in keeping up Brahmacharya. It makes you an Urdhvaretas. The seminal energy is transmuted into Ojas Spiritual Shakti. This is also called sex-sublimation. You will not have wet dreams or spermatorrhoea. In Urdhvareta Yogi the seminal energy flows upwards into the brain and get stored as spiritual energy which is absorb for contemplative activity (Dhyana). When you do this Asana, imagine that the seminal energy is being converted into Ojas and it moves through the Chakras in the spinal column, then into the brain for storage.

Sirsasana is really a Blessing and Nectar. Words will fail to adequately describe its beneficial results and effects. In this Asana alone, the brain can draw plenty of Prana and blood. This acts against the force of gravity and draws an abundance of blood from the heart. This leads to natural Pranayama and Samadhi by itself. No other effort is necessary. If you watch the breath, you will notice that it becomes finer and finer. It greatly helps to achieve meditation after Sirsasana. You can

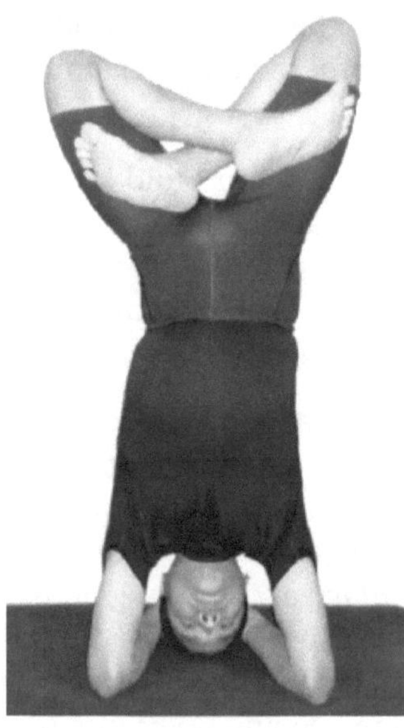

hear Anahata sounds quite distinctly. Young, robust persons should perform this Asana. The advantages that are derived from this Asana are incalculable.

This is a panacea, a cure-all asana for all diseases. It brightens the psychic faculties and awakens Kundalini Shakti. It removes various diseases of the intestines and stomach and improves mental power. This is a powerful blood purifier and tonic for nerves. All diseases of the eyes, nose, head, throat, stomach, urogenital systems, liver, spleen, lungs, renal colic, deafness, gonorrhoea, diabetes, piles, asthma, consumption, syphilis etc. can be managed effectively. It augments the digestive fire (Jatharagni). Many uterine and ovarian diseases are cured. Sterility disappears. facial wrinkles and grey hairs will disappear. According to Yoga Tattva Upanishad, "he who practises this for three hours daily conquers time".

Precautions: It is not recommended to start practice with this posture. Sirsasana is contraindicated in some conditions viz.

high blood pressure, heart condition, glaucoma, detached retina, conjunctivitis, brain diseases, neck, brain, back injury, headache and menstruation. You can practice sirsasana in pregnancy, if you are experienced with this posture. However, if your a beginner, do not practice Sirsasana after you become pregnant.

SHAVASANA/MRITASANA/KAYOTSARGA
(Corpse Pose)

The name comes from the Sanskrit words Shava meaning corpse and Asana meaning posture. Mritasana is another name for this pose. This asana looks very simple to practice but is actually very difficult. To keep the body in a corpse like state is the external position and is not so important. What is most important in the success of this asana is to have the mind focused on relaxing every part of the body. To be able to do this, the body needs to be in a comfortable and soothing position.

The aim of this asana is to reduce any strain and give the muscles complete rest and relaxation that they urgently need. All the muscles cannot be relaxed immediately after being in Shavasana position; therefore one has to deliberately relax each muscle. When you go into this asana, the motor neurons that innervate the skeletal muscles are still firing nerve impulses. As the breath becomes deep, regular and relaxed the nerve impulses slowly begin to drop. The deep and rhythmical movement of breathing in the process leads to deeper relaxation and eventually the nerve impulses are minimized.

Shavasana is perhaps the most important part of yoga practice. The whole body is relaxed on the floor with an awareness of the chest and abdomen rising and falling with each breath. After taking this position, the whole body is scanned for muscular tension of any kind, which is consciously released as it is found, optionally with a small repetitive movement of the area. In addition, it's important to pacify the sense organs. Soften the root of the tongue, the wings of the nose, the channels of the inner ears and the skin of the forehead, especially around the bridge of the nose between the eyebrows. Let the eyes sink to the back of the head, then turn them downward to gaze at the heart. Release your brain to the back of the head. After relaxing the whole body turn the mind to the direction of the breath. Do not allow the mind to control the breath but let it be slow and relaxed. The more the body relaxes, the slower the breath will become. In the final position the whole body is completely relaxed, the breath is very slow and the mind is stable, calm and quiet.

Procedure

- Lie flat on your back.
- Spread the legs keeping them two feet apart, the toes are turned outwards, the heels facing each other.
- Let the toes remain separated.
- Move your arms away from the body, palms turn upward.
- Close your eyes and breathe slowly.
- Receive auto suggestions to relax the whole body.
- Feel the whole body being completely relaxed.
- Now, bring your awareness on your right leg.
- Give auto suggestion to relax your toes. Gently vibrate

your toes and relax them.

- Feeling comfortable, bring your awareness to your soles and relax.
- Now bring your awareness to your heel and gently vibrate it. With auto suggestion to relax, feel the comfort level and leave it.
- Bring your awareness to your ankle giving auto-suggestion to relax. Vibrate it. Feeling comfort let it relax there.
- Bring your awareness to your calf and relax.
- Bring your awareness to knees and relax. Vibrate and feel the comfort.
- Come to your thighs, relax and feel the comfort and then let it be there.
- Bring your awareness to hip and hip joint. Relax, vibrate to feel the comfort.
- Enjoying the comfort as you realize your right leg being totally relaxed from the tip of the toes to the hip and hip joint.
- Similarly relax your left leg from toes to hip joint.

- Now bring your awareness to your torso and relax each and every vertebrae, joints, nerves and muscles from the bottom of spine to the top.
- Feeling comfort gently vibrate the region, enjoy the liberating effects and let them be there.

- Now bring your awareness to the trunk region (abdominal region and chest region).
- With autosuggestion, relax each and every organ of the trunk viz. kidney, adrenal, liver, gallbladder, pancreas, spleen, stomach, small intestine, large intestine, urinary system, lungs, heart and ribs etc.

- Give auto suggestion to relax them.
- Feel the comfort there with deep breath and enjoy the liberation.

- Now bring your awareness to your right hand and relax your right hand starting from your thumbs, fingers, palms, wrists, elbows, arms and shoulders.
- Give auto suggestion to relax and vibrate them to feel the comfort.
- Enjoying the comfort and liberation bring your awareness to your left hand and relax your left hand from thumb to the shoulder.
- Once again bring your awareness to your shoulders of both hands and with auto suggestion to relax, bring gentle movements to feel the comfort.
- Now realize that your whole body is liberated up to the shoulders from the tips of the toes.

- Bring your awareness to your neck and throat and relax.
- Feeling comfort gently turn your head right to left and come to the centre.
- Now bring awareness to face and relax each and every parts of it with autosuggestion to relax viz. your chin, mouth, nose, cheeks, ears, eyes including eyeballs, eyelids, eyebrows, forehead, and upper head as well as the back of the head. Enjoy the comfort.

- Now bring your awareness once again to the whole body to realize total liberation.
- Breathe gently in and out. Let the diaphragm be relaxed.
- Feel that the body becoming lighter and lighter as if it is floating in space.

- Feel nothing but a centre of consciousness moving in space.
- This is our eternal nature. Enjoy the Divine within.

Duration: It should be practiced whenever the body becomes tired, before and after asanas. Stay in this position for 5 minutes for every 30 minutes of intensive yoga practice. It may also be practiced separately during the day, when needed, after a hard day's work or before going to sleep.

Releasing: In this period, activation of anabolic state of metabolism accelerates maintenance and repairing. To come back to active conscious state requires the body to switch back to the highly active catabolic state of metabolism therefore it should be reintroduced sensitively as the two states do not coexist well.

Gently vibrate your toes and fingers. Bring both your legs together. Take left turn gently with deep exhalation. Keep your knees folded slightly. Place both your hand as a pillow and inhale 3 deep breaths. Exhaling sit up pressing your hands against the floor and lifting your torso first and then lastly your head.

Sit for a few seconds. Rub your palms to create warmness in your palms. Place your palm on your eyes. Gently massage your eyebrows and rub your palms on your face in down to up motion, then on the whole body. Rub your palms once again to make it warm. Make cups of palms and cover your eyes. Open your eyes with blinking within the cup of your palms. Slowly bring your hands down.

Tips To Achieve Savasana: Mat should not be too soft as this will induce sleep. If the ground is slanted then let the head be lower, this prevents a drop in blood circulation to the brain and other vital organs. For those with lower back pain a light cushion can be placed under the lower back. Also, some may need a small cushion under their knees also. If you are prone to falling asleep then keep the legs a little closer together. This will give a mild moola bandha which will prevent sleep. If it is consistently difficult for you to relax then try a sequence of tensing and then relaxing the muscles. First the legs, then the pelvis, lower back and abdomen, followed by the chest and upper back then arms the facial muscles. Finish by tensing the whole body and then relaxing.

Precautions: Comfort is essential in this asana. Do not wear tight fitting clothing while practicing savasana. If you have back injury or discomfort, do this pose keeping the knees bent and your feet on the floor, hip distance apart; either bind the thighs parallel to each other with a strap (taking care not to position the heels too close to the buttocks) or support the bent knees on a booster. Raise your head and chest on a booster in pregnancy to do savasana. Avoid going to sleep as this will prevent the decrease in nerve impulses as well as the deep relaxation. Keep the spine in a straight line. Avoid moving the body parts during savasana as even the slightest movement will use many muscles and increase the nerve impulses. If thoughts arise, do not stress about them but let them pass. Keep the eyes closed throughout.

Benefits: Shavasana combines asana and meditation. It gives rest not only for the body but also the mind and soul. Relaxation is a very important factor in muscular exercises. During intense muscular activity, the metabolism is increased. Metabolism is the Anabolic and Catabolic changes that take place in the body. Anabolic changes are constructive and catabolic changes are destructive. During metabolism all the muscular tissues are supplied with fresh oxygenated blood or plasma through capillary oozing and carbon dioxide is taken back through the veins to the right auricle of the heart. This is termed tissue-respiration. Just as interchanges of oxygen and carbon dioxide takes place in the lungs, interchanges of carbon dioxide and oxygen takes place in the tissues also. Mark the wonderful creation and working of the internal mechanism of the body! How marvelous is the machinery! Thank God for this wonderful mechanism of the body. Enter into silence. The whole mystery of creation will be revealed unto you through His Grace.

After the exertions, the practices of Shavasana allows the body a chance to regroup and reset itself. Even the deepest muscles will have the opportunity to let go and shed their regular habits, if only for a few minutes. Along with numerous Physiological benefits, it decreases in heart rates, respiration, blood pressure, muscle tensions, in metabolism, and oxygen consumption. It reduces anxiety, infrequency of panic attacks, increase energy levels and general productivity. Enhances concentration, improve memory power, increase focus, decrease fatigue, coupled with deeper and sound sleep as well as improve self-confidence. It gives the nervous system a chance to integrate neuromuscular information before it is forced once again to deal with all the unexpected stress factors inherent at present in today's Lifestyles.

Practitioner's awareness is turned inwards and purifies the sensory distractions. In a state of sensory withdrawal it becomes easier to be aware of the breath and of the state of the mind itself. Though not the best position for prolonged meditative contemplation; it helps to achieve silence necessary to achieve deeper state of meditation. Normally Shavasana is the beginning of deeper, meditative Yogic practices.

It leads to a relaxed mind which allows you to see and relate to the world in a more realistic light, be more efficient in work and give greater happiness to life. It integrates the feeling of relaxation into the conscious and super conscious awareness. It removes disturbing thoughts and tensions and relieves stress and fatigue of the body and mind so that they get rejuvenated. It improves functioning of the brain and mind. It relaxes the muscles which lead to a decrease in the demand for blood and oxygen, giving the circulatory and respiratory systems a break. When the body is relaxed the awareness of the mind increases and this leads to the development of Pratyahara. According to studies twenty minutes of Shavasana helps to produce almost same amount of melatonin that is produced in two hours of sleep thus it reduces the requirement of sleep. It helps to cure insomnia as well. Last but not the least, this is one of the most useful processes for people with stress related diseases viz. headache, migraine, fatigue, high blood pressure, heart diseases, stress, anxiety and insomnia etc.

Benefits for Women: Shavasana is useful for everyone and helps to improve the functioning of every systems of the body but there are some benefits especially for women. It is very useful during menstruation to control irritation, fatigue, tiredness, anger and stress as it provides deep rest and relaxation to the muscles as well to the mind. Savasana helps to rebalance the irregularities in the menstrual cycle which are often indicative of a larger problem. Shavasana can also give relief to any lower back or pelvic pain. During pregnancy it is a great practice to do at any time of the day, especially if feeling tired or emotional. It is greatly useful to control the manifestation of menopausal symptoms; emotional disturbances, stress, anger, depression, frustrations, redirecting the energy and provides emotional bliss, calm and peace.

SURYA NAMASKAR

(Complete Yogic Exercise for Better Fitness)

Surya Namaskar is a Sanskrit word which means obeisance or prostrations (Namaskar) to the Sun (Surya). It has been around for thousands of years and has withstood the test of time.

History of Surya Namaskar

The Sun Salutation (Surya Namaskar) became central to our modern practice in the early 20th century; however, it is rooted further back in time. New research by Chris Tompkins discovered the series of movements in Tantra tradition (450–1200 CE). The Pasupats incorporated linked poses inspired by the sacred dance tradition described in the commentary on the Indian arts called the Natya Shastra.

Tantra integrated Surya Namaskar into a larger cycle of everyday rituals performed by householder. We find variant chants for Surya Namaskar in the Vedas (c. 1500 BCE). Daily sun worship was meant to fortify the body and mind for a householder's affairs.

How Surya Namaskar was re-integrated into Hatha yoga in the early 20th century is told in Mark Singleton's revolutionary book on modern yoga history, Yoga Body (2010). He tells us that, in the mid-1930s, "Suryanamaskar was not yet considered a part of Yogasana."

Classic Surya Namaskar is a rite of sun worship. It includes 12 points of prostration, each with its own pose and mantra connected to the 12 houses (or dasas) of the sun. The sun salutation is a nitya vidhi practice (nitya, "eternal, daily, obligatory," and vidhi). Hence, it is meant to be practiced every morning before or as the sun rises. Though it was a householder practice, the Indian epic, which gained centrality in the tradition as early as 400 BCE granted the sun salutation magical powers. In the epic poem, the Ramayana, the story of the Rama's fight to reclaim his wife, Sita, the Aditya Hridayam form of Surya Namaskara is taught to Lord Rama by the sage, Agastya, before his fight with Ravana (his wife's kidnapper). It is described in the Yuddha Khanda section of the tale.

Modern Surya Namaskar

- Samarth Ramdas (1608-1681) respected Guru of the great Marathi King Shivaji, developed a muscular style Sun prostration to train troupes in defending against the Muslim invasion.

- Sri Bhawanrao Pant Pratinidhi, the Raja of Aundh (1868-1951,) a small state in Maharashtra, modifies Ramdas's Surya Namaskar for fitness and health and publishes a book on Surya Namaskar in Marathi in 1908, triggering a spreading of the practice throughout his state and eventually, all of India. He introduced it into schools and encouraged ordinary men to be physically fit by performing surya namaskar every day. Some Western scholars classify surya namaskar as a modern physical exercise invented by Raja of Aundh.

- In 1929 the Rajah published Surya Namaskars for Health, Efficiency & Longevity in English and other related publications followed. This begins the spread of Surya Namaskar on a global level. It develops into the world's most famous "yoga" exercise as other teachers of hatha yoga within India develop their own variations.

- In the modern movements of the Sun Salutation practice, popularized in books by Swami Sivananda beginning in the 1920s, may be centuries or millennia old.

- Krishnamacharya, the guru of Iyengar and K. Pattabhi Jois, was one among many prominent teachers who were using the sun salutation in their yoga routines in the 1930s, but he changed the form to the one best-known today. It comes to the modern world through Jois' Ashtanga Vinyasa yoga and integrates the familiar danda ("stick") movements (updog, downdog, plank and chaturanga). Krishnamacharya learned these dandas from Indian wrestling and taught them to Jois and others. Jois made them world-famous through his international teaching of Ashtanaga Vinyasa yoga which began in 1975 with a teaching trip to Encinitas, California. Today's creative vinyasa flows that use the dandas, Warrior One, and other familiar movements ending in Tadasana (the simple standing pose), can be traced back to Jois' Ashtanga style. He incubated the systems of poses he learned from Krishnamacharya (making only small changes) for over 40 years before beginning to teach them outside India. Krishnamacharya detailed these Surya-Namaskar-based vinyasas in his books Yogasanagalu (1941) and Yoga Makaranda (1934).

- In the 1980s, the Ashtanga teacher, Tim Miller, and the Iyengar teacher, Roger Cole, working in Southern California, began mixing and matching Jois' Surya Namaskar elements and this began the modern Vinyasa yoga revolution.

Why to Practice Surya Namaskara?

It is considered the best exercise for this human body. Surya Namaskar consists of important Yoga asanas and Pranayama. The advantages of Pranayama are skilfully incorporated in Surya Namaskar. The Mantras chanted in the process are very useful as well. On the one side, practicing Surya Namaskar is the perfect beginning to a great day ahead and on the other side ending the day with surya namaskara followed yogic relaxation called Savasana and Yoga Nidra is fantastic for many reasons. Often, after a hard day's work, we would just flop down on the couch apparently relaxing our body but it is NOT so. The stagnant energies remain locked up and the organs remain de-oxygenated to a large extent. It has a deep effect in detoxifying the organs through oxygenation and has a deeper relaxing effect. Surya Namaskar is the best way to burn the calories and reduce weight. It is often recommended for obesity. Sun salutation is an appreciated exercise among people of all ages from kids to old age people.

Procedure to Practice Surya Namaskar

Surya Namaskar or Sun Salutation is a set of 12 steps consisting of 7 or 8 asanas (Some teacher practice with Parvatasana insted of Plank Pose in step 5); one asana following another, in a fixed, cyclic order to ensure improvement and good health in one's digestion, agility, rejuvenation, beauty and longevity. These alternating backward and forward bending postures flex and stretch the spinal column through their maximum range giving a profound stretch to the whole body.

Step 1: Namaskar Asana/ Pranamasana (Prayer Pose)

Breathe: Exhale
Concentration: Anahata Chakra
Mantra: OM Mitraya Namah
(ॐ मित्राय नमः)

Procedure

- Stand straight with chest out and spine erect, heels together and toes slightly going out, looking forward with palms together in front of the chest.

- Distribute your weight evenly over both feet and slowly establish a steady rhythm of your breath.

- Once you start doing the routine, you spend about one second in this pose, and the others that follows. You may take this a little slower if you are weak or aged, or if you are new to the routine.

Benefits: This asana helps you in finding balance in your body and improve our posture.

Step 2: Hasta Uttanasana/Urdhva Hastasana (Upward Hand Pose)

Breathe: Inhale
Concentration: Vishuddhi Chakra
Mantra: OM Ravaya Namah (ॐ रवये नमः)

Procedure

- While inhaling, raise your arms up in the air keeping the palms together.

- Arch your body backwards as far as you can go, forming a crescent -like curve from your feet to the hands.

- Hold the breath to a comfort level.

Benefits: As you inhale and stretch your body, this posture helps you to increase the capacity of your lungs and lets you breathe in full. This posture helps retain the flexibility of the spine.

Step 3: Pad Hastasana/Padangusthasana (Standing Forward Bend Pose)

Breathe: Exhale
Concentration: Swadhisthana Chakra
Mantra: OM Suryaya Namah (ॐ सूर्याय नमः)

Procedure

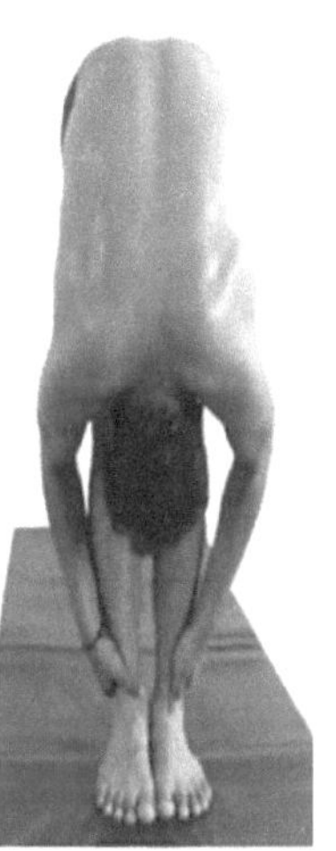

- While exhaling, bring your hands down to your feet bending forward at the waist, while keeping the legs as straight as possible.

- Keep your legs firmly engaged without loosening them even for a moment.

- In the beginning, you may not be able to touch your feet or touch your nose to the knees.

- Try to bend as much as possible without bending in knees.

- The best position is to bring the hands flat to the mat on either side of your feet, while keeping the head as close to the knees as you can.

Benefits: Regular practice would bring in more flexibility and in achieving the complete posture of this asana. The most important aspect of this pose is that it squeezes the stomach and assists in digestion to extract many vitamins and nutrients in one's food, which helps to turn it into blood. It also loosens any fat that has accumulated there. This posture is very good for your back and helps in stretching and opening your hamstrings. If you have back pain already you may bend your knee while going down so that initially you'll be able to protect you back.

Step 4: Ashwasanchalan Asana (Equestrian or High Lunge Pose)

Breathe: Inhale
Concentration: Ajna Chakra
Mantra: Om Bhanave Namah (ॐ भानवे नमः)

Procedure

- While inhaling, put your hands on the mat and lower your hips and stretch your right leg back as far as you can.

- Keep Right Leg Straight and off the mat resting on the toes. (You can touch the mat with your knee with foot flat if needed.)

- The left leg is bent at 90 degrees from the knee keeping the thigh parallel to the floor.

- Keep your hands flat on the mat, your arms straight.

- Look upwards, giving a nice stretch to your neck.

Benefits: This posture helps you to stretch the hamstrings as well as the hip joints. It helps ensure flexibility of the spinal cord and immunity from diseases in the back, side, leg muscles and ligaments.

Step 5: Utthita Chaturdand Asana (Plank Pose)

Breathe: Exhale
Concentration: Manipura Chakra
Mantra: Om Khagaya Namah (ॐ खगाय नमः)

Procedure

- Exhale slowly and take the left leg back.
- While going in Plank bring your body parallel to the mat.
- Keep your palms flat on the mat keeping them shoulder-width apart and your feet at hip distance.
- Make sure your stomach is in and tight; navel pulled in towards the spinal cord.

Benefits: This posture is good to improve stamina and strength in your arms. It is great for your abdomen as you make it tight to hold this position.

Step 6: Ashtanganaman Asana (Eight Limbs Pose)

Breathe: Suspend or hold
Concentration: Manipura Chakra

Mantra: Om Pushne Namah (ॐ पुष्णेय नमः)

Procedure

- While holding your breath, bend both hands from the elbows and touch the mat with your knees, chest and forehead.

- Keep both elbows close to the chest.

- The forehead, chest, both palms, toes and knees should touch the mat, rest of the body not touching the mat.

- Since only eight parts rest on the ground, it is called Ashtanga position.

Benefits: This is again a challenging posture for your abdomen and helps in improving your stamina.

Step 7: Bhujangasana (Cobra Pose)

Breathe: Inhale
Concentration: Swadhisthana Chakra
Mantra: Om Hiranyagarbhaya Namah (ॐ हिरण्य गर्भाय नमः)

Procedure:

- Inhale and straighten the elbows.
- Stretch your shoulders back, opening up the chest nicely (stretching it out as much as possible) while looking up.
- Make sure your shoulders are not hunched towards the ears.
- Press the waist downwards keeping your navel on the mat.
- Keep the knees and toes on the mat.
- Look up and stretch your throat.
- Keep your heel and toes together while pointing your toes out.

Benefits: Bhujangasana is very good for your lower back and also opens up your shoulders and chest, thus improving your posture at the same time.

Step 8: Parvatasana/ Adhomukh Shwanasan (Mountain Pose / Down Dog Pose)

Breathe: Exhale

Concentration: Vishuddhi Chakra

Mantra: Om Marichaye Namah (ॐ मरीचये नमः)

Procedure

- Exhale slowly and curl your toes in.
- Raise your waist upwards, while your palms and feet are firm and flat on the mat.
- Make sure your heels touch the mat and are not in the air.
- Tilt your chin down to press the throat.
- Push the body backwards.
- Do not move the palms on the mat.

Benefits: This is an excellent posture to improve flexibility in your legs by stretching the hamstrings and it also gives a good stretch to your back.

Step 9: Ashwa Sanchalanasana
(High Lunge / Equestrian Pose)

Breathe: Inhale
Concentration: Ajna Chakra
Mantra: Om Aditya Namah (ॐ आदित्याय नमः)

Procedure

- While inhaling, bring your right leg forward between both hands.

- Let the foot of left leg rest on the toes keeping the knee in the air or touching the ground.

- Bend your right leg with 90 degrees angle keeping your thigh parallel to the mat.

- Keep your hands flat on the mat, your arms straight.

- Arch your head upward and back so you are looking at the ceiling or sky.

Benefits: This posture helps you to stretch the hamstrings as well as the hip joints. It helps ensure flexibility of the spinal cord and immunity from diseases in the back, side, leg muscles and ligaments.

Step 10: Pad Hastasana / Padangusthasana (Standing Forward Bend Pose)

Breathe: Exhale
Concentration: Swadhisthana Chakra
Mantra: Om Savitre Namah (ॐ सवित्रये नमः)

Procedure

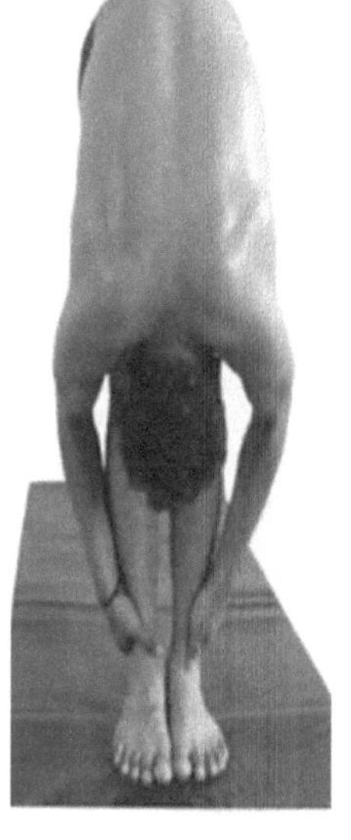

- Exhale and bring the left leg forwards and place it beside the right.

- Keep your palms touching the mat, fingers pointing forward, thumbs at 90 degree angle and legs straight.

- Place both your legs between both arms.

- Try to touch the forehead to the knees.

- Relax the neck.

Benefits: Regular practice would bring in more flexibility and in achieving the complete posture of this asana. The most important aspect of this pose is that it squeezes the stomach and assists in digestion to extract many vitamins and nutrients in one's food, which helps to turn it into blood. It also loosens any fat that has accumulated there. This posture is very good for your back and helps in stretching and opening your hamstrings. If you have back pain already you may bend your knee while going down so that initially you'll be able to protect you back.

Step 11: Hasta Uttanasana / Urdhva Hastasana (Raised Arms Pose)

Breathe: Inhale
Concentration: Vishuddhi Chakra
Mantra: Om Arkaya Namah (ॐ अर्काय नमः)

Procedure

- While inhaling, raise your arms up in the air keeping the hands together.

- Arch your back as far as you can.

- Feel a renewed sense of energy as you draw your arms over head into Urdhva Hastasana.

Benefits: As you inhale and stretch your body, this posture helps you to increase the capacity of your lungs and lets you breathe in full. This posture helps retain the flexibility of the spine.

Step 12: Namaskar Asana / Pranamasana (Prayer pose)

Breathe: Exhale
Concentration: Anahata Chakra

Mantra: Om Bhaskaraya Namah (ॐ भास्कराय नमः)

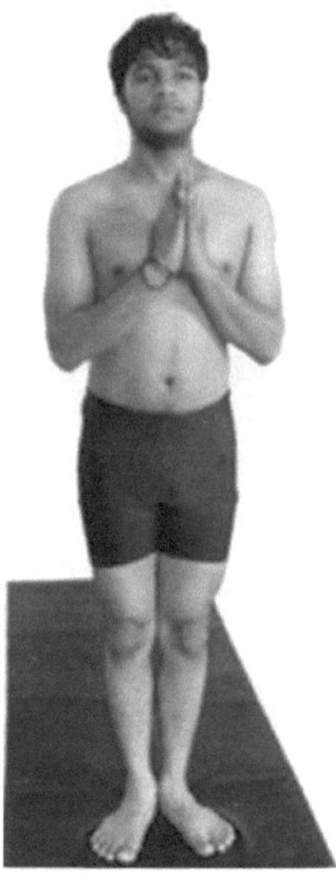

Procedure

- Exhaling bring your hands down to place them in front of your chest in Namaskar Mudra, your initial pose.

- Remain here for a few breaths, feeling the movement of energy through your body, or continue on to your next round.

Benefits: This asana helps you in finding balance in your body and improve our posture.

Note: This is only a half round, you need to complete the sequence, switching left to right and right to left to complete a full round. The transition from posture to posture is facilitated by either an inhalation or an exhalation. As you move through the sequence, monitor your breath closely. Slow your pace or stop and rest entirely if during them you become breathless. Always breathe through your nose, not your mouth - nasal breathing filters and warms incoming air and slows your breathing down, thereby lending the sequence a meditative quality and reducing the risk of hyperventilation.

You may do each posture separately the first time you do this to familiarize yourself with each one. Then begin to do it from one posture to the other, through all postures. Do it as a cycle of 108 Surya Namaskars, or even more, if you can. You will certainly notice the difference in your health, weight, flexibility, energy level, and even overall attitude.

Some more important Benefits of Sury Namaskara Practice

Surya Namaskar is a holistic practice. It not only brings physical and mental health but also helps to achieve emotional and spiritual health. It renders the body suppleness and strength coupled with mental peace. It removes psychosomatic tensions, ensuring a calm mind. It increases concentration power and your entire physiology is invigorated.

It improves breathing patterns and increases oxygen intake and accelerates blood circulation. It is an ideal warm-up and conditioning exercises for the entire body and mind. It prepares you to encounter the challenges of the competitive era. The entire muscular system becomes stronger that includes the muscles of the eyes, neck, shoulders, arms, hips and legs. All the joints get loosened and become stronger. The

Endocrine system is balanced and harmonized. The heart and the lungs get energized due to controlled breathing. Blood circulation improves to all organs and parts of the body. The spine gets good stretching that will make it supple. Spinal pains and aches are relieved. Spinal cord disorders and deviations are corrected. It stimulates all nerves and improves the health of nervous system. The abdominal exercises relieve the abdominal viscera by stretching and contracting movements of the abdominal area. It stimulates the peristalsis and thereby helps in regulating bowel functioning. It reduces abdominal flab. The fat in other parts of the body like thighs, waist, abdomen and arms is reduced.

You can cure ailments like sciatica, diabetes, blood pressure, mental tension, backache and indigestion among others. It tones up the organs and limbs. The limbs become symmetrical while the internal vital organs become more functional. It improves digestion, absorption and assimilation of nutrition out of food consumed. It facilitates the excretion of the digestive and metabolic waste. It works as yogic cardio that increases metabolic rate by increasing heart and respiration rate as a result it reduces body fat. It improves strength, stamina, stability, efficiency with improvement in posture. It is relaxing and rejuvenating.

KEY POINTS

Success depends on commitment and regularity. An everyday practice would be the best. If possible, don't skip more than a couple of days in a row or you might end up back to square one. Start your practice slowly with 4 - 5 rounds to gradually build up your stamina to 108 rounds. You can pace the sequence briskly to generate heat and cleanse the body and mind or more moderately to create a moving meditation.

Precautions

All the Asanas should be in sync with your breath. If you get breathless while doing Surya Namaskar take rest till your breathing gets normal. It is not suggested for patients of Hernia. If you have back pain, don't do forward bending instead come down 90 degrees (forming 90 degree angle with your waist and hips) and keep your hands on your knees. To transit into the next posture, bend your knees and sit in a squat and then take your leg back. For people with High Blood Pressure, the Sun Salutation should be carried out in slow pace accompanied with deep breathing. Pregnant women should not practice this after third month of pregnancy. Women should avoid practicing Surya Namaskar during their menstrual cycle or do it less aggressively and as per the strength in them during those days.

Secret : 4

SCIENCE OF BANDHAS

Bandha is Sanskrit word which means 'to lock or tighten'. The bandha is a sustained contraction of a group of muscles that assists the practitioner not only in retaining an asana but also in moving in and out of it. In Bandhas, the breath is locked and concentrated in a particular area of the body. This locking of life force has a lot of beneficial effects.

Energy or Life force is keeping us alive. It regulates the functions of our body and mind. Life force has to flow through our body and provide a certain amount of energy to each of our cells. Our unhealthy diet, lifestyles, and negative thinking disturbs this flow. Irregularity in this flow or pattern leads to various ailments. Certain parts of our body get either too much or too less energy. The energy may not be reachable in some places and at other parts there might be stagnation of energy. Such imbalances lead to headaches, backaches, constipation, sexual disorders, stomach ailments or any other disorder depending upon imbalances. Besides Pranayama, Bandha is another yogic practice to regulate this life force. Bandhas help in massaging the internal organs and removal of stagnant blood. The practice of Bandhas regulates the nervous system, delays aging, increases vitality and leads to spiritual development. Bandhas help to release the psychic knots and opens the door to spiritual successes. According to yoga philosophy, there are three bandhas; namely Moola, Uddiyana, Jalandar which are considered as internal body locks.

Precautions

Bandhas should be done with care and some precautions. You must listen to your body during the practice and stop at any indication of discomfort. Patience and practice will lead to wonderful and blissful results. Adults suffering from high blood pressure, peptic and duodenal ulcers or heart ailments should not practice Bandhas. Pregnant women should practice only Jalandhara and Moola Bandhas.

MOOLA BANDHA (ROOT LOCK OR ANUS LOCK)

Moola Bandha is a Sanskrit compound term: Moola and Bandha. Moola denotes root, base, beginning, foundation, origin, basis or source. Bandha denotes bondage, posture, joining together and catching hold. Moola Bandha got first literary mention in oldest Jain canon Acharanga Sutra. - BKS Iyengar's book Light on Yoga (1976: p.525) defines

In Moola Bandha muscles from the anus to the navel is contracted and lifted up towards the spine. The actual muscle contracted in this process is neither the sphincter muscle nor the muscle which helps in cessation of urination, but the muscle equidistant between the two.

Moola Bandha Method

- Sit comfortably in Vajrasana or Padmasana (cross legged) with knees touching the floor.

- Place palms on knees.

- Inhale deeply, filling your lungs. Hold your breath and contract muscles of the perineum/cervix area by drawing them upwards.

- Hold the lock as long as comfortable. Feel the tightening of your muscles.

- Release contraction and exhale slowly.

- Repeat this 10 times and gradually increase to 30.

- Moola Bandha may also be done in conjunction with Chin Lock as well.

Benefits

Moola Bandha has many benefits. It helps in managing problems of sexual organs, constipation and hemorrhoids (piles). It tones the pelvic area. It also strengthens the sphincter muscles of the anus and stimulates the intestinal peristalsis. Spiritually- It is helpful in awakening Kundalini. Moola Bandha helps the Apana Vayu (Prana in the lower abdomen whose course is downward) to flow up to unite with Prana Vayu, which has its seat within the region of the chest.

UDDIYANA BANDHA (ABDOMINAL LOCK)

Uddiyana bandha comes from Sanskrit word. It is the abdominal lock employed in Hatha Yoga. It involves pulling the abdomen in and up under the rib cage while holding the breath, after exhaling all the air out and then releasing the abdomen after a pause. Uddiyana bandha, as classically described, is to be performed after the complete exhalation (Rechaka) with external retention (Kumbhaka). Exhalation facilitates the navel area, abdominal muscles to move inward toward the spine because the organs of the upper abdomen are drawn upward and out of the way by the lifting of the diaphragm. This is the standard and classical Uddiyana Bandha.

Uddiyana Bandha Method

The Uddiyana Bandha, often described by bringing the navel close to the spine, is a contraction of the muscles of the lower abdominal area.

Procedure

- Sit in a meditative pose. (Beginners can stand and lean forward keeping the spine straight.)

- Exhale the air drawing the diaphragm upward so that the front of the abdomen can move toward the spine as the breath is exhaled.

- Hold the breath out in external retention (Bahya Kumbhaka).

- Retain the Bahya Kumbhaka with extension and with Moola Bandha in order to increase the effect.

- Release the Bandha before there is a strong feeling to gasp air, letting the navel come back to normal position and allowing the diaphragm to come down, keeping the back and torso straight.

- Let the breath come back to normal and repeat as above.

- Uddiyana Bandha can be mastered in a couple of weeks if practiced daily.

Benefits

Uddiyana is used in Kunjal, Nauli Kriya, Agnisara, Tri-Bandha, Advanced Mudras, Pranayama, Meditation and Yoga Asanas (especially in forward bends). It tones the abdomen. It increases the gastric fire and stimulate the entire Manipura Chakra which improves digestion, absorbtion, assimilation and immunization. It opens blockages in the Manipura Chakra and thus connects the Water centre (Swadhisthana Chakra) with the Air centre (Anahata Chakra). It often occurs spontaneously in those whose natural vital energies are active (have not become repressed). It is a great purifier of the entire abdomen.

It is considered the most important bandha as it supports our breathing and encourages the development of strong core muscles.

JALANDHARA BANDHA (CHIN LOCK)

Jalandhara Bandha is a Sanskrit word. Jala means web or net and dhara means holding. Jalandhara bandha is the chin Bandha described and employed in Hatha Yoga.

Method

It is performed by dropping the head slightly so that the chin is tucked close to the collarbone and the tongue pushes up against the palate in the mouth. Jalandhara Bandha is good to practice in all the yoga postures except when the head is turned during twisting movements and backbends.

Procedure

- Sit comfortably in any meditative posture.

- Place your palms on knees.

- Inhale deeply, filling your lungs. Retain and hold your breath inside.

- Now keeping your back straight, tilt your head forward, so that the chin touches the notch between the collar bones. Keep the chin tightly pressed to create the lock.

- Straighten the arms, so that the arms too are tightened.

- Hold the lock as long as you are comfortable. Feel the pressure of air and the flow of blood in your chest.

- Then relax the shoulders, bend the arms, release the chin lock, slowly raise the head and exhale.

- Never exhale or inhale during the chin lock. Do so only after release of lock and with head upright.

- Practice 5 rounds with breath retained inside (after inhalation with lungs filled) and then 5 rounds with breath retained outside (after exhalation with lungs empty)

Benefits of Jalandhara Bandha

Jalandhara Bandha has many benefits. It helps in managing throat problems, excess mucus and thyroid imbalance. It also improves the quality of voice and stammering. It helps in management of anger and stress. It helps to achieve spiritual experience by stimulating the Vishuddhi Chakra.

Secret : 5

SCIENCE OF MUDRAS

The Mudra is made of two words. First one is 'MUDA' and second one is 'DRA'. In Sanskrit, 'muda' means happiness and 'dra' means drawing. It means 'drawing happiness'; and this is the literal meaning of Mudra. In other word Mudra means gesture. So we can conclude that the Mudra means the gesture that draws happiness or something good is called Mudra in yoga practice.

Since time immemorial, yogis have been doing sadhana with profound knowledge (Jnana) and contributing in the process of human civilization in the whole world. Our learned ancient sages proclaimed that knowledge is the only path to attain salvation. They observed, perused and studied Mother Nature and dedicated priceless gems of knowledge in the form of Vedas, Upanishads and Darshanas for the benefit and welfare of all living beings. Science of Mudra is one of the branches of the study given by them for the greater good of humanity.

Types of Mudra

Since Mudra is part of Yoga, they are called 'Yoga Mudras'. Nerves and energy centres are creating energy that is flowing in the inner and outer parts of the human body. This lively vital energy can enter back into the body and optimize the whole system when we practice Yoga Mudra. Mudras done using hands are called Hasta Mudra. Hasta Mudra can be practiced individually or as a series of hand gestures flowing one into the next.

While practicing yoga Mudra, each Mudra should be felt like an offering to the Divine. This naturally calms the mind. The hands express our thoughts and feelings. We see this in communication with one another. The hands move to further communicate the feeling. The hands also move reflecting the state of mind even when one isn't speaking. For example, when one is nervous, the fingers often fidget or when one is upset the hands normally begin to clutch. If anger intensifies the hand becomes a fist that is used to attack. The opposite of such intense negative emotion are feelings of caring, loving emotions. For example, when we meet one another we either greet with Anjali mudra, hands placed together at the heart level, or with a handshake.

From ancient times, the placement of hands during meditation has been practiced. The photos or Murtis (statues) of all deities have their hands in a precise gesture. From this hand gesture, one can understand the aspect of that Divine that is being represented.

Fundamental Basis of Mudra Science

The universe is made of 5 Elements - Fire, Air, Space, Earth and Water. Similarly, the body is made of 5 elements – Earth, Water, Fire, Air and Space. When these 5 Elements are not in balance we get various physical and psychological ailments. The energy from the body radiates out mainly through the tip of the nose, lips, fingertips and toes. When the thumb is in contact with the other fingers, energy is directed back to vitalize various parts of our body which are related with that particular Mudra. This is called a circuit bypass.

We must ensure balance among the 5 elements to stay healthy. Electromagnetic waves are sent to our brain when we join any one of the tips of fingers with our thumb. This energy will reach the brain and incite the nerve centres which will make this energy reach different organs of the body to activate them in a right manner.

Connection between 5 Fingers and 5 Elements (Tatwas)

5 Elements	5 Fingers	Attributes	5 Sense	Chakra
Aakash (Space)	Middle Finger	Sound	Ear	Visuddhi, Aagna, Sahasrara
Vayu (Wind)	Index Finger	Sound + Touch	Skin	Anahat
Agni (Fire)	Thumb	Sound + Touch + Form	Eye	Manipura
Jal (Water)	Little Finger	Sound + Touch + Form +Taste	Tongue	Swadhisthan
Prithivi (Earth)	Ring Finger	Sound + Touch + Form +Taste + Smell	Nose	Muladhar

The Fire element is the most important one and when this Fire element goes weak, various ailments enters the body and death sets in when the Fire element dies. Joining the Fire element (thumb) with other elements (other fingers) help to vitalize the other elements also. Thumb gives basic foundation to other fingers on the hand to make the body healthy. Fire element helps other elements to keep them in right proportion. The way fingers connect with each other have the potential to increase the pranic flow in body.

Influences of Fire Element on other Elements

i.   When the tip of the thumb joins the tip of other fingers, respective tatvas get balanced in the body.

ii.   When the tip of the thumb joins the base of other fingers, respective tatvas get increased in the body.

iii. When the tip of the fingers are brought to the base of the thumb, respective tatvas get decreased in the body.

1. Gyan Mudra (Mudra of Knowledge)

This is the mudra, most people are familiar with. As it is a Mudra of knowledge, it enhances knowledge. The tip of the thumb represents the centres of Pituitary and Pineal glands. When we press these centres by index finger the two glands get activated and start working actively.

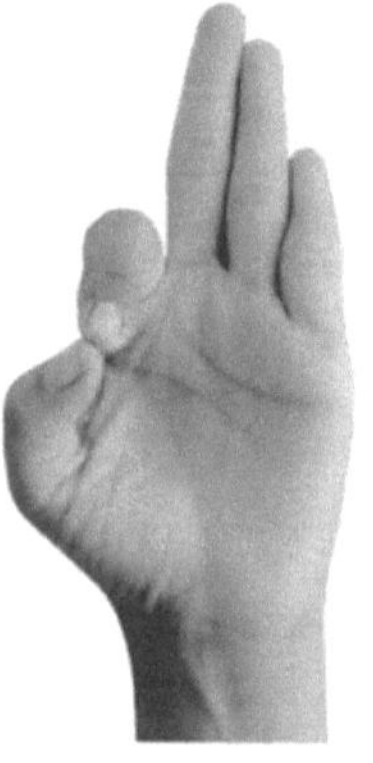

Method: Join the tips of the thumb and Index finger, keeping the other three fingers stretched out.

Time duration: This can be done any time and at any place. There is no time limit for practicing this Mudra. You can practice for longer period also.

Benefits: Great thinkers such as Buddha, Mahavir, Jesus and Guru Nanak are generally depicted in this Mudra. Its practice ensures mental peace, concentration and improves spiritual development. This Mudra energizes Pituitary and Pineal glands; increases memory power and sharpens the brain. It enhances concentration and decision making capacity. It cures Insomnia and mental disorders; and dissipates tension, depression and drowsiness. This is good for people having frequent headaches and sleeplessness. If we practice it regularly, it will cure all psychological disorders like mental hysteria and anger. This is a must for those who aspire to develop telepathy or wish to acquire extrasensory abilities. Stubborn nature, fickle mindedness, short temper will not be found in the dictionary of Yoga-sadhakas who practice Gyan Mudra; instead life will become blissful.

2. Vayu Mudra (Mudra of Air)

This mudra harmonizes all 5 upa-pranas: Naga (belching), Kurma (blinking), Krikala (sneezing), Devadatta (yawning), Dhanajaya (preserving the body for a while after death). Vayu Mudra prevents all diseases that occur due to the imbalance of Air element.

Method: Fold the index finger to the base of the thumb and place the thumb over it. Keep other fingers straight. This mudra controls Vayu Tatva in the body.

5 Upa-Pranas

- Naga (burping, belching and hiccup)
- Kurma (eyes opening, blinking)
- Krikara (sneezing, induces hunger & thirst)
- Devadatta (yawning)
- Dhananjaya (closing and opening of heart, preserving the body for a while after death when the dhananjaya leaves the body decomposition starts)

Time Duration: The practice of this mudra for 45 minutes reduces the severity of the disease in 12 to 24 hours. For better results practice it for two months.

Benefits: This is particularly beneficial for people with Vata Dosha – rheumatism, arthritis, gout, gas problems, body ache and bulging stomach. This improves concentration. It is useful in meditation. It is effective in managing Parkinson's disease and Paralysis. It is useful in Cervical Spondylitis also.

3. Akasha Mudra (Mudra of Space)

Method: Join the tips of the thumb and middle finger. Keep the other fingers straight. Place your hands on your knee. Place your palm facing up.

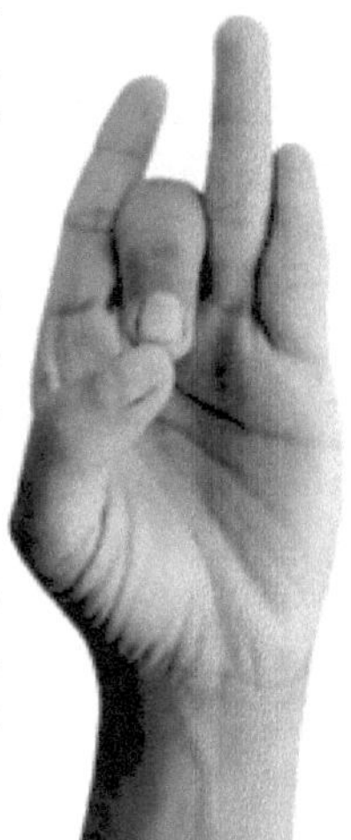

Time Duration: It has no specific time duration. You can practice it according to your convenience. It is better to practice for long before meditation to yield best result.

Benefits: Akasha mudra balances the Space element inside the body. Rotating Japa Mala on middle finger makes the heart strong. It strengthens the bones. It improves hearing.

4. Shunya Mudra (Mudra of Emptiness)

This Mudra reduces the Akasha tattva in the body. It is ideal for ailments of the ear, and also helps those of the nose and the throat. Even five minutes of this Mudra will help with ear ache.

Method: Bring the middle finger down to touch the palm and bring the padding of the thumb on top of it. Keep other fingers straight. Place your hands on your knee and keep your palm facing up.

Time Duration: Do this for 20 to 30 minutes daily until you cure your disease.

Benefits: When Akasha element (tatva) increases, it creates problems on the efficiency of ears. Practice of Shunya Mudra can rectify hearing. It is useful for the deaf and mentally challenged as well. It improves hearing ability, speech clarity and reduces stammering. Ear pains, leakage in ears and other ear problems can be overcome by practicing this Mudra for 20 to 30 minutes followed by Prana Mudra for 10 minutes. It relieves an ear ache within 4 or 5 minutes. There are examples where ear problems of children are cured when they do this Mudra followed by Prana Mudra. Vertigo is caused due to increase in Akasha 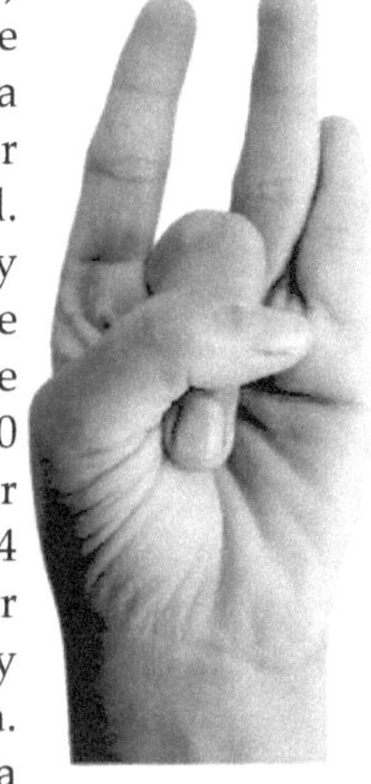 element which can be corrected by the practice of Shunya Mudra. It reduces dullness in our body.

5. Prithvi Mudra (Mudra of Earth)

In our body, muscles, bones, hair, veins and skin are made of Earth element. Shabda (sound), Rupa (form), Rasa (Taste), Gandha (smell), Sparsha (touch) are forms of the Earth element. This Mudra harmonizes all the organs of knowledge.

Method: Prithvi Mudra is formed by joining the tip of the ring finger to the tip of the thumb, keeping other fingers straight and placing hands on the knees.

Time Duration: It has no particular time duration. You can practice it any time you want. Practice this for 30 to 40 minutes daily.

Benefits: Prithvi Mudra reduces all physical weaknesses. It helps to increase weight in weak people. It improves skin complexion and makes the skin glow. It makes the body active by keeping it healthy. Body weight becomes proportional to height. Mind becomes calm and peaceful. It removes lethargy. Excretion becomes normal. Regular practice normalizes the deficiency of the Earth element and any disturbances caused by this deficiency; thus bringing the body to its natural equilibrium. Five Jnanendriyas (senses- ear, eyes, nose, tongue and skin) get activated. It gives peace of mind and increases glow and lustre of body. It gives sadhakas a surprising amount of tolerance and patience.

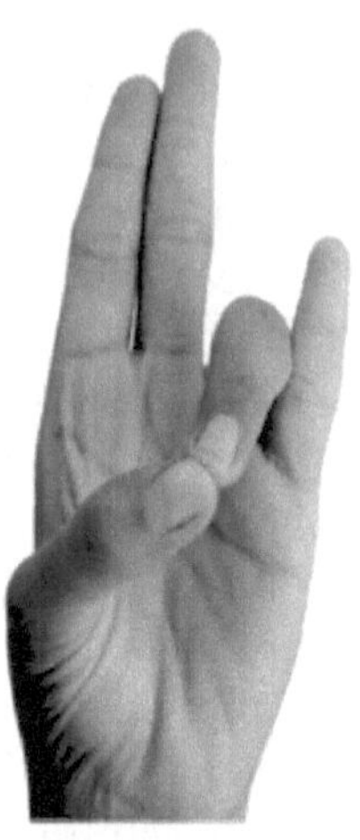

Blood circulation becomes normal. Bowels movement becomes regular and mind becomes calm and quiet.

6. Surya Mudra (Mudra of Sun)

Method: Bend the ring finger and bring it to the base of the thumb and place the thumb above the ring finger. Keep the other fingers straight and place the hands on the knees and palms facing up. This can be done while walking also.

Time Duration: Do this for 20 to 30 minutes followed by Prana Mudra for 10 minutes.

Benefits: Surya Mudra reduces and controls the Prithvi tatva in the body. Cholesterol accumulated in the body will vanish. This reduces anxiety. Problem of phlegm in the body (Kapha dosha) sinusitis, cold, pneumonia, TB, asthma and other breathing problems can be cured. Do this Mudra followed by Linga Mudra for 7 to 8 minutes for better results. It improves digestion. It helps to burn fat and weight loss. You will live in enthusiasm. It improves efficiency of the Thyroid gland.

Caution: Persons with weakness should not do this Mudra for long.

7. Apana Mudra (Mudra of Digestion)

Apana Mudra plays an important role in our health as it regulates the excretory system.

Method: Join the middle finger and the ring finger with the tip of the thumb; keep the index finger and the little finger straight.

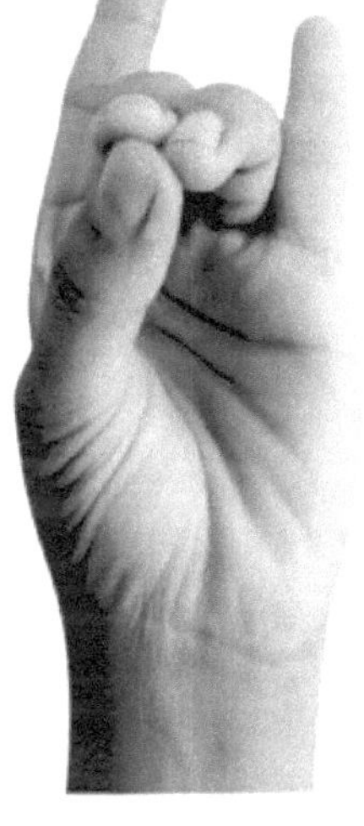

Time Duration: Practice it daily for 45 minutes. Practice for longer time yields more benefits.

Benefits: Improves digestion and excretion. It controls diabetes. It is a quick remedy for stomach ache and tooth ache. It cures constipation and piles. It helps excreting normal waste regularly. It improves eyesight and hearing problems as well. Prana Mudra must be done following this Mudra. It provides relief in urinary problems and eases difficulty in labour. It facilitates the discharge of waste matter from the body and purifies the system.

8. Apana Vayu Mudra or Mritsanjeevini or Hridya Mudra (Mudra of Heart)

It is a combination of 2 Mudras. When you do Apana and Vayu Mudra together, it becomes Apana Vayu Mudra or Hridya Mudra.

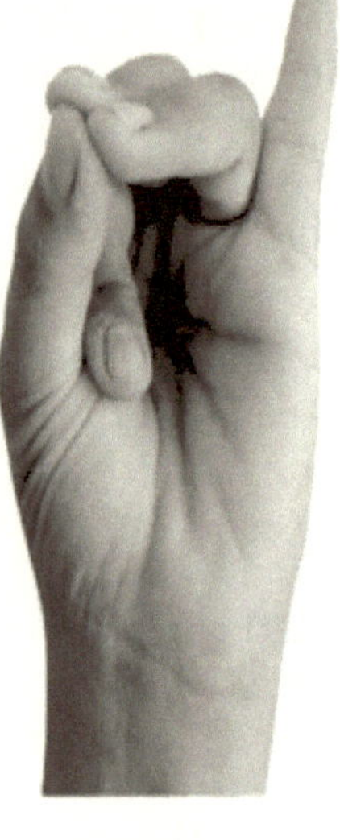

Method: Place the tip of the index finger at the base of thumb and join the tip of the thumb with the tips of middle finger and ring finger. Keep your little finger straight. Place your hand on your knee palm facing up.

Time Duration: Practice it as many times as you can. Heart patients and BP patients can practice it for 15 minutes twice daily for greater results.

Benefits: In case of heart attack this Mudra saves life. This Mudra rectifies heart palpitations. Doing this Mudra every morning and evening for 15 minutes can prevent heart attacks. It regulates excretory system. This Mudra cures stomach ache, acidity and constipation problems. It regulates complications of the heart. This Mudra is also called Sanjeevini (Life Saver) Mudra and Jeevandayee (Life Giver) Mudra. This can prevent the erratic throbbing of heart. This will have impact on preventing more perspiration in hands and legs. Passing of urine will be easier. Toothache will vanish. It helps to cure Piles. When you are awake in the night, or when worried or while doing laborious job, practice this Mudra without fail.

Note: Before stepping on stairs, climbing hills and mountains, practise this Mudra for 2 minutes to gain energy. At times of quarrel, psychological pressure, this Mudra can prevent heart attack. If you don't get cured from wind related diseases by practicing Vayu Mudra, then practice Hridaya (Heart) Mudra.

9. Varun Mudra (Mudra of Water)

Varun Mudra balances the water content and prevents all diseases which occurs due to lack of water in the organs.

Method: The Varun Mudra is formed by joining the tip of thumb with the front part of little finger keeping other fingers straight. Place your hands on the knees and palm facing up.

Time Duration: It has no specific time duration. You can practice it according to your convenience but practice at least 5 minutes to experience the effects.

Benefits: It retains clarity in blood by balancing water content in the body. It prevents pains from Gastroenteritis and muscle cramps. It is very good particularly for people with dry skin, dry cough, burning sensation in eyes and dryness of nose. Regular practice ensures an optimum level of water in the body and heals all ailments connected with dehydration. Blood circulation improves. Blood gets purified and skin diseases are cured. There will not be wrinkles on the skin. In case of itching, practice this and you will be surprised by getting rid of it. It enhances physical beauty and decreases dryness in the body. Fainting persons can regain consciousness in a moment when the fore parts of the thumb and little finger are rubbed.

Important: While walking in the sun, caught in a crowd practice this mudra and avoid thirst, faintness and dry cough.

10. Jalodar Nashak Mudra

Method: Fold the small finger and bring it to the base of the thumb. Place the thumb above the small finger. Keep other fingers erect. Place your palm facing up. Practice this for 20 to 30 minutes.

Time Duration: It has no specific time duration. You can practice it according to your convenience.

Benefits: Excessive water in the body causes various illnesses. Phlegm, cold and sore throats related problems occur when there is more water content in the body. With the Fire tatva above the Water tatva, this problem is solved. It removes water retention. Pain and swelling is cured. Frequent urination can be avoided by practicing this Mudra.

11. Linga Mudra (Mudra of Heat)

Method: Interlock the fingers of both hands and keep the thumb of the left hand vertically straight encircling it with the thumb and the index finger of the right hand.

Benefits: Since many acupressure points are pressed simultaneously; efficiency of heart, pituitary and thyroid glands, liver and throat will improve. If you do this during winter, body will get heated in a few minutes. It stops the production of phlegm and strengthens lungs. It cures severe cold and bronchial infection. It invigorates the body. It helps to cure diseases like cough, cold, sinus, asthma, pneumonia and TB. Diseases that recur during weather changes will vanish. Cholesterol and proteins are melted which help in decreasing body weight. Do this followed by Surya Mudra to control increasing body weight. Solar plexus will come to its original place and digestion will be normal. It is beneficial for people working in air conditioned offices. It is beneficial for women with problems during periods. It helps to digest fats quickly.

Time Duration: Practice it any time you want. Do this for 5 to 6 minutes. Don't practice it a lot, as it produces heat in the body. It can cause sweating even in winter if you practice it longer.

Note: It generates heat in our body. Take milk, ghee, more water and fruit juices in addition to practice of this Mudra for greater benefits.

Caution: People suffering from Pitta (Bile) related problems should NOT do this Mudra. Please note that those who suffer from acidity, head swings, and ulcer should not practice this Mudra.

12. Yoni Mudra

This hand gesture is believed to invoke the primal energy inherent in the womb as a source of creation. Practicing yoni Mudra helps balancing the energies in the body through the interlacing of the fingers. The joining of the

thumb and index fingers intensifies the linked flow of prana. This is an excellent Mudra to practice during meditation to boost concentration while also encouraging relaxation. This is a special practice for women to celebrate the female aspect and enhance it. This is used as part of mind control practices is also a powerful spiritual practice.

Method: Lock all fingers of both hands together, except index fingers and thumb. Join the index fingers and thumbs with index fingers pointing downwards. Draw the thumbs back toward the body, creating the shape of a yoni or womb. Place your hands at navel level. Close your eyes. Focus on the soft movement (up and down) of your breath at the abdomen.

Benefits: This mudra is particularly beneficial for women. It removes problems associated with menopause. This improves women's health overall. It is very de-stressing. It helps to control chronic ailments like BP, headaches, migraines etc. It helps in higher evolution and personal growth.

Thumbs of fire element and index fingers of vayu element joining each other will have good impact on womb. Mothers and sisters who suffer pain during periods can heave a sigh of relief immediately after doing this Mudra without consuming any medicine.

Time Duration: Do this for 10 minutes followed by Prana Mudra for 5 minutes for better results.

13. Anjali Mudra (Namaskar Mudra)

Method: Place your 2 palms together in front of your chest resting one upon another.

Benefits: 5 Elements -Tattvas (Earth, Water, Fire, Air and Space) are harmonized in the body. It increases strength in the body. Peace, harmony and politeness increases. This mudra cures headaches.

Note: For everything, the starting point is the belief and confidence that it works. Have confidence or belief and surrender yourself to the practice, you will have great results.

Important things to know about the Mudras:
- Hasta Mudra can be done by anyone and at anytime.
- As far as possible, the palms should face upwards while doing the mudras.
- Doing the mudras on both hands is more beneficial.
- Mudras can be done for few seconds, 10 minutes, half an hour or 50 minutes. If done for 50 minutes, desired results will be faster.
- While doing the mudras, only the tips of the fingers are used. Pressing the fingers is not needed. Other fingers should be straight.
- There is no side effect in this. They can also be done while you are in meditation.
- If you practice Prana, Apana, Jnana and Prithvi mudras everyday for 5-15 minutes, your health will improve significantly.

- Mudras improve not only physical health but also mental health by liberating you from addictions, reducing anger and increasing calm and peacefulness.
- Chikitsa mudra should be stopped after one's health has improved.
- During Mudra practices, chant 'Om' or 'Gayatri Mantra' or any 'Nama Japa' of your choice or do breathing exercises with closed eyes to derive early desired results.
- Jnana mudra can be practiced throughout by everyone for entire lifetime.

Secret : 6

PRANAYAM
(Yogic Breathing)

The term Pranayama has been coined from two Sanskrit words Prana+Ayama. Prana can be explained as the vital life force that regulates all activities in this universe. In other words Prana is the Universal Life Force that enters the body with each breath. Ayama has a wide range of meaning; the most appropriate ones are Regulation of Breaths, Control of Vital Forces and Channeling the Pranas (vital body force) in the right direction. This prana is inter-linked with consciousness (Chitta) both at the Cosmic and Individual levels. Pranayama is devised to create a synergy between the self-energizing life forces and individual mind-body-spirit by scientific regulation of Prana.

It is both the Art and Science of Breath Control. Pranayama purifies the channels along where the life streams of 'Prana' flows. It helps to prevent and cures a variety of physical and mental ailments. It increases one's overall immunity and resistance to diseases.

Pranayama is the fourth limb (Anga) of Patanjali's Eightfold Path of Yoga. It consists of conscious Inhalation (Puraka), Retention (Kumbhaka), and Exhalation (Rechaka). At an advanced state, breath retention occurs spontaneously for longer periods of time. There are various methods of regulating Prana with rhythmic control of the breath.

तस्मिन् सति श्वासप्रश्वासयोर्गतिविच्छेद: प्राणायाम:

tasmin sati shvasaprashvasayorgativichchhedah pranayamah (PYS 2.49)

According to Maharshi Patanjali, Controlling and expanding the flow of breathe is called pranayama.

बाह्याभ्यन्तरस्तरम्भवृत्तिर्देशकालसंख्याभि: परिदृष्टो दीर्घसूक्ष्म:

bahyabhyantarastambhavrittih deshakalasankhyabhih paridrishto

dirghasookshmah (PYS 2.50)

बाह्याभ्यान्तरविषयाक्षेपी चतुर्थ:

bahyabhyantaravishayakshepi chaturthah (PYS 2.51)

There are 4 types of Pranayama according to Maharshi Patanjali: Bahyavritti, Abhyantarvritti, Sthambhvritti and Bahya Abhyantar Vishayakshepi.Bahya (Rechak- Exhalation), Abhyantar Vritti (Purak-Inhalation), Sthambh Vritti (Kumbhak-Retention) are three pranayama which are practiced making them deep and subtle possible. The forth pranayama is beyond inhalation and exhalation (breathless state).

तत:क्षीयते प्रकाशावरणम्

Tatah kshiyate prakaasha aavaranam (PYS 2.52)

धारणासु च योग्यता मनस:

Dhaaranaasu cha yogyataa manasaha (PYS 2.53)

When pranayama is achieved, the practitioner will be able to overcome the barriers of life energy and mind so that the practitioner can achieve the state of Dharana.

Atha saptasadhanalaksanam :

षट्कर्मणा शोधनं च आसनेनभवेद् दृढम्।।
मुद्रया स्थिरता चैव प्रत्याहारेण धीरता

प्राणायामाल्लाघवं च ध्यानात्प्रत्यक्षमात्मनि।

समाधिना च निर्लिप्तं मुक्तिरेव न संशय:

Satkarmana sodhanam ca asanena bhaved drdham
Mudraya sthirala caiva pratyaharena dhirata (1.10)
Pranayamal laghavam ca dhyanat pratyaksam atmanah
Samadhina nirliptam ca muktir eva na samsayah (1.11)

According to Gherand Sanhita, Purification of the body is acquired by the regular performance of Shatkarma, Dridhata or strength is acquired by the practice of Asana, Sthirata or steadiness is acquired by the practice of Mudras, Dhirata (calmness) is acquired by the practice of Pratyahara, Laghima (lightness) is acquired by the practice of Pranayama, Pratyaksha (perception of self) is acquired by the practice of Dhyana and Nirliptata (isolation or ultimate liberation) is achieved by the practice of Samadhi. (GS 1.10 & 11)

Gherand Samhita explained Pranayma as Kumbhaka. There are 8 kumbhaka explained in Gherand Samhita: Sahita Suryabheda, Ujjayi, Sitali, Bhastrika, Bhramari, Murccha and Kevali. (G.S./5.46/)

Kind of Kumbhaka

सहित: सूर्यभेदश्च उज्जायीशीतली तथा।

भस्त्रिका भ्रामरी मूच्छी केवली चाष्टकुम्भका:

Sahitah suryabhedas ca ujjayi sitali tatha
Bhastrika bhramari murcha kevali castakumbhikah (GS 5.46)

Kumbhaka or retention of breath is of eight kinds: Sahita, Suryabheda, Ujjayi Sitali, Bhastrika, Bhramari, Murccha and Kevali.

Hatha Yoga Pradipika also explained Pranayma as Kumbhaka.

There are 8 kumbhaka explained in Hatha Yoga Pradipika: Suryabheda, Ujjayi, Sitkari, Sitali, Bhastrika, Bhramari, Murccha and Plavini. (HYP/2.44/)

सूर्यभेदीनमुज्जायी सीत्कारी शीतली तथा

भस्त्रिका भ्रामरी मुच्छी पप्लाविनीत्यष्टकुम्भकाः

Suryabhedanam ujjayi sitkari sitati tatha

Bhastrika bhramari murccha plavinilyastakumbhakah (HYP 2.44)

WHAT IS THE OBJECTIVE OF PRANAYAMA?

The objective of Pranayama is to awaken, regulate and direct the vital forces that exist in the body. It is designed to help the master to control the breath and to infuse the body with prana. Even simple Yogic Breathing like deep and quiet breathing can reduce mental stresses and strains. Pranayama balances the Pranic Forces in the body with regular practices by restoring emotional, mental and physical inconsistencies. Pranayama reduces the need of oxygen and the production of carbon dioxide reducing respiratory rate.

Pranayama is the best amongst all the methods of treatment in yoga therapy. Regular and systematic practices cure many diseases in the nervous system, stomach, nerves, bones, muscles and many organs. It activates all bodily systems. It increases life energy and strengthens the Endocrine glands. Regular practice of pranayama along with Asanas is helpful for all round development and improve memory power.

Heart has a close connection with breathing and blood circulation systems. This relation is dependent on mental activities. If mental strain increases, our breathing rate is affected. In Pranayama, with controlled breathing, heart beats is slower, which reduces the strain on heart muscles; in response lowers heart beats in Diastolic and Systolic ratios.

This increases the stability of mind and mental faculties; hence all activities are controlled. It is advisable to practice Pranayama followed by meditation.

General Cautions and Contraindications for Pranayama:

- Pranayama should always be practiced with suitable asanas (asanas that increases the volume of the lungs and free the muscles of the ribs, back, and diaphragm) or yogic posture for its effectiveness.

- The breathing techniques of Pranayama should be first taught and practice under the supervision of an experienced teacher.

- Simple breathing techniques can be used at the start of a session to help calm and focus the mind and body. The practice of Pranayama is highly recommended before relaxation and meditation at the end of a session.

- The practitioner should not exhaust himself in the process.

- If you feel any kind of discomfort or symptoms such as dizziness or nausea as you practice Yogic Breathing just relax with deep breaths or a few recovery breaths. If discomfort persists, do not continue your practice until you get advice regarding your symptoms.

- Those who suffer from chronic shortness of breath or other breathing disorders, they should not attempt Pranayama without proper guidance.

- Breathing should always be done in an almost empty stomach.

- Breathing should not be done in haste, nor should it be jerky or irregular. Breathing should always be smooth and steady otherwise the whole purpose of Pranayama is lost. Uneven exhalation is held to be a sign of present or impending illness.

WHAT IS THE RIGHT TIME TO DO PRANAYAMA?

It can be done any time you can manage but maintain a gap of at least 2-3 hours between food intake and Pranayama. Obviously early in the morning after waking, rising, when your stomach is naturally empty is the best time. It is advisable to do Pranayama after the neuromuscular integration exercises and before meditation.

EFFECTS OF PRANAYAMA ON DIFFERENT SYSTEMS

Pranayama is a Scientific and controlled way of Yogic Breathing. Practice of Pranayama not only strengthen and balance the Pranas but also cleanse the body and mind. Pranayama cause different effect in different organs and systems to maintain physical, mental, emotional, intellectual, psychological, and spiritual health. Yogic Breathing stimulates disease preventative effects, supply curative power and promotes greater health to all organs of the body. Pranayama facilitate optimum health benefits in most systems.

Nervous system: Nervous system is a communication channel among different organs of the whole body. It plays a vital role for many activities of an individual. Pranayama enhance the nervous system releasing stress and tension that relaxes the entire body. Pranayama provides holistic health supplying the nervous system with healthy, clean, disease free with pure energy. Pranayama purify Ida, Pingala and Sushumna Nadis maintaining perfect coordination and union which is miraculously effective.

Blood circulation: Blood circulation is facilitated through Pranayama. Pranayama purifies the blood supplying more oxygen and removing carbon-dioxide along with other toxic elements. Purification of blood and proper circulation of purified blood to every organ keeps them healthy.

Endocrine System: It balances the secretion of all the Endocrine glands. Helps to increase stress resistance capacity.

Muscular System: Brings soothing and relaxing effect in the muscular system as the level of oxygen increases and level of toxin decreases in blood circulatory systems.

Respiratory System: It corrects the breathing patterns. Optimum utilization of lungs capabilities with the help of Pranayama will increase oxygen intake, detoxify carbon dioxide and other toxic gases.

1. UDGEETH PRANAYAMA (OM CHANTING)

In Sanskrit Udgeetha means singing in a loud pitch. Literally Udgeeth Pranayama means chanting OM in a loud pitch. The letters A, O, M collectively represent this word. The collective powers of Brahma, Vishnu and Mahesh are included in this word. OM is not a figure or expression of any individual person, but it is a Divine Energy, Sound; which regulates the entire functioning of our Cosmic Universe. God has fashioned the shape of brows like AUM. Every Individual Being with the Universal Cosmic Being is filled with this mantra sound. OM chanting has been widely used traditionally as a meditation technique since Creation in all Ages.

Method

- Sit in comfortable position.
- Close your eyes and observe your breath.
- Inhale deeply and start chanting OM.
- Concentrate your mind on Chakra centers; Coccyx to Heart centre while chanting O, from Heart centre to Neck centre, while chanting U, then concentrate on Forehead (3rd Eye) centre while chanting M.

- With practice, try to lengthen each breath to one-minute including inhalation and exhalation.

Benefits of Udgit Pranayama

Chanting is yet another way of changing the vibrational level of the body so that stress and diseases are controlled. Practicing these simple chants increase your vibrational level, this naturally prevents diseases. Also this cures diseases of stomach; chest and brain respectively. It is useful for improving memory power. It increases mental strengths. This is a very relaxing technique. It prevents insomnia by deepening the quality of sleep and relieving bad dreams. It assists the mind to be more focus and facilitates the practice of conscious sleep (Yoga Nidra).

2. BHASTRIKA PRANAYAMA

Bhastrika Pranayama engages rapid movement of the belly like the bellows of a blacksmith hence it is also called Bellow Breathing. This breathing exercise increases the flow of air into the body and produces inner heat at the physical and subtle level. This Pranayama burns up toxins and removes diseases of all the Doshas: Kapha (Phlegm-Water), Pitta (Bile-Fire) and Vata (Wind-Air). The rapid exchange of air in the lungs, practiced in this technique improves the metabolic rate, produces heat and flushes out wastes and toxins.

Method

- Sit in any comfortable posture with your spine straight.

- Inhale deeply filling the lungs up to the diaphragm and exhale with full force emptying the lungs.

- In this Pranayama equal emphasis should be laid on inhalation and exhalation.

- The inhalations and exhalations should be done with

slow speed or medium speed or fast speed depending on your practice, capacity and state of health.

- You can practice this Pranayama for 2 to 5 minutes as per your level of comfort.

Precaution: People with a weak heart or weak lungs should do Bhastrika with slower speed.

Benefits of Bhastrika Pranayama

Health improves when the brain gets pure life energy. The pranas and mind become stable, nervous weaknesses and memory power improves. It cures Tridoshas (Vata, Pitta, Kapha) and problems arising from the brain. This cures forgetfulness. It improves appetite. It is beneficial in case of low blood pressure, depression, sleeplessness, knee pain, headache, diabetes, obesity, loss of appetite and asthma. It cures thyroid and tonsils and other related diseases. It strengthens the heart and lungs. This is the best thing for diseases like cold, cough, allergy, asthma and respiratory problems of all kinds. Hence it also cures diseases of the throat like thyroid, tonsils and other ailments of the throat.

3. KAPALBHATI PRANAYAMA

Kapalbhati is one of the popularly practiced Pranayama that promises to cure various ailments over a period of time. In Sanskrit Kapal means head and Bhati means shining or glow; thus literally this breathing technique brings glow to the forehead of the practitioner. Apart from bringing glow and enhancing beauty this Pranayama has various other benefits.

Methods

- Sit in comfortable position with spine straight.
- Take two or three deep inhalations and exhalations.

- Inhale deeply to exhale sharply and forcefully through both nostril, drawing the belly in as you exhale and producing a puffing sound.

- Let the inhalation be passive, and continue this cycle of forceful exhalation and passive inhalation at a fast pace, so that the belly is pumping continuously.

- At the same time, receive autosuggestion about increased flow of blood circulation, detoxification and vitalization of the vital organs viz. kidney, small and large intestines, prostate gland, liver, gallbladder, pancreas, spleen and lungs etc.

- Practice this process for 5-15 min. You may take short breaks; if you feel tired initially. Over the period of time you will develop the capacity to do it for 15 minutes continuously.

Benefits of Kapalbhati

Kapalbhati Pranayama supplies pure life energy to the brain. It increases the blood circulation gradually in the brain and removes blood clots thereby improving memory power. Other than this the toxins and foreign substances from the body are evacuated. It cures cold, sinusitis, allergy, tension and other diseases. It is very useful in case of phlegm, skin diseases, asthma, heart diseases, low blood pressure, depression, tiredness, laziness, sleeplessness, migraine, joint pains, obesity, diabetes, constipation, indigestion, acidity, gastric problems and other diseases pertaining to kidneys and prostate gland etc. It cleanses the lungs and entire respiratory system, purifies the blood, increases the supply of oxygen to all cells, improves digestion, strengthens abdominal muscles, energizes the mind for mental work, reduce obesity. It cures diabetes, brain, lungs, thyroids, infertility, hormonal imbalances, PCOD, PCOS, problems. As a result the whole body becomes healthy and disease free.

4. Agnisar Pranayama/ Agnisar Kriya

This cleansing technique draws its name from the words 'Agni' (Fire), Sar (Essence) and Kriya (Action). Fire is the essential element of digestion and this cleansing action stimulates this fire for the digestive system to work at its optimum level.

Method

To Practice as a Kriya while Standing: bend slightly forward from the waist while keeping the back straight.

To Practice as a Pranayama:

- Sit comfortable, keeping your spine erect.

- Take support by resting your hands on your knees so that the back is not strained. Make sure the arms are straight.

- Now, breathe in deeply and exhale fully contracting the abdomen and lungs so that all the air is expelled.

- Put your chin down to do chin lock.

- While holding the breath in this position, contract & release your abdominal muscles in and out.

- This should be done rapidly while holding the exhaled position without inhaling. Do this as many times as possible and then take a slow, deep breath inside.

- This is one round of the practice.

- Release the chin lock.

Benefits of Agnisar

It is excellent for the health of abdominal organs and the digestive system. Works wonders on a sluggish liver and kidneys. It also removes several gastrointestinal complaints, such as excessive gas, hyperacidity, indigestion etc. It massages the abdominal organs. This is an excellent practice to develop control over those sluggish abdominal muscles and diaphragm.

Precaution: Practitioners with High BP, heart diseases or internal ulcers of any kind should avoid this process.. Also, those with hyperthyroidism or chronic diarrhea should avoid this Pranayam.

Bahya Pranayama (with Mahabandha)

It is also called Tri Bandha. It is a method of retention of the breathing process after exhalation. Mahabandha is a process of applying all three bandhas of the body. There are three types of bandhas (locks) in Pranayama. The first one is Jalandhara Bandha (touching the chin on the pit located near the base of throat), second is Uddiyana Bandha (pulling the stomach in so as to touch the back) and third is Mula bandha (pulling up the perineum by contracting the anus and tightening the lower abdomen). In the position of Mahabandha all three bandhas are applied simultaneously.

Method

- Sit in one of the meditative postures keeping your spine erect.

- Breathe in and fill your lungs up to diaphragm.

- Breathe out with full force and suspend the breathing process.

- Apply the Mahabandha in sequence starting from Uddiyana Bandha, Mula 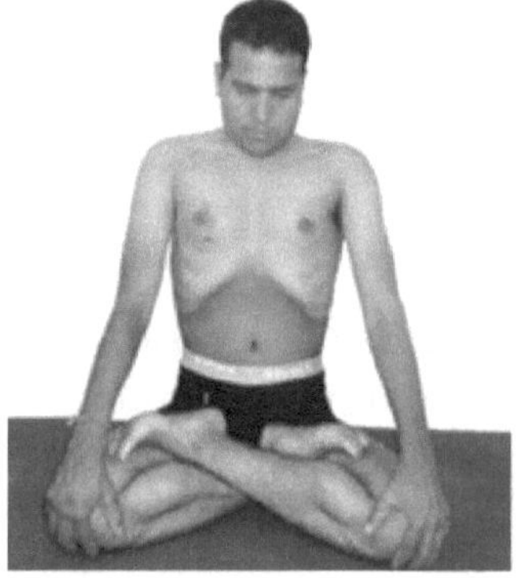 Bandha and finally Jalandhara Bandha again.

- Now exhale and release the three bandhas gradually in a sequence starting from Jalandhar Bandha,

- Uddiyana Bandha and finally Mula Bandha.

- It completes one cycle of this breathing technique. A minimum of three such cycles is recommended.

Benefits of Bahya Pranayama

This Pranayama stops the fluctuations of the mind. Sharpens intelligence, cleanses the entire body, causes seminal fluids to rise up and cures several abnormalities. It is very effective for improving health of the thyroids, adrenal and gonads glands. It improves digestion. It is beneficial in all kinds of abdominal ailments. It is especially beneficial for people suffering from problems related with stomach, hernia, uterus and urinary systems.

Precaution: Not for heart and high BP patients.

6. Anulom Vilom (Alternate Breathing) Pranayama

Anuloma-Viloma is an Alternate Nostril Breathing Technique of Yoga. In many people, the natural rhythm of breathing is disturbed. Anuloma Viloma balances the rhythms of breathing, restores, and equalizes the flow of Prana in the body. It is the best technique to soothe the nervous system and calms the mind.

Method

- Sit in a comfortable position and relax your body.

- Rest the back of the left wrist on the left knee performing Jnana Mudra.

- Block the right nostril with the right hand thumb & inhale slowly through left.

- Block the left nostril with middle and ring fingers & exhale through right.

- Inhale through right nostril. Block your right nostril with right thumb & exhale through left.

- Repeat this exercise alternately with deeper breaths. Continue alternate breathing for 2-15 minutes.

Benefits of Anulom Vilom

The respiratory passage is cleansed. This prepares practitioners for practices of other Pranayama Breathing methods. Becomes easy and regulated. It cleanses and energizes the body with the flow of prana. 72,000 nadies are supposed to be the carriers of prana to different parts of the body. It helps to make heartbeat rhythmic, calms the mind, removes its disturbances and makes it conducive for meditation. It aids in enhancing concentration, memory and other mental faculties.

It ensures the proper supply of oxygen and removes carbon dioxide effectively. Normal breathing becomes efficient with increased flow of oxygen per breath. It purifies the blood. It is very effective for stress management. Reduces anxiety, depression and other mental illnesses. Balances Ida and

Pingala removing all blockages from these energy channels, which may lead to spiritual awakening. It gives perfect benefits for deeper breathing as well.

Last but not least, this Pranayama is ideal for patients suffering from high BP, heart blockage (30 - 40%blockages can be reversed within 3-4 months), depression (can be reversed with positive thinking, enthusiasm) arthritis, cartilage problem, bent ligaments, Parkinson, paralysis, nervous systems related problems, migraines, asthma, allergy and sinus.

The Scientific Confirmation of Alternate Nostril Breathing

Medical science has recently discovered the nasal cycle, something that was known by the Yogis thousands of years ago. Scientists have recently found that we don't breathe equally with both nostrils, that one nostril is much easier to breathe through than the other at any particular time and that this alternates about every three hours. The Yogis claim that the natural period is every two hours, but we must remember these studies were done on people who do not have an optimum health level.

Secondly, Scientists discovered that the nasal cycle corresponds with brain function. The electrical activity of the brain was found to be greater on the side opposite the less congested nostril. The right side of the brain controls creative activity, while the left side controls logical mathematical and verbal activities. This research showed that when the left nostril was less obstructed, the right side of the brain was predominant. Test subjects were indeed found to do better on creative tests. Similarly when the right nostril Medical science has not quite caught up with the Ancient Yogis as yet. The Yogis went one step further. They observed that a lot of diseases were due to the nasal cycle being disturbed; that is, if a person breathed too long through one nostril. To prevent and correct this condition, they developed the alternate nostril breathing technique. This clears any blockage to air flow in the nostrils and re-establishes the natural nasal cycle. For example, the Yogis have known for millenniums that prolonged breathing through the left nostril only (over a period of years) will produce asthma. They also know that this so-called incurable disease can be easily eliminated by teaching patients to breathe through the right nostril until the asthma is cured, and then to prevent it recurring by doing the alternate nostril breathing technique. The Yogis also knew to a large extent that diabetes is caused by breathing mainly through the right nostril.

7. Nadi Shodhan Pranayama

It is the same Anulom Vilom with retention of breath after every inhalation and exhalation for 10-20-30-45-60 seconds.

Method

- Sit in a comfortable position.

- Close your right nostril with your right thumb.

- Inhale slowly through the left nostril as deeply as possible.

- Retain the inhaled air according to your capacity.

- Do Mula Bandha and Jalandhara Bandha simultaneously.

- After keeping yourself in this position unlock Jalandhara Bandha and breathe out slowly and completely through the right nostril.

- Keep your breath out for some time and then inhale slowly through the right nostril. Hold your breath with Jalandhara Bandha for as long you are able to hold your breath. Open your Jalandhara Bandha and slowly exhale through left nostril.

- Repeat the exercise for 2-10 min.

Benefits of Nadi Shodhan Pranayama

Nadi Shodhan Pranayama controls and develops the Pranic flow. The blood in the whole body receives a larger supply of oxygen than normal breathing. You feel refreshed, your mind becomes still and your nerves are calmed and purified. It produces optimum function to both sides of the brain; that is creativity and logical verbal activity. This also creates a more balanced personality. This is considered as one of the best technique to calm the mind and the nervous system.

Precaution: High BP patients should do it only under supervision of a Yoga Guru.

8. Sitali Pranayama (Tongue Hissing Without Kumbhaka)

Shitali means a cool breath. It is one of the cooling breaths that lowers the fire energy called Pitta that is associated with catabolic processes in the body.

Method

- Sit in a comfortable cross-legged position.
- Take two or three deep breaths through the nose to prepare.
- Roll the tongue, curling the sides in towards the center to form a tube.
- Stick the end of the tongue out between your lips. If you can't roll your tongue, just purse the lips making a small "o" shape with the mouth.
- Inhale through the tube of the tongue.

- Raise your chin as you inhale (like a straw), feeling the cool air over the tongue.
- On exhalation, slightly lower your chin, place the tip of your tongue behind your front teeth, close your lips, and exhale through your nose.
- Repeat 5-10 times as you feel the cooling effect.

Benefits of Sitali Pranayama

This breathing exercise will lower the body temperature, and make the saliva cool. It also helps to quench thirst, and improves digestion, absorption, and assimilation. It is very useful to calm down the body temperature in hot weather conditions or high fevers. It helps to alleviate nausea.

9. Sitkari Pranayama (Teeth Hissing)

Like Sitali, Shitkari is also a breath cooling Pranayama that removes excess heat from the body.

1st Method

- Sit in comfortable position.
- Join your teeth together.
- Touch your teeth with the tip of your tongue and palate with the middle part of tongue.
- Keep your lips separate.
- Now suck in the air with an audible. Si..S..Si. Sound.
- Then retain the breath as long as possible.
- Finally exhale the breath through both nostrils.

2nd Method

- Sit in a comfortable position.
- Part your jaws slightly keeping small gap between your upper and lower teeth.

- Roll the tongue upward touching the upper palate and its mid part touches the lips.
- Now inhale through your teeth, with the air passing over your tongue.
- The air should feel cool as it moves over the surface of your tongue during inhalation.
- Retain the breath as long as possible and then exhale through left nostrils by blocking right nostril with right thumb.
- Repeat it for 2 minutes.

Benefits of Sitkari Pranayama

Sitkari Pranayama removes symptoms like hunger, thirst, laziness and sleep. It prevents bile from increasing. It removes hardness from the tonsils. Increases the mental and physical powers of the performer. It also cures diseases like acidity and hypertension. It harmonizes the secretions of reproductive organs and all the Endocrine systems. It is an aid to improve digestion. It purifies the blood and control High Blood Pressure.

10. Ujjayi Pranayama

This soothing technique can be applied while holding Yoga postures. It helps to increase lungs capacity. So that, more oxygen is absorbed into the bloodstream. It generates internal heat. It also helps to achieve a state of calmness and mental clarity.

1st Method

- Sit in a comfortable position preferably in Padmasana.
- Inhale by contracting the throat with snoring like sound.
- The air should not have friction with the nose but with throat. This friction produces a sound.

- Lock your neck by pressing your chin down.
- In the beginning do not practice Kumbhaka (retention) and practice only Poorak (Inhalation) - Rechak (Exhalation).
- After inhalation gradually equate the duration with Kumbhaka and after few days double the duration of Kumbhaka.
- Then do Jalandhara Bandha (neck lock) and Moolbandh (anus lock) to hold as long as you can.
- Open your locks.
- Close the right nostril and exhale with left nostril.

Precaution: The above should be practiced under expert guidance for special benefits.

2nd Method

- Sit in any comfortable position.
- Partially close the back of your throat.
- Inhale and exhale through your nose and let the air passes through a narrower air passage in your throat.
- Inhaling and exhaling should be slow, long, deep
- As the back of throat is partially closed a sound is produced at inhalation and exhalation by contracting the muscles in the back of your throat.

Note: This variation can be used while performing yoga asanas and also while holding the postures.

Benefits of Ujjayi Pranayama

Ujjayi Pranayama is especially beneficial to children. It cures lisping problems among children. They may never suffer from cold, cough, catarrh, tonsils, thyroid, sleeplessness, mental tension, blood pressure, indigestion, arthritis, fever, spleen and other problems. Regular practice gives a healthy throat and sweet voice. It also affects carotid sinus, which help reduce BP. Ujjayi Pranayama balances the Pranic flow of energy in the body.

11. Bhramari (The Bee Breath) Pranayama

In Sanskrit, Brahmari means Bee. In this Pranayama a buzzing sound is produced similar to the buzzing of the bee hence the name Bhramari was given. Bhramari is an excellent breathing technique that helps to clear and strengthen the respiratory system and improve vocal resonance. It has a calming effect on the body, uplifts the spirit, stimulates the brain, clears and invigorates the mind and thought processes.

Method

- Sit comfortably in any asana with your spine straight.
- Keep your lips gently closed and teeth separate.
- Block your ears with thumbs, eyes with middle & ring fingers and place your index finger on your forehead.
- Breathe in till your lungs are filled with air.
- Concentrate your mind on Ajna Chakra (between eyebrows).
- Begin slow exhalation, making buzzing sound of a bee with mental recitation of AUM.
- Try to make this sound as sweet as possible.
- When the process of exhalation is complete the bee sound will stop for sometime.
- Keep inhaling and exhaling to produce the sound.
- Repeat the Exercise for 5 to 21 times depending upon your capacity and time.

Benefits of Bhramari Pranayama

It cures brain related problems, tension, worries, anger, sleeplessness, depression and other problems. It improves memory power. It cures anxiety and is useful in case of restlessness, high blood pressure, heart disease etc. It is good for diabetes, obesity, asthma, nervous weakness. It is beneficial in case of gynecological diseases. It cures Vata, Pitta, Kapha and related problems. It is also beneficial in case of headaches, colds and catarrh. This will help you to merge your individual consciousness with the divine Cosmic Consciousness.

Secret : 7

DHYANA
(Meditation)

Literally Meditation is a process of giving attention to one thing and do not think about anything else. The purest Eastern definition of the word 'meditation' means not thinking at all, rather focusing consciousness on the cosmic whole or mental state of effortless consciousness. Meditation can be defined as the art of consciousness being aware of itself on a grand cosmic scale. Meditation is one of the most powerful tools to help you restore the harmony within. It gives you access to your body's inner intelligence. In meditation, you rediscover the silence in your mind and make it a part of your life. Silence is the birthplace of happiness. It is where you get your burst of inspiration, your tender feelings of compassion and your sense of love. Meditation is a journey to freedom and self-knowledge. Meditation has been used by many to relieve stress in the body and mind. It relaxes the body, clears the mind and creates inner peace.

According to Maharshi Patanjali, effortless concentration on specific subject or subject of concentration is called meditation. It is the next stage of Dharana in Asthanga yoga. Ultimate and advanced state of Meditation is Samadhi. Collectively Dharanan, Dhyana and Samadhi is called Samyam.

According to Maharshi Patanjali Yoga Sutra

देशबन्धश्चित्तस्य धारणा

deśa-bandha cittasya dhāranā (PYS 3.1)

Harmony with thoughts and the ability to concentrate are attained by aligning the mutable aspects of humankind with a specific subject.

तत्र प्रत्ययैकतानता ध्यानम्

tatra pratyaya-ikatānatā dhyānam (PYS 3.2)

Allowing your thoughts to flow in an uninterrupted stream results in contemplation (dhyana).

तदेवार्थमात्रनिर्भसं स्वरूपशून्यमिव समाधि: (PYS 3.3)
tadeva-artha-mātra-nirbhāsa svarūpa-śūnyam-iva-samādhi

Insight (samadhi) occurs when only the subject matter of the orientation shines forth without any being affected by the person in question.

त्रयमेकत्र संयम:

trayam-ekatra samyamah (PYS 3.4)
The three processes of dharana, dhyana, and samadhi, when taken together, are the components of meditation (samyama).

तज्जयात् प्रज्ञालोक:

tajjayāt prajñāloka (PYS 3.5)
Mastery of this meditation gives rise to absolute knowledge of all that can be perceived.

Gheranda Samhita is a step by step detailed manual of seven fold yoga (Saptanga Yoga or Shashthopadesha) taught by sage Gheranda which includes:
1. Shatkarma for body cleansing
2. Asana for body strengthening
3. Mudra for body steadying
4. Pratyahara for mind calming
5. Pranayama for inner lightness
6. Dhyana for inner perception and
7. Samādhi for self liberation and bliss.

According to Gherand Samhita, dhyana is of three types: 1. Sthula 2. Jyotirmaya and 3. Sukshma

स्थूलं ज्योतिस्थासूक्ष्मं ध्यानस्य त्रिविधं विदुः।

स्थूलं मूर्तिमयं प्रोक्तं ज्योतिस्तेजोमयं तथा ।

सूक्ष्मं, विन्दुमयं ब्रह्म कुण्डली परदेवता (GS **6.1**)

Sthula Dhyan (Gross Meditation) is absorptive contemplation on a divine form, more specifically, the image of personal god (ishtadeva) or guru firmly established in one's being. Jyotirmaya Dhyan (Radiant Meditation) is focusing on the individual soul (jivatma) or on the supreme Self, radiating light (tejomaya brahma) in the cavity of the heart. With practice, the sadhaka is able to see flashes of light in the primal sound reverberating within. Sometime, focus is made on luminous objects, like the flame of a candle or an earthen lamp (diya) or on the sun, moon or a star as advised by the spiritual teacher.Sukshma Dhyan (Subtle Meditation) is done on something abstract like a sacred mantra, geometrical form (yantra), inner sound (nada) the vital energy or the serpent power (kundalini shakti) that lies coiled up at the base of the spinal column. It is best performed in shambhavi mudra with eyes half-open, and focused within.

According to Gheranda Samhita, jyoirmaya dhyana is a hundred times better than sthula dhyana, and sukshma dhyana a million times better than jyotirmaya dhyana. As dhyana reaches its peack, the seeker discovers the entire universe in his/her body. Yogis believe that the inner cosmos (brahmanda) lies on the royal road (maha marga) from the tongue (jihva) to the hollow place in the crown of the head, called brahmarandhra or dashma dvara (tenth door). Kundalini-shakti is active in this region. Gheranda suggests that the seeker should be totally absorbed in the meditative process for divine experience.

WHY TO MEDITATE?

The world is increasingly becoming a global village with the wide use of technology, where there is tough and neck breaking competition. Doctors are increasingly citing stress as a major factor in illnesses like depression, anxiety, high blood pressure, cardiac diseases, insomnia, diabetes, ulcers, colds, fever, asthma, arthritis and alcoholism. Research has shown that meditation contributes to reducing stress and achieving deep relaxation and a profound state of rest. Meditation has important benefits for a wide range of health problems. It allows the mind and body to function with maximum efficiency by reducing stressful factors.

Meditation is perhaps the only permanent source of tranquillity available to human beings. All other forms of serenity are temporary and dissolve into conflicts and chaos over time. The euphoria of drugs quickly leads to misery and self-destruction. The comfort of wholesome love and beauty is relatively short lived. Meditation brings a sense of fullness and completion. Meditation changes and reverses chaos to divine natural order by universal forces!

Meditation is an adventurous path of self-discovery. You may identify yourself as a person with your name if someone asks you who you are during the day. But ask yourself who you are when you are in deep sleep, unconsciousness and without even a dream to prove that you exist at all. Ask yourself who you were ten months before you were born and who you will be just one moment after your body dies. You need to know the fact that is actually going on behind your own eyes to experience the ultimate realisation. Meditation is the gateway for the journey within.

Effects of Meditation in different dimensions of Personality

You will reconnect with your essence in meditation. This connection extends into your daily life and can result in improved health, more fulfilling relationships, enthusiasm for life and increased creativity. According to World Health Organisation, "Mere absence of disease can't be considered health. Health is a state of physical, mental, emotional, and socio-economic well-being." Meditation is a holistic yet scientific practice that optimizes the physical mental, emotions, intellectual as well as spiritual dimensions of our personality. When physical, mental and emotional health is in balance, health of the individual is achieved. This in turns gives rise to social health. All the four interdependent constitute as a whole is spiritual health.

Effects on Physical Level

Our body is made of different systems, systems are made of different organs, organs are made of different tissues and tissues are made of different cells. Cell is the smallest unit in the human body. Our body is made of 60 to 110 trillion tiny cells. This is the level up to where medical science is working. Effects of meditation goes beyond the cellular level to energy level thus renew each cell to rejuvenate, increasing flexibility of muscles by facilitating digestive, respiratory, circulatory as well as the other bodily processes.

Effects on Mental Level

During meditation your mind becomes quiet allowing your body to gain the deep rest necessary to release stress and fatigue. It relaxes the whole body by activating parasympathetic nervous system and de-activating sympathetic nervous system. Meditation is a methodology to train the mind to liberate by controlling the swirls of the mind. It is an effective way to treat psychosomatic diseases without drugs. It works as an efficient tool to control addiction.

Effects on Emotional Level

Meditation helps to control the swirls of mind with realization of self and its true worth. It assists the practitioner to be bold enough to resist ups and downs in life. Harmonization of the Nervous system and Endocrine system results in control and eradication of anger, fear, lust, jealousy and hatred ultimately that makes the practitioner strong from within.

Effects on Social Level

As a social being, we must adjust our natural instincts to progress in society. Physical, mental and emotional harmony leads to social harmony and spiritual awakening. It gives freedom from anguish and infatuations. Awakening of the spiritual wisdom leads to attainment of our blissful state.

CAN I DO MEDITATION?

People of any age, educational level, culture and from other Religious Faiths can learn and practice Meditation. It does not require specific beliefs or a change in lifestyle. The only change or adjustment needed is a regular schedule to meditate.

Methods of Meditation

There are various kinds of Meditational Techniques for people with different temperaments. You might wish to try several techniques to discover which one is the most suitable for you if you have never practiced meditation before. You can try soft instrumental meditation music in the background, if you respond to music. You can start with Trataka if you are a visual learner. In any case, get into the habit of meditating by setting aside quiet time each day. You may try Mantra Chanting. When you silently repeat your mantra, your awareness gently moves away from the non-stop activity of your mind to the stillness of your spirit. This soothes your entire physiology of mind, body and soul. These meditations are best experienced by practicing under guidance every day at a special time.

General Preparation to Meditate

Position:

Begin by finding a quiet spot where you will not be disturbed. Remove the home phone off the hook. Turn off your mobile phone, radio, and television, as well as any unnecessary electrical equipment in the area of immediate surrounding space where you will be meditating.

Sit in a comfortable position with Gyan Mudra or Anjali Mudra with priority. If difficulties, you may have back rest or sit in an arm chair with back straight, feet flat on the ground, and hands resting on thighs with palms flat. If even this is not possible, lie down either on the ground with feet shoulder width apart, back straight and hands resting gently to the sides, or on a bed in the same position.

Gently close your eyes with focus outside. Loosen your jaws keeping your chin down. Relax your body and concentrate on your breath with total awareness. When you inhale, you know you are inhaling and when you exhale, you know you are exhaling. Experience the breath that is going deeply within your body. Feel that your inhale breath is cooler than your exhale breath. Your exhale breath is hotter than your inhale breath. It will prepare your mind for meditation.

Pledge: Pledge will help you channelize your energy better. So, it is good idea to start meditation with pledge but it is not compulsory.

Mentally recite 5 times without moving lips and tongue; "I pledge within myself to practice meditation".

OM MEDITATION

Technique-1:
Close your eyes and focus your attention on the point between the eyebrows. Chant 'OM' for a few minutes until a peaceful feeling touches you. Fill the mind with faith in the divine that protects and directs your being.

"SO HUM" MEDITATION
With perception of breath, mentally recite "So" with inhale and "Hum" with exhale. Practice this process as long as possible. Retain silence and look at your body and mind with Ajna Chakra "Third Eye". Develop your awareness within (inside) and without (outside). Slowly open your eyes.

SOUND MEDITATION
Sound meditation is centred on the idea of relaxing and non-doing. When you are thinking, you may hear but you

cannot truly listen. As you centre your awareness in music, chanting, or natural sounds, you experience the essence of the sounds, giving yourself the experience of emptiness, clarity and receptivity.

Procedure: Carefully listen, every sound coming around. Be attentive to the sound coming from every direction. Be aware of the sound coming from outside. Awaken your pin drop attention, so that you will be able to witness the minute sound of pin and clip as well. Continue the practice for at least 5 - 20 minutes. Slowly, open your eyes feeling good and wide awaken.

INTERNAL TRIP MEDITATION

Procedure: Imagine that your spine is like a transparent tube. That is filled with grey and white matter (fluid). Visualise the grey and white fluid going to the tail bone along with inhale breath and coming up to the brain along with exhale breaths. Continue the process for 5 -15 minutes.

Gradually bring your awareness to breaths, body and the surroundings. Feeling energized, joyful and relaxed slowly open your eyes.

AWARENESS (WITNESSING) MEDITATION

Witnessing is the purest form of meditation. It is interesting to notice our moment-to-moment thoughts in a constant complete neutral position.

Procedure: Simply start watching the thoughts that come and go without judging or commenting. Be aware of every activity happening inside and outside. Do this for 5-20 minutes. You'll reach to ultimate silence and state of thoughtlessness over the period of time. Slowly open your eyes.

VIPASSANA MEDITATION

Vipassana means to see things as they really are. Vipassana is one of India's most ancient techniques of meditation. It was rediscovered by Gautama Buddha more than 2500 years ago and was taught by him as a universal remedy for universal ills (which is explained in the form of Four Noble Truths which comprise the essence of Buddha's teachings. They are 1. the truth of suffering 2. the truth of the cause of suffering 3. the truth of the end of suffering and 4. the truth of the path that leads to the end of suffering). This technique aims for the total eradication of mental impurities and the resultant highest happiness of full liberation. Vipassana is a way of self-transformation through self-observation. It focuses on the deep interconnection between mind and body, which can be experienced directly by disciplined attention to the physical sensations that form the life of the body and that continuously interconnect and condition the life of the mind. It is this observation-based, self-exploratory journey to the common root of mind and body that dissolves mental impurity, resulting in a balanced mind full of love and compassion.

Procedure: Focus on the rise and fall of the breath. While the mind is engaged in focusing on your breathing it cannot focus on its usual distractions. Just allow it to be the focus where your mind is centred and enjoy the feeling of witnessing and breathing rather than concentrating on it. Start with 20 minutes and gradually increase the time.

Ending: Slowly develop your awareness of the body and surroundings. Open your eyes with the feeling of silence and peace.

ZEN (ZAZEN) MEDITATION

Zazen means "just sitting." It is the basic meditation of Zen Buddhists for whom the path of enlightenment is everyday life lived with awareness and totality. Zazen is a tool to help rediscover the purity, simplicity of daily life as we did as children. Transient thoughts are paper tigers and that paying attention to them only gives them more energy. Zazen helps to gain the feeling of sitting and experiencing the fact that you are not the mind and can ignore its chatter at will. If your mind is particularly rebellious, you can give it a distraction to play with, such as concentrating on the breath.

Procedure: Close your eyes and allow whatever happens to happen. Simply release all thoughts of the mind. Do not get distracted with any past and present concerns which may arrives to take your awareness away from fully experiencing the moment. If you find any distractions, bring your mind back to neutral state again without getting disturbed or with feeling any regret. Continue this process as long as you can or wish.

Ending: Bring your awareness to the body and the whole surroundings. Open your eyes with the feeling of the divine bliss.

MANTRA MEDITATION

In Sanskrit Language, 'MAN' means Mind'' and 'TRA' means Vehicle or Instrument or Protection. In mantra meditation, you produce the sounds, loud or to yourself; either way, the sounds will produce an internal effect. The repetition of a ''mantra or sound' evokes a deep and peaceful reaction in your body and mind. Mantras are energies that are thought to have always existed in the universe. The mantra leads the way to meditation and to a state of non duality. A mantra can be anything that you enjoy repeating. For example: OM (I am), So-Hum (I am that), Om Namah Shivaya (Salutations to God within) or any of your choice. It should be repeated slowly, sounding each syllable: Om-Na-Mah-Shi-Va-Ya. You can choose a mantra that was given by a Guru with Initiation or any mantra that 'Resonate with Your Soul'. You can chant it in silence, loud or repeat it sub-vocally.

Procedure: Chant mantra with sounds with a small pause in every chant for 5-20 minutes. Chant mantra without sound (without moving lips and tongue) with small pause in every chant for 5-20 minutes.

Ending: Slowly bring your awareness to your whole body and surroundings. With a feeling of greatness and divinity, slowly and softly open your eyes with smile, feeling calm and light than before.

WAVES OF LIGHT MEDITATION

Process: Close your eyes. Take a deep breath, hold it in and tense up every muscle of your body, exhale and release the tension. Repeat this twice. Visualize your muscles becoming relaxed and saturated with a brilliant, white light. Start at your toes and work your way up to the top of your head, pay particular attention to the shoulders, jaw and facial area and any other area of your particular concern. If you hear sounds such as cars passing by, people talking, dogs barking etc; just let these sounds pass over you. Do not judge these sounds, simply allow them to occur and fade away with gentle deep breaths.

Visualize the white light that soaks your body starting from the top of your head to the tips of your toes. Visualize these waves starting very small and gradually building in intensity to a level that you feel comfortable with. Visualize the waves washing away negative thoughts or negative energies if any. These thoughts or energies can be visualized as black clouds which are covered by the white-light and gradually disappear. Be aware of cleaning effects with the waves of healing energy. When you feel sufficiently 'Cleansed' by the white light waves, visualize them gradually decreasing in intensity, until once again the white light is as calm as the surface of a pond. Gradually and gently bring your attention back to your surroundings and slowly open your eyes. Peace is with you.

PRAYER MEDITATION

Process: Reflect on how you could add one form of light hearted activity to your life, such as: showing patience; being kind; allowing another to express themselves without interruption; adopting an attitude of seeing a glass half full rather than half empty; doing a volunteer activity; helping a person in need. Continue your visualization for 10-20 minutes.

Ending: Finish your meditation with a prayer or affirmations of well wishes for family, friends, community and world peace. Take a deep breath, open your eyes, relax and stand. Be ready to move ahead with positive and energetic mind set.

LIGHT MEDITATION

Process: Visualize a tiny light somewhere in the distance. Begin to move toward that light. The light may be clear or hidden by a misty fog that creates an aura around it. As you get closer and closer, the light becomes more significant and more brilliant. Imagine that the Holy Spirit is at the centre of the light. All the Wisdom and Holiness of God is also in that light, which is presently intensely glowing whiter. Keep your mind focused on the light. Feel it is glowing brighter as you approach nearer to it. You are totally immersed in its wondrous golden glow. Now move into the centre of the light and feel it entering in your being, moving all around and through you. Feel the presence of God's Love within it and realize it is your love. Feel the embrace of the Spirit of God. Surrender to the Love and become one with it. Delight in the presence of God and feel His warm embrace as you connect with His Love. Understand, it will always be with you. Relax, knowing that you are one with this Creative source.

Now, feel all this light that was surrounding you and flooding through you, begin to gather inside your being as if you are a magnet, pulling all that light inside, so that you become the light itself. You are a being of pure light. You contain God, the Holy Spirit, and the entire essence of love.

Now, collect all this light together, allowing it to focus in the centre of your heart- where it disappears from sight, but still glows with the same intensity as before. It will burn brightly there forever as it always has, but now you will be aware of it.

Slowly develop your awareness in the room. Be aware of this light that is forever with you and seen in your eyes as a gentle radiance that is shown as a radiant beauty on your face; which everyone will know you came into contact with. Realise, the God's Divine presence is within you and open your eyes with smile.

GOLDEN LIGHT MEDITATION
Process: Visualize the flow of the waves of golden light as a river from the top of your head to the toes removing all the worries, tensions, strains and stressors. The light is spreading out to the whole room, the Universe and Infinity. Be one with the flow. Continue your visualization for 20 minutes.

Bring your awareness to the body and your surroundings. Feeling full of joy and blessings, gently open your eyes. Turn around with smiles and move ahead with full of positive vibrations that bring perennial peace, health, happiness and prosperity in your life.

POINT TO POINT BREATHING

Point to point breathing technique is a wonderful practice. It is especially useful when the mind is fatigued and when the body feels lethargic and heavy.

Procedure: Lie down flat on Shavasana (corpse pose) and allow the body to become still. Establish relaxed diaphragmatic breathing and observe it.

- Inhale while witnessing the effects of your breath going all the way through crown of your head, down to your toes and exhale back to the crown of the head. Repeat this 3 times.
- Inhale while witnessing the effects of your breath from the crown, down to the ankles and exhale back to the crown. Repeat this 3 times.
- Inhale witnessing the effects of your breath from the crown, down to the knees and exhale back to the crown. Repeat this 3 times.
- Inhale witnessing the effects of your breath from the crown, down to the hip joints to bottom of the spine and exhale back to the crown - repeat this 3 times.
- Inhale witnessing the effects of your breath from the crown, down to the navel centre and exhale back to the crown. Repeat this 3 times.
- Inhale witnessing the effects of your breath from the crown, down to the heart centre and exhale back to the crown. Repeat this 3 times.
- Inhale witnessing the effects of your breath from the crown, down to the throat and exhale back to the crown. Repeat this 3 times.
- Inhale witnessing the effects of your breath from the crown, down to the eyebrow centre and exhale back to the crown. Repeat this 3 times.
- Reverse the order; first the throat, then heart centre, to

navel centre, to hip joints, to knees, to ankles and to the toes.

- Breathe as if the whole body is breathing. Visualize that you are lying in the centre of a wave of energy and bliss. Let your breathing remain deep and watch it as you relax your body and mind. Slowly open your eyes with smile.

TRATAKA MEDITATION

Preparation: Decide an object on which you gaze to do Tratak. Object can be candle (you can gaze at the flame of candle) or idol of your choice or black spot etc. Place the object at eye level maintaining 3-5 feet distance.

Procedure: Start with fast breathing. Go for rapid inhalation and exhalation. Do it faster and faster as if it is your last breath. Focus more on exhalation. You may have small pauses but do not stop for a longer time. Best process is to do it continuously for 5-10 minutes.

Now, come back to normal breathing. Open your eyes and keep eyes focused on the object. Constantly keep your eyes focused until you have tears in your eyes. Once the tears come in your eyes, close your eyes and visualise the object in your mental screen. The moment, object of visualization disappears from you mental screen, open your eyes to gaze again for some time. Close your eyes and repeat the visualisation. Do this for 5-20 minutes.

Rub your palms to make them warm. Cover your eyes with palms and gently massage. Blink your eyes and gently open with smile.

COLOUR MEDITATION - BALANCING CHAKRAS

This meditation will bring all healing colours and light into your spiritual being. It helps you to cope with different aspects of your life in a more meaningful way. You will be more peaceful and your life will make more sense. You will be spreading your Rainbow of Light to the people around you and they will respond to you in a more positive way.

Process: Begin by visualizing the white Light swirling around you in a clockwise motion, starting at your feet, and moving up towards your head. Picture this motion of white light going around you three times, each time starting at the bottom of your feet and moving upwards.

Crown Chakra (Situated at top of the head)

Visualise a purple light swirling around Crown-Chakra. Move the flow of light clockwise. Now visualise the Purple light swirling around your body, swirling down toward your feet and back up going in a clockwise motions. The Purple light may be moving with ease or feel heavy and stuck. The heavy or stuck feeling means that this chakra is unbalanced but the more you work at this on a daily basis, the more it will open up, gets balanced and begins to move with ease.

Ajna Chakra (Third Eye & Intuitive Chakra)

Now, move to the Forehead Centre, which is called Third Eye Centre or Intuitive Centre. Visualize Indigo Colour light swirling around the Ajna Chakra. Move the flow of light clockwise. Picture it moving until you feel that it is clear or moving in an easy motion. Now, visualize the indigo light swirling around your body, in a clockwise motion down to your feet and back up to your head.

Vishuddha - Throat Chakra

Bring your awareness to the Throat Chakra which regulates anger and the ability to speak up for oneself.

Visualize blue colour light swirling around the Throat Chakra. Move the flow of light in clockwise motion. Picture it moving until you feel that it is clear or moving with an easy motion. It may take several times before the chakras will change and become clear and balanced and the colour moving with ease. Now, visualize the blue light swirling around your body in a clockwise motion down to your feet and back up again to your head.

Anahata - Heart Chakra

The chest area or the heart chakra is the centre of love for self, and being able to love. Visualize a green or pink colour light moving clockwise around the Anahata chakra. Now, visualize this light moving around your body, in a clockwise motion down to your feet and back up to your head.

Manipura Chakra - Below Breastbone Stomach

The Manipura centre, which is the diaphragmatic area located right below your breastbone. Visualise the yellow colour that relates to emotional issues. Once again picture the yellow colour going clockwise motion. Now, visualise the yellow light moving around your body in a clockwise motion down to your feet and back up to your head.

Swadhisthana Chakra - Below Belly Button

The colour of this chakra is Orange and it relate to our gonads -procreation and sexuality. Visualize the orange colour moving around swadhisthana chakra in a clockwise motion. Now, visualise the orange light moving around your body, in a clockwise motion down to your feet and back up to your head.

Mooladhara - Chakra (Root)

Lastly the Root chakra colour is red and located in the pelvic area. Root Chakra relates to safety, security, and stability in all aspects of life. Visualise the red colour light in the chakra area moving around clockwise motion.

Now, visualize the red colour moving around your body, in a clockwise motion down to your feet and back up to your head.

Ending: Visualize the energy within and outside. Feel the peace and comfort within and outside. Slowly open your eyes feeling energized and peaceful.

PREKSHA MEDITATION

Preksha Meditation (PM) means to see; See deep being free from ego, attachment and hatred. Preksha Meditation is a technique of meditation that aims at bringing about positive attitudinal and behavioral changes through overall transformation in the personality. Although, the technique of Preksha Meditation is derived from the wisdom of ancient philosophy, it is based on scientific principles. PM emphasises more on the concentration of thought because perception is more important than thinking for the realisation of the truth. Several experiments such as deep breathing, alternate breathing, perception on different parts of the body, meditation, colours, relaxation, contemplation etc. are conducted in the Preksha Dhayana. All these processes have direct impact on physical, mental and emotional plane and spiritual synergy's are enhanced and enriched. This technique was developed by Acharya Tulsi and Acharya Mahapragya.

The main purpose of the Preksha Meditation is to purify the mental state. A human mind is constantly exposed to contaminating urges, emotions and passions. Therefore, it is essential to remove these obstacles. Peace of mind appears with the disappearance of the impure thoughts. In addition, balanced mind, equanimity and well-being are also experienced simultaneously. Uncontrolled emotions like anger, greed etc. are not only the hurdles in spiritual progress but also becomes the cause of disaster in social life. PM can cure and even protect us from several psychosomatic disorders that result from mental stress and tension.

Preparation

Posture: You may select a posture of meditation in which you can sit comfortably and steadily for a long period. The posture of meditation may be 'full lotus-posture,' 'half lotus-posture,' 'simple cross-legged posture or Vajrasan (diamond-posture).

Mudras: Position of the Hands There are two alternatives: one position is called Jnana Mudra and other is Brahma Mudra (Vitrag Mudra).

Jnana Mudra: Keep your right hand on the right knee and left hand on the left knee, keeping the palms turned up. Let the tip of the index finger touch the tip of the thumb with a slight pressure between them. Keep the other fingers straight.

Brahma Mudra (Vitrag Mudra): Keep both the hands on your lap one above the other by keeping the palms upturned. Let the left palm remain under the right one. Keep your eyes softly closed.

Recitation of Arham: Start the meditation session with the repeated recitation of the mantra Arham. Exhale fully and inhale completely. By slow exhalation begin the intonation of the mantra. Concentrating your mind on the navel, produce the sound "A" for about two seconds, while concentrating your mind on the Centre of Bliss situated near the heart, produce the sound "Rha" for about four seconds and lastly taking your mind upward from throat to the Centre of Knowledge situated at the top of the head, produce the sound "mmm" for about six seconds. Inhale deeply again and repeat the same exercise 9 times. Visualize that the sound waves are criss-crossing and weaving an oval-shaped web of armour all around you, protecting yourself from the evil effects of the external vibrations.

Recitation of the Mahaprana Dhvani: Alternatively start meditation with the repeated recitation of the Mahaprana Dhvani. Exhale fully and inhale deeply as long as you can. By slow exhalation, produce the sound "mmm" through the nostrils like buzzing of a bee, while concentrating your mind on the Centre of Knowledge situated on the top of the head and keeping the mouth closed. Inhale deeply again and repeat the same exercise nine times.

The Aphorism of the Aim: "Sampikkhae Appaga Mappaenam" Perceive and realize the deepest and highest levels of your consciousness by your conscious mind. See yourself through yourself. For perception and realization of the self, practice preksha meditation.

Resolve for Meditation: "I am practicing preksha meditation for the purification of my mind (psyche)". (Repeat three times)

First Step- KAYOTSARGA

The first step of meditation is Kayotsarga that is relaxation with self-awareness. Keep your body steady, relaxed and free from tension. Keep your spine and neck straight but without stiffness. Relax all the muscles of your body. Let your body become limp.

Practice steadiness of body at least for five minutes. Keep your body completely steady, as motionless as a statue. Do not allow the limbs of your body to move. No movement at all. Kayotsarga has two implications: complete relaxation of the body and self-awareness. For achieving complete relaxation of the body, mentally divide it into several parts and concentrate your mind on each part of the body one by one from feet to head. Allow your mind to spread in the whole part; allow it to undertake a trip in the whole part; use the technique of auto-suggestion to relax the whole part and experience the resulting relaxation. Experience that each and every muscle, each and every nerve has become relaxed. And in the same way attain the relaxation of the whole body. Use deep concentration and remain completely alert.

Detailed Instructions for Relaxation: Starting with the big toe of your right foot, concentrate your mind on it. Allow your mind to spread throughout the big toe. Suggest to the muscles and nerves to relax. Relax..... Relax..... Relax..... Experience that they are relaxing. Experience that they have become relaxed. In the same way, attain relaxation of the other parts of the right limb; the other toes, sole, heel, ankle, upper part of the foot, calf-muscles, knee, thigh, up to the hip-joint. In the same way relax the left limb up to the hip-joint. Experience that the whole of the lower portion of the body has become completely relaxed.

Now achieve the relaxation of the middle portion of the body from the waist up to the neck. Concentrate your mind on each part one by one starting with the lower abdomen, relax the front, the back, the right side, the left side, the outside and the inside of your lower abdomen. Similarly relax the upper abdomen—the front, the back, the right side, the left side, the outside and the inside of your upper abdomen. Now through your navel enter the abdominal cavity and relax the large intestine, the small intestine, the kidneys, the spleen, the liver, the pancreas, the stomach and the diaphragm. Use autosuggestion and achieve relaxation. Then concentrate your mind on the chest and relax the entire ribcage.

Beginning with the lowest rib, relax each and every rib in turn. Relax the front ribs, the back ribs, the right ribs and the left ribs. Now enter the chest and relax the right lung, the left lung and the heart by auto-suggestion. (Those who have got any heart trouble should pause here for a few minutes and by autosuggestion slow down the heart to remove stress.)

Now achieve the relaxation of the neck muscles in the front and in the back. Then concentrate your mind on both the hands and arms one by one; starting from the thumb, relax the fingers, the palm, the wrist, the lower arm, the elbow, the upper arm and the shoulder. Experience that the whole of the middle portion of your body has become completely relaxed.

Now achieve the relaxation of the upper portion of body from throat up to the head. Here we have come to a bit more difficult part of the exercise. So far you were relaxing large muscles which respond quickly to your suggestion. But now we have to relax a large number of small and tiny muscles which are difficult to relax. First unclench your teeth and unlock your jaws and let your tongue go limp. Keep your lips softly closed. Now relax all the facial muscles; beginning with the chin, relax the lips, the inner portion of the mouth including the teeth, the gums, the palate and the tongue; then relax the cheeks, the nose, the ears and the temples, both the eyes, the forehead and the scalp, through auto-suggestion.

Experience that the whole of your upper portion of the body has become completely relaxed.

Again allow your mind to travel from the head up to the feet and from the feet up to the head; this time rather quickly and see that there is no tension anywhere in the body. Experience that the whole body from the feet up to the head has become completely relaxed. Maintain the posture of Kayotsarga throughout the meditation session. Try to keep your body completely steady and motionless.

Now practice inner silence at least for five minutes through relaxation of the vocal cords (voice box). Concentrate your mind on the voice box inside the throat and completely relax it. Observe complete inner silence.

Internal Trip (Antaryatra)

The second step of Preksha meditation is the practice of internal trip through the spinal cord. Take your mind to the lower end of the spinal cord, called the Centre of Energy. Allow your mind to go upward inside your spinal cord up to the top of the head called the Centre of Knowledge. Again allow it to come back through the same path to the Centre of Energy. Again and again repeat the same process. Let your mind continuously undertake the trip inside the spinal cord and perceive the subtle vibrations of the vital energy, taking place inside the spinal cord, or whatever sensation you get there. Simply perceive them without any reaction. Concentrate your entire consciousness on the spinal cord. You may synchronize your internal trip with the process of breathing. During exhalation, undertake the upward trip and during inhalation, undertake the downward trip. Use deep concentration and complete awareness. Practice the internal trip through the spinal cord. Allow your mind to rise and fall inside the spinal cord just like mercury rising and falling inside the instrument used for measuring blood pressure.

PERCEPTION OF BREATHING

The third step of preksha meditation is perception of breathing. Regulate your breathing; make it slow, deep and rhythmic. Let the vibrations of each breath reach your navel. Allow your abdominal muscles to expand during inhalation and contract during exhalation. Now concentrate your mind fully on your navel. Practice deep, slow and rhythmic breathing, by allowing each breath to take the same time. Perceive each inhalation and exhalation through the expansion and contraction of the abdominal muscles accompanying each inhalation and exhalation respectively. Continuing the slow, deep and rhythmic breathing, now shift your attention from the navel and focus it inside the nostrils at the junction of both the nostrils. Perceive each incoming and outgoing breath. Remain fully aware of each and every breath. Continuously practice slow, long and rhythmic breathing, inhale and exhale each breath while remaining fully aware of it. Fully occupy your mind in perception of breathing. If you are distracted by any thought, do not try to stop it forcefully, but also perceive it and then again start perceiving your breath. If the distraction is frequent, you may hold your breath for a few seconds without causing any discomfort. Maintain the continuity of the awareness of breathing. Merely perceive it without like and dislike.

PERCEPTION OF BRIGHTWHITE COLOUR

The fourth step of Preksha meditation is perception of bright white colour on the Centre of Enlightenment. Concentrate your mind on the Centre of Enlightenment, situated in the middle of your forehead. Allow your mind to penetrate inside and perceive bright white colour there. You may visualise as if the bright white light of the full moon is spreading throughout the portion or visualise the bright white colour of the snow or any other white thing. Practice concentrated visualisation of bright white colour on the centre of enlightenment. Perceiving the bright white colour; experience through auto-suggestion that all your passions and emotions are being pacified. All your excitations are subsiding. Your anger is waning away. Now allow your mind to spread throughout the whole portion of your forehead and perceive the bright white colour there. Visualise that the particles of bright white light are permeating the whole portion of the forehead, covering the emotional area in the frontal lobe of your brain. Continuously perceive bright white colour and experience complete tranquillity, complete mental peace and bliss. Conclude the meditation session with two or three long breaths.

THE APHORISMS OF WISDOM
Appana Sachchamesejja, Mettim Bhuesu Kappae
Search truth yourself and befriend all living beings. ...3 times

Ahamsu Vijjacharanam Pamokkham
For emancipation from sufferings, practice knowledge and conduct. ...3 times

THE APHORISM OF TAKING REFUGE
Arahante Saranam Pavvajjami
     I seek refuge in the adorable ones.
Siddhe Saranam Pavvajjami
     I seek refuge in the emancipated ones.
Sahu Saranam Pavvajjami
     I seek refuge in the saints.
Kevali Pannattam Dhammam Saranam Pavvajjami-
     I seek refuge in the religion propounded by the omniscient ones.

Now adopt the posture of obeisance, that is kneel and bow, pay obeisance to truth. With folded hands first inhale fully and then during exhalation, pronounce the Aphorism of Faith.

"Vande Sachcham"…3 times

"I pay my obeisance to Truth" by bowing down to ground. Repeat it three times.

Meditation session concludes.

THE CHAKRA SCIENCE

Chakra is a Sanskrit word that literally means Wheel. Chakras are the powerhouses in the way it generates and stores energy. It signifies the basic energy centres in the body that correspond to nerve ganglia branching out from the spinal column and endocrine glands. There are major 7 Chakras located in our Aura (Etheric body). There are 3 bodies according to yogic philosophy: 1. Sthula Sarira (gross body) 2. Sukshma Sarira (Subtle body or astral body) and 3. Karana Sarira (Causal Body). Chakras are located along the spinal column from the base of spine to the top of the head. Cosmic energy from the Cosmos pulled in more strongly at these points. The main Nadis viz. Ida, Pingala and Sushumna run along the spinal column in a curved path and cross one another several times. At the points of intersection they form strong energy centres known as Chakras.

The word Chakra literally translates as wheel or disk and refers to a spinning sphere of bioenergetics activity emanating from the major nerve ganglia branching forward from the spinal column. Generally, ·six of these wheels are described, stacked in a column of energy that spans from the base of the spine to the middle of the forehead and the seventh which is beyond the physical region. It is the six major chakras that correlate with basic states of consciousness."

The 3 Major Nadis (rivers) and the 7 Chakras (wheels of energy)

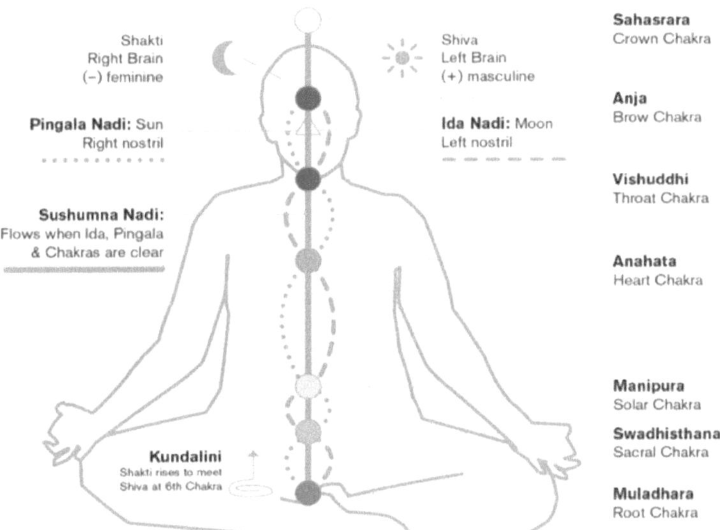

Modern interpretation of the chakras by Anodea Judith: "A Chakra is believed to be a centre of activity that receives, assimilates and expresses life energy.

According to yogic philosophy, there are three types of energy centres in human body. The Lower or Animal Chakras are located in the region between the toes and the pelvic region indicating our evolutionary origins in the animal kingdom. The human Chakras lie along the spinal column. Finally, the higher or divine Chakras are found between the top of the spine and the crown of the head.

HISTORY

Original information on Chakras comes from the Upanishads. They are believed to have been passed down orally for approximately thousands years before being written down for the first time between 1200–900 BCE.

SCIENTIFIC BASIS OF CHAKRA

The Chakras interact with the body's ductless (Endocrine) glands and lymphatic system by feeding in good bio-energies and disposing of unwanted bio-energies. Chakras are responsible for the states of consciousness, developmental stages of life, representative elements, body functions, colours and sounds. They form a profound formula for wholeness, when they are in balance and harmony. If Chakras are imbalanced, it is manifested in the form of hormonal imbalances, emotional disturbances or other physical disorders.

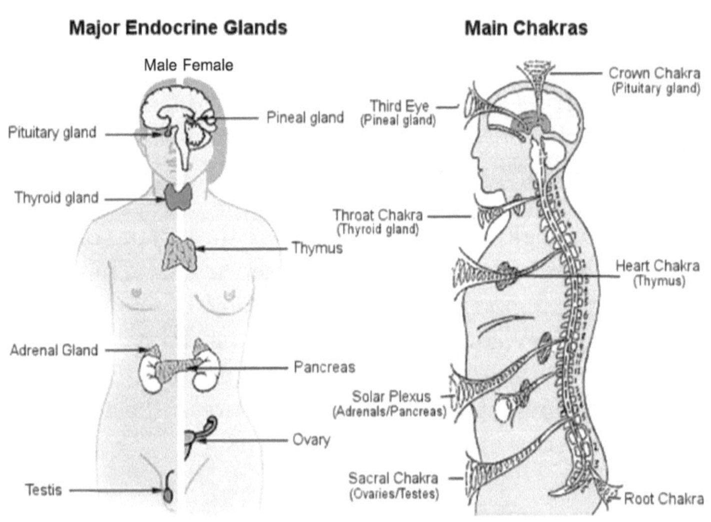

Functions of Chakra

Function of these chakras depends upon the person's physical, mental, emotional, intellectual and spiritual health. Some may be sluggish, under active, hyper active because of different reasons. Good news is that there are yogic techniques to bring balance and harmony among them by channelizing the energy that flows all over the body through the Nadis.

Nadis

Nadi literally means stream or channel. In Yoga, Nadis are considered as the channels of Kundalini energy. There are gross as well as subtle Nadis in our body. Gross channels are visible as vessels, tubes, nerves, arteries, veins, lymph including acupressure meridians. When we talk about Nadis in Yoga, they are channels of Mind and Chitta or being. According to Ayurveda there are over 72,000 Nadis in our body. Tantra yoga identifies 14 principal Nadis (Ida, Pingla, Sushumna, Gandhari, Hastajihva, Yashasvini , Pusha, Alambusha, Kuhu, Shankini, Sarasvati, Payasini,Varuni, Visvodara) of which Ida, Pingala and Sushumna are the most important.

THE SEVEN CHAKRAS

MULADHARA (ROOT CHAKRA)

It is the centre of all the vitality, physical energy and self-preservation. It is the location of the resting Kundalini– the serpentine energy coiled inside every human being. Kundalini is released and drawn up through the Muladhara Chakra. Spiritual awakening begins after its purification. It is related to our survival instincts, stillness and our sense of grounding and connection to our bodies as well as the physical world. It activates and strengthens our will, assists in living on the physical plane and stimulates the life-sustaining energies. Ideally, this Chakra brings us health, prosperity, security and dynamic presence.

Location: Located at the base of the spine in the lower pelvic floor between the anus and sexual organs, this Chakra forms our foundation.

Symbolism: A Lotus flower of four deep red petals. At the centre of the flower is a glowing yellow square. Within this yellow square, there is an inverted red triangle with its apex pointing down. This is Shakti – symbol of creative energy.

Visualization: Internally focusing on the red triangle within the yellow square enhances inner balance and integration of creativity and stability. Muladhara is concerned with survival viz. food, shelter and clothes.

SVADHISHTHANA (SACRAL) CHAKRA

It is the second Chakra. This is the dwelling place of deep-rooted instincts and all Samskaras viz. mental and emotional impressions of the past. It is concerned with health, recreation and secondary sexual character. It influences the emotions, relationships, procreation, pleasure, desire and sexuality as well as creativity and intuition. It connects us to others through feeling, sensation and movement. It stimulates the creative life force required for existence on the physical plane. Ideally this chakra brings us fluidity and grace, depth of feeling, sexual fulfilment and the ability to accept change.

Blockage of this chakra causes emotional problems or sexual guilt. The gonads include the ovaries in women and testes in men, are related with Svadhisthana Chakra. They connect energetically to the heels, ankles and lower legs and support the Homolateral Push.

Location: Above the Muladhara Chakra, directly behind the genitals or hypo-gastric plexus and 4 inches below the navel.

Symbolism: A Lotus flower of six deep crimson petals and a bluish- white crescent moon sits within the lower half of the Lotus circle. It symbolizes Moon's influence on ocean's tides and human emotions.

Visualization: Concentrating on an image of bluish-white crescent moon above a deep open ocean helps to restore emotional calm and balance and frees us from compulsive behaviour and unhealthy habitual pattern of the past.

MANIPURA (SOLAR PLEXUS/NAVEL) CHAKRA

Manipur Chakra is known as the power chakra as well. It is the centre of inner power, intellect astral force, energy, ambitious drive and assertiveness as well as desire and emotions based on intellect, and touch. It is the seat of emotions, ego identity and self-definition. It regulates metabolism.

It contains a protective energy, protecting against any negativity. When healthy, this chakra brings us energy, effectiveness, spontaneity and non-dominating power. Blockage of the chakra manifests as anger or a sense of victimization.

Manipura Chakra is related with the adrenals & the pancreas. The Adrenals are situated like little hats on top of the Kidneys. They are associated with instinct for survival, physical courage based instinct and its counterpart – fear. They connect energetically to the knees, femurs and sacroiliac joints. The Adrenal gland underlies courageous instinct and relate to Manipura Chakra. The Pancreas is a base of support for the heart which has qualities of love and being there for others. It also gives energetic support to the head, feet, tail, hands and the Homologous Push. The pancreas underlies social instinct and relates to the Solar Plexus and Manipura Chakra.

Location: It is located behind the navel or solar plexus, below the breastbone.

Symbolism: A Lotus flower of ten petals. Within the circle of the lotus is a downward pointing fiery-red triangle – like a gleaming ruby, signifying energy and power.

Visualization: Visualizing a golden light radiating from the fiery triangle and spreading throughout the body cultivates physical, mental and psychic energy, dynamism and vitality. The navel Chakra is related to energy and self-esteem.

ANAHAT (HEART) CHAKRA

Anahat means "the unstruck sound" - this refers to the cosmic sound which does not arise from two objects being struck (as is the case to produce all other sounds) but is always present in the heart. From this centre, internal vibrations and pulsing of heart can be heard. This Chakra is called the heart Chakra as well.

The Anahata Chakra unifies the loving energy of the heart and the analytical energy of the intellect. It is the integrator of opposites in the psyche: mind and body, male and female, persona and shadow, ego and unity etc. A healthy Anahata Chakra brings unconditional love, compassion, understanding of equality and brotherhood as well as sense of peace. Blockage can manifest as immune system or heart problems or a lack of compassion.

Energetically the heart centre supports gestures where there is opening and embracing with the arms and also reaching out through hands and eyes. The function of the heart centre is therefore one of 'giving and receiving'. They support the forearms, wrists and the Homologous Push. The Thymus Gland is part of the lymphatic system which relates to issues of defence and boundaries. The Thymus gives support and freedom in movements of the shoulder girdle and shoulder joints and openness across the chest. The function of this Chakra is to give courage based on love and beyond instincts or duty.

Location: The Heart Chakra is located in the centre of the chest behind the sternum, level with the heart.

Symbolism: This Chakra is symbolized by a Lotus flower of twelve petals. A six-pointed star is at the centre of the Lotus, like a hexagram, which consists of two triangles. The upward and downward pointing triangles denote the mid-way balance of lower Chakras of physical existence and upper Chakras of spiritual transcendental levels. The star contains a gentle burning flame – the symbol of individual soul (Jivattama).

Visualization: Focusing on steadiness of this inner flame of the heart connects us to our individual soul, internal truth and compassion, which remain steady and undisturbed by the external activities of the world.

VISHUDDHI (THROAT) CHAKRA

 This is the wheel of purity. This chakra is related to communication, expression by thought, speech & writing, sound and creativity. Here, we experience the world symbolically through vibration, such as the vibration of sound representing language. You will feel pressure when you are not communicating your emotions properly. It helps to accept all dualities, polarities and dichotomies of opposites within us without judgement that helps us to move forward.

The Parathyroid and the Thyroid glands relate to Vishuddhi Chakra. The Thyroid and Parathyroid glands underline creative expressions. The Thyroid supports vocal expression and gives energetic support to the elbows and humours.

Location: The Throat Chakra is located at the neck behind the wall of the throat, or the Pharyngeal Plexus.

Symbolism: A Lotus flower of sixteen violet petals. Within the Lotus flower is a white circle like a silvery full moon with a teardrop shape of nectar at its centre. This symbolizes the harmonizing and purifying of all polarities and opposites.

Visualization: Visualizing and sensing a sweet tear-drop of nectar-like calming balm at the level of your throat and your breath is said to resolve our internal conflicts of heart and mind. This helps to cultivate understanding and non-judgemental attitude to mind and heart.

AJNA (THIRD EYE/ BROW) CHAKRA

 Ajna Chakra means the "Command Centre". This energy centre is the gateway to our Intuition. Here communication and commands from the internal Guru are heard. At this point, the links between mental and psychic aspects of our being are created.

It is the centre of psychic power, higher intuition, energies of the spirit, magnetic forces and light. It enables focus on the higher intuitive information. It will assist in the purification of negative tendencies and elimination of selfish attitudes and desires.. It opens our psychic faculties and our understanding of archetypal levels. When it is healthy it allows us to achieve clairvoyance with increased psychic abilities, imagination, visions, and dreams.

Pituitary and Pineal glands are associated with Ajna Chakra. The Pituitary Gland supports the functions of eyes, intelligence, imagination and conceptual thoughts. It brings altruism and compassion. The Pineal Gland is associated with the sense of hearing and the vestibular/ balance mechanisms of the inner ear. It harmonizes patterns of rest and activity, the circadian rhythms. It also underlies the integration of the soul and relates to Ajna Chakra.

Location: The Third-eye Chakra is located above the eyebrows at the centre of the forehead behind the space in between the eyebrows, midbrain at medulla (Pineal Plexuses). Because of its location at the "Third Eye", it may also be referred to as Gyan Chakshu ("Eye of Wisdom").

Symbolism: A two-petaled silver Lotus – one petal representing the Sun (Pingala) and one the Moon (Ida). The circle of the Lotus is of a silvery-white shade with a lingam in its centre. This is placed within a downward pointing triangle, which is a symbol of Shakti, the feminine principle.

Visualization: Focusing on a glowing circle of light at the centre of your eyebrows, radiating wisdom and intuition enhances insight and inner knowledge.

SAHASRARA (CROWN) CHAKRA

Crown Chakra is the dwelling place of our highest awareness. It is the union of all consciousness and all energy. It is the centre of spirituality, enlightenment, dynamic thought and energy. It is our connection to the greater world beyond time and space.

The Hypothalamus is part of the brain and is not an endocrine gland. Hypothalamus is not usually included in comparisons of the Chakras with the endocrine system. It is found that if you focus on it, breathe into it and visualize it, you will get a sense of white light at the crown of your head which seems to have an affinity with meditation.

Location: The Crown Chakra is located at the crown or the top of the head or skull.

Symbolism: A circular Lotus blossom of a thousand shining petal lying over one another. Inscribed on each petal is a letter of the Sanskrit alphabet. In the centre of the Lotus, is a full moon; within the Full Moon is a Jyotirlinga – a Lingam of light shining upward, symbolizing pure consciousness.

Visualization: It is said that the experience of Sahasrara is beyond words and all definitions. It has to be felt to be understood. It is the Buddha Nirvana, or the Yogic Samadhi. This state is the perfect merging of all things. It is Yoga itself.

CHAKRA HEALINGS

The health of an area of the physical body and the condition of its associated chakras are considered interdependent e.g. when a chakra is clear and vital the associated portions of the body should also be in the optimum state. When a healer clears the chakras, the body becomes revitalized to make efforts for realizations of dreams and desires. It is important to balance Chakras in Chakra Healing.

BALANCING THE CHAKRAS

Chakras can be opened, activated and balanced by a variety of methods. One method is Aura cleansing. When stimulated, developed and cleansed, it enables one to see the truth concerning illusory ideas, materialistic pursuits, self-limiting concepts, pride and vanity; it further allows one to experience continuous self-awareness and conscious detachment from personal emotions. It brings us knowledge, wisdom, under-standing, spiritual connection and bliss.

There are different yogic process that includes Asana, Pranayama and Meditation to balance the Chakras. Systematic regular practice of these processes can purify the Chakras and facilitate the Pranic flow throughout the body. As a result, one can achieve optimum physical, mental, emotional and psychological health and wellness.

BALANCING FINANCIAL ENERGY WITH CHAKRAS

The chakra system can greatly influence every dimensions of life and its relationship to money and financial aspect. By applying this sacred system to your financial life, you can LEARN TO BUDGET while supporting major life areas to flourish with money. It is simply an example. It can be applied in every field of life. Here are list of life areas associated with each chakra that seek financial attention; you can certainly add your own special areas that are unique to you.

The Chakra Money Balance Sheet (Budget)

1. Muladhara Chakra

This energy center is located at the base of the spine. It manages physical health, body maintenance, and survival-related bills (food, shelter, clothes). Pen in the approximate amount of money you allocate to each item (on monthly basis), unless indicated otherwise:

Food: ________ Home/Rent: ________ Clothes: __________

Other chakra one expenses: ________________________

2. Swadhisthana Chakra

This energy center is located 4-5 inches below navel connected back with spine. It manages health, emotion, relationships, recreations and entertainment. The items listed here are not necessities like those listed for chakra one, rather they are the privileges that comes with having extra money. Approximately, how much money do you give to this chakra (on monthly basis), unless indicated otherwise?

Doctor (yearly): __________ Health & Hygiene: __________

Club Membership: ____________ Sports: ____________

Car/ Motorcycle: ____________________________

Vacation (yearly): ____________________________

Dining Out & ___________________ Parties: ___________________

___________________ Shopping: ___________________

Other costs: ____

3. Manipura – Chakra

This energy center is located at the solar plexus (navel centre). It manages personal savings. How much money do you put aside for yourself, monthly?

Money you put in a savings account? ___________________

Money you put in a retirement account? ___________________

Money you put in an investment portfolio? ___________________

Money you put in real estate? ___________________

Other investments: ___________________________________

4. Heart Chakra

This energy center is located at the heart region. It manages compassion. How much money do you give/donate to charities (on monthly basis)? ___________

Other costs (e.g., financially helping a friend or a family member): ___________________________________

5. Vishuddhi Chakra

This energy center is located at the throat region. It manages self-expression. Approximately, how much money do you spend on expressing yourself through creative outlets, (on monthly basis)?

Drawing & Painting: _______ Writing: _________ Crafts: _______

Music & _______ Dancing: _________ Gardening: _________

Photography: _______________________________________

Other costs for hobbies that exhibit your creative expression:

6. Ajna Chakra

This energy center is located on the forehead between the eyebrows. It manages your dream and social vision. How much money are you giving to actualizing your dream (onto the physical plane, a dream that is also serving humanity in the positive direction)? For example, are you opening your own organic farming? Organic Restaurant? School? Clinic? Yoga Studio? Job Website Service? Retail Outlet? Health Store? What amount of your money are you using to materialize your dream? _______________________________________

Other costs: _______________________________________

7. Crown Chakra

This energy center is located on the crown of your head. It manages your spirituality (i.e., your connection to Source Energy), learning and brain functioning.

Meditating:_________________ Praying: _________________

Taking classes on higher mind-body disciplines (e.g., yoga, tai-chi) or higher philosophies (e.g., Buddhism, Mysticism, Hinduism etc.): _______________________________________

Other costs: _______________________________________

EXPLANATION

When you look at the monetary values for each chakra you'll notice the chakra(s) that is not balanced. For example, if you are controlled by money and most of your money is tied up in chakra one (survival needs) then the rest of your chakra system is not getting proper financial attention. By contrast, a person who has money evenly distributed in all seven chakras is a person who is a master of money, not a slave to money, no matter the size of his/her income. This person's thinking is different than a person controlled by money. How rich or poor you live your life is a matter of your thought process. This puts the creation of poverty and wealth into your hands and is your responsibility. There is no one to blame for your crippled financial state.

Paying into Your Chakra System

Let's go through an example of setting up the chakras to receive money. Assume that you make Rs 2,00,000 a year.

You give survival chakra Rs 1, 00,000 yearly (rent, food, clothes).

You give pleasure centre, chakra, Rs 42,000 yearly (car, entertainment, fun).

To saving chakra, you save Rs 1,500 a month (Rs 18,000 for the year).

The remaining Rs 40,000 is unaccounted for, as you don't know what you spend it on other than on life's unexpected events.

You can plug that floating money into the upper chakras so as to activate your higher financial centres. For example: allocate money to helping, to self-expression, to your vision and to higher learning. Money invested in these upper chakras serve to develop your character into a more complete and balanced person. Wholeness is success. When you radiate success, you magnetize more of it to you. When you are finished with the worksheet, proceed to the visualization exercise.

Abundance Visualization Meditation

According to Quantum physics, "the energy realm controls the physical realm of life". Given that fact, use visualization to see money (as energy) being deposited into all your chakra energy centres. Do the visualization now and every day hereafter. Create strong associations within your brain between the thought of depositing money into each chakra centre and the feelings (gratitude, joy, excitement) of receiving money for each centre. These feelings serve to generate the physical manifestation of money being deposited into each chakra—and may even open unexpected doorways to more income.

Muladhara (Root) Chakra: In your mind, imagine money (e.g., Rs 10,000, or you pick an amount believable to you) immediately being deposited into your first financial centre located at the base of your spine. Feel that all of your health and survival needs are taken care of with ease and abundance. See yourself having more than enough money to pay for your house, utility bills and organic groceries.

Swadhisthana Chakra: In your mind, visualize money (e.g., Rs 10,000, or you pick an amount) immediately being deposited into your second financial energy centre, located at your belly button. Feel that all of your relationships are secure and all of your pleasures are met. For example, you are able to go to any entertainment event you want. For all of your health needs such as yoga, health club membership as well as doctor and dentist appointments. Your vehicle is paid off. You enjoy all the pleasures of life, effortlessly.

Manipura Chakra: In your mind, imagine money (e.g., Rs 10,000, or you pick an amount) immediately being deposited into your financial balancing centre located at your solar plexus. Feel the joy and security of watching your savings account accumulate into great wealth. See your investment portfolio expanding as you fund growing and lucrative options.

Anahata (Heart) Chakra: In your mind, visualize money (e.g., Rs 10,000, or you pick an amount) immediately being deposited into your fourth financial energy centre. Feel the love and gratitude from the people whom you have freely given some of this money in order to help them improve their quality of life. See the positive karmic consequences of your financial help.

Vishuddhi (Throat) Chakra: In your mind, imagine money (e.g., Rs 10000, or you pick an amount) immediately being deposited into your fifth financial energy centre located at your throat. Feel the liberation your body and mind as money is helping you to nurture your hobbies and talents.

For example, you have the financial means to express yourself whether that means cultivating your own garden or developing your culinary skills or enhancing your artistic abilities—whatever is important to you.

Ajna (Third Eye) Chakra: In your mind, visualize money (e.g., Rs 10,000, or you pick an amount) immediately being deposited into your sixth financial energy centre located on your forehead between your eyebrows. Feel the excitement of having more than enough resources to turn your dream into a reality. For example, your ideal home is being developed or your business venture is being embraced and supported you have been able to run a reputed school.

Crown Chakra: In your mind, imagine money (e.g., Rs 10,000, or you pick an amount) immediately being deposited into your seventh financial energy centre located on the top of your head. Feel your divine connection to the Source of Life and allow this bliss to fill up your every cell. You are joyful and thankful for all that you are, for all that you experience and for your abundant life that is supported by this Source.

CONCLUSION

Visualize all your seven chakras filled with money abundance and that abundance protruding outward to the external reality. Now getting fine and better and better bring your awareness to your body, breathe and surroundings. Open your eyes with joyous feeling and with gentle smiles.

(7) CROWN CHAKRA
LOCATION: Top of the head **COLOR :** Violet **ELEMENT:** Thought/will (Spirit)
FUNCTION : Vitalizes the upper rain (cerebrum) **GLANDS/ORGANS:** Pinal Gland, Cerebral Cortex, Central nervous system, right eye. **QUALITIES/LESSONS:** Unification of the Higher Self with the human personality. Oneness with the Infinite. Spiritual will, inspiration, unity, divine wisdom and understanding, Idealism, selfless service, Perception beyond space and time. continuity of consciousness. **NEGATIVE QUALITIES:** Lack of inspiration, confusion, depression, alienation, hesitation to serve, senility.

(5) THROAT CHAKRA
LOCATION: Throat area **COLOR :** Sky blue
ELEMENT: Akasha/ether
FUNCTION : Speech, sound, vibration, communication
GLANDS/ORGANS: Thyroid, parathyroid, hypothalamus, throat, mouth
FOOD: Blue/pumple, fruits and vegetables.
QUALITIES/LESSONS: Power of the spoken word, True communication. Creation expression in speech, writing and the arts, Integration, peace, truth, knowledge, wisdom, loyalty, honesty, reliability, gentleness, kindness
NEGATIVE QUALITIES: Communication and/ or speech problems used unwisely ignorance, Depression, thyroid problems.

(3) SOLAR PLEXUS CHAKRA
LOCATION: Above the navel, below the chest **COLOR :** Yellow **ELEMENT:** Fire
FUNCTION : Vitalizes the sympathetic nervous system. Digestive processes, metabolism, emotions
GLANDS/ORGANS: Pancreas, adrenal, stomach, liver, gallbladder, nervous system, muscles.
QUALITIES/LESSONS: Will, personal power, authority, energy, mastery of desire, self-control, Radiance, warmth, awakening, transformation, humor, laughter, immortality.
NEGATIVE QUALITIES: Taking in more than one can assimilate and utilize. Too much emphasis on power and /or recognition. Anger, fear. Digestive problems.

(1) ROOT OR BASE CHAKRA
Location : Base of the spine (Coccyx)
COLOR : Red (secondary color is black)
ELEMENT: Earth
FUNCTION: Give vitality to the physically body. Life-force, legs, bones
GLAND/OR GANS: Adrenal, kidneys.
FOODS: Proteins (meat and dairy products not recommended) Red Fruits and vegetables.
QUALITIES/LESSONS: Matters relating to the material world, success the physical body, mastery of the body. Grounding individually, stability security, stillness, courage, patience.
NEGATIVE QUALITIES: Self-centered, insecurity, violence, greed, anger. Overly concerned with one's Physical Survival.

(6) AJNA CHAKRA (Third Eye)
LOCATION: Center of the forehead, between the eyebrows.
COLOR : Indigo (Dark blue) **ELEMENT:** Light
FUNCTION : Vitalizes the lower brain (cerebrum) and central nervous system, vision.
GLANDS/ORGANS: Pituitary Gland (some sources say pineal gland), left eye, nose, ears.
FOOD: Blue/pumple, fruits and vegetables.
QUALITIES/LESSONS: Soil, realization, intuition, insight, imagination. Clairvoyance, concentration, peace of mind. Wisdom, devotion, perception beyond duality.
NEGATIVE QUALITIES: Lack of concentration, fear, cynicism, tension, Headaches, eye problems, bad dreams, detached from the world.

(4) HEART CHAKRA
LOCATION: Center of the chest
COLOR : Green (Secondary color is pink)
ELEMENT: Air
FUNCTION: Anchors the life-force to the Higher Self, energizes the blood and physical body with the life-force. Blood circulation.
GLANDS/ORGANS: Heart, thymus gland, circulatory system, arms, hands, lungs
FOOD: Green fruits and vegetables.
QUALITIES/LESSONS: Divine/ unconditional love. Forgiveness, compassion, understanding, balance, group consciousness, oneness with life. Acceptance, peace, openness, harmony, contentment
NEGATIVE QUALITIES: Repression of love, emotional instability, out of balance. Heart problems, Circulation problems.

(2) NAVEL CHAKRA (Sacral Plexus)
LOCATION: Lower abdomen to navel area.
Color: Orange **ELEMENT:** Water
FUNCTION: Procreation, assimilation of food, physical force and vitality, Sexuality.
GLAND / OR GANS: Ovaries, testicles, prostate, Genitals, spleen, wom, bladder.
FOODS : Liquids, Orange fruits and vegetables.
QUALITIES / LESSONS: Giving and receiving, emotion s, desire, pleasure, sexual / passionate love, change, movement, assimilation of new ideas. Health, family tolerance, surrender. Working harmoniously and creatively with others.
NEGATIVE QUALITIES: Over-indulgence in food sex, Sexual difficulties. Confusion purposelessness. Jealousy, envy, desire to posses. Impotency uterline and / or bladder problems.

CHAKRA TABLE

Chakra	Root	Sacral	Solar Plexus	Heart	Throat	Thrid Eye	Crown
Colour	Red	Orange	Yellow	Green	Blue	Indigo	Violet
Complementary Colour	Blue	Indigo	Violet	Red/Pink	Red	Orange	Yellow white Golden
Gland	Adrenal	Gonads	Adrenal Pancreas	Thymus	Thyroid Parathyroid	Pituitary	Pineal
Connected To	Physical self	Emotional self	Mental self	Unconditional Love	Holistic Thought	Unconditional self	Spiritual self
Personality Traits	Strong Willed, Impulsive	Extroverted, Happy	Intellectual, Practical	Nature, Loving, Romantic	Caring, Curious	Wise, Truth Seeker	Intuitive Creative, Inspiring
Qualities	Vitality, Courage, Strength, Security, Will-Power	Joy, Resourcefullness, Removed Inhibitions & Limitation	Wisdom, Clarity, Self-Esteem, Curiosity, Awareness	Balance, Self-control, Harmony, Renewal, Understanding	Knowledge, Health, Decisiveness, Truth, Loyalty, Communication	Intuition, Understanding, Fearless, Idealist, Fulfilment	Self-Sacrificing, Creativity, Visionary
Affirmation	"I Will"	"I Feel"	" I can"	"I Love"	"I Speak"	"I See"	"I know"
Element	Earth	Water	Fire	Air	Ether	Light	Spirit
Sense	Smell	Taste	Sight	Touch	Hearing	Intuition	Knowing-ness
Day of the Week	Tuesday	Wednesday	Sunday	Friday	Thursday	Saturday	Monday
Physically Gives Energy To Help	Legs, Feet, Vagina & Urinary Organs, Tiredness, Anaemia, Blood Disorders	Respiratory, Spleen, Kidney & Gall Bladder, Recharges Etheric Body/Aura	Digestion, Liver, Diabetes & Lungs, Arms Skin, Poor Digestion & Nervousness	Heart, Bronchia, & Legs, Chromic Disease and Hyper-tension	Neck & Voice, Reduces Fevers, Hyper-activity, Insomnia & Menstrual Problems	Pineal Gland & Nervous System, Increases Psychic Abilities, Heals Body/Aura	Lymphatic System, Kills Bacteria & Heals Skin Rashes, Emotional Issues

REFERENCES

- Raja Yoga By Sri Swami Sivananda, The Divine Life Society.
- Practice Lessons in Yoga By Swami Sivananda, The Divine life society, India
- Bless Divine By Sri Sivananda The Divine Life Society
- Autobiography of Swami Sivananda, The Divine Life Society
- Karma Sannyasa – By Swami Satyasangananda Saraswati, Yoga Publications Trust, Munger, Bihar, India
- Nawa Yogini Tantra- By Swami Muktanand, Yoga Publications Trust, Munger, Bihar, India
- Yoga for Digestive System, Dr Swami Shankardevananda, Yoga Publications Trust, Munger, Bihar, India
- Guru Shishya Sambandh By Swami Satyananda Saraswati, Yoga Publications Trust, Munger, Bihar, India
- Dynamics of Yoga, By Swami Satyananda Saraswati, Yoga Publications Trust, Munger, Bihar, India
- Yoga Education for Children Swami Satyananda Saraswati, Yoga Publications Trust, Munger, Bihar, India
- Nine Principal Upanishads Swami Satyananda Saraswati, Yoga Publications Trust, Munger, Bihar, India
- Taming the Kundalini Swami Satyananda Saraswati, Yoga Publications Trust, Munger, Bihar, India
- Steps to Yoga Swami Satyananda Saraswati, Yoga Publications Trust, Munger, Bihar, India
- Yog Nidra Swami Satyananda Saraswati, Yoga Publications Trust, Munger, Bihar, India
- Moola Bandha Swami Buddhananda, Yoga Publications Trust, Munger, Bihar, India
- Yoga Darshan By Swami Niranjananda Saraswati,
- Yoga Publications Trust, Munger, Bihar, India
- Samkhya Darshan By Swami Niranjananda Saraswati, Yoga Publications Trust, Munger, Bihar, India
- Meditations and Mantras By Swami Vishnu Devananda, Motilal Banarsidass Publishers
- Hatha Yoga Pradipika By Sivananda Yoga Vedanta Centre, Motilal Banarsidass Publishers
- Yogasana Vigyan By Dhirendra Brahmachari, Dhirendra Yoga Publications

- Yogic Sukshma Vyayama by Dhirendra Brahmachari, Dhirendra Yoga Publications
- Yoga Darshan By MDNIY, India
- Yogic and Naturopathic Treatment for Common Diseases By CCRYN, Delhi
- Research Methodology in Naturopathy & Yoga By CCRYN, Delhi, India
- Ayurveda, Its Principles and Philosophies- By Acharya Balkrishna, Divya Prakashan, Haridwar
- Maharshi Patanjali Yog Darshan by Swami Ramdev, Divya Prakashan, Haridwar
- Yog Science By Swami Ramdev, Divya Prakashan, Haridwar
- Sadhana and Siddhi By Acharya Mahapragya, Jain Vishwa Bharati , Ladnun
- Prekshya Dhyan Theory and Practice, By Acharya Mahapragya, Jain Vihawa Bharati, Ladnun
- Mahavira's Scripture of Health By Acharya Mahapragya, Adarsh Sahitya Sangh (Churu)
- Abstract Thinking By Acharya Mahapragya, Jain Vishwa Bharati, Ladnun
- Neuroscience & Karma By JL Zaveri & Muni Mahendra Kumar, Jain Vishwa Bharati, Ladnun
- Jeevan Vigyan By Muni Kishalal & Subhakarn Surana, Jain Vishwa Bharati, Ladnun
- An Introducion to Preksha Meditation By Mukhya Niyojika Sadhvi Vishrut Vibha, Jain Vihawa, Bharati, Ladnun
- Yoga for Hypertension & Heart Diseases, By HR
- Nagendra, Swami Vivekananda Yoga Prakashan, Banglore
- Yoga, The Path to Holistic Health By BKS Iyengar, By Dorling Kindersley (DK)
- Light on Yoga- By BKS Iyengar, Harper Collins Publishers -1996
- Light on Pranayama-By BKS Iyengar, Harper Collins Publishers-1998
- Pranayama, The Art and Science By HR Nagendra, Swami Vivekananda Yoga Prakashan, Banglore
- The Secret of Action By HR Nagendra, Swami Vivekananda Yoga Prakashan, Banglore
- Raj Yoga, The Path of Will-power, By HR Nagendra, Swami Vivekananda Yoga Prakashan, Banglore
- Integrated Approach of Yoga Therapy, By HR Nagendra, Swami Vivekananda Yoga Prakashan, Banglore
- Yoga for Arthritis, By HR Nagendra, Swami Vivekananda Yoga Prakashan, Banglore
- Natural Health and Yoga By Dr Brij Bhushan Goel, All India Nature Care Federation
- Health Diagnosis By Dr Brij Bhushan Goel, All India Nature Care Federation
- Uttam Jivan Jine Ki Kala By Dr Brij Bhushan Goel, All India Nature

Care Federation
- Anatomy of Hath Yoga By H David Coulter, Motilal Banarsidass Publishers
- Lifestyle and Health By Dr H.K. Chopra, Sterling Publishers, New Delhi, India
- In the Light of Meditation By Mike George, Brahma Kumaris,
- Anatomy and Physiology of Yogic Practices By Dr Makarand Madhukar Gore, New Age Book, India
- Yogic Exercises, By S Dutta Ray, Jaypee Brothers Medical Publishers, New Delhi
- Health in Your Hands By Devendr Vora, NavNeet Publication, India
- Kaun Banega Swastha Rakshak, By INO, Surya Foundation, India
- The Ten Principal Upanishads By Shree Purohit Swami & WB Yeats, Faber & Faber, London
- How to Read The Aura By Ted Andrews, B Jain Publishers, New Delhi, India
- Yoga Fun for Toddlers, Children & You By Juliet Pegrum, Cico Books, London
- Yoga for Suits By Edward Vilga, Running Papers
- Yoga for Young Mothers, By Seema Sondhi, Wisdom Tree, Delhi, India
- The Forceful Yoga By Pancham Singh, Rai Bahadur Sirsa Chandra Vasu, Motilal Banarsidass Publishers.

MESSAGES

I have been doing yoga with Yogaguru Dr Mohan since 2004. I was 94 Kg. and now just 73kg. I could overcome number of health complications viz. Neuropathy, Nephropathy and Retinopathy. Fluctuating BP & Sugar are now stable with yoga. He helped me to cure Slip Disk, Cervical Spondylitis & Back Pain. I am sure this book from him with his authentic knowledge and vast experiences will be a great help for the readers.

N.M. KEJRIWAL
Chairman—Kejriwal Group of Company

Yogaguru Mohan helped me to cure my chronic Parkinson disease at the age of 82 through Yoga & Naturopathy. I feel as if I have got new life. Some of the tests show wonderful response viz. Lipid profile blood test, BP and Sugar. I feel rejuvenated with complete servicing of my body. I hope his book will give light of hope to many people.

PC SHARMA
President—Bharat Vikas Parishad, New Delhi

Dr. Mohan Kumar Karki is a multiple Therapist with specialization to cure all diseases, particularly chronic through Yoga, Pranayama and Naturopathy. He has done so in a number of cases of Paralysis, Cervical Spondylosis, Insomnia, Asthma and Heart Diseases. I am impressed by his competence, devotion and multiple qualifications. I wish him best of luck in his noble pursuit of public interest work extended to actions.

DR. TILAK TALWAR
Convener, Thinkers Group, (1998), India
Nominated for Nobel Peace Prize - 2007

I have been to almost all the senior yoga therapist in India mainly in Delhi. I have never seen any teacher with this much caring way of teaching like Mr Mohan. He is really the best teacher. He has a capacity to make miracles happen to any patient.

YP VERMA
Chairman—Beltek Group of Companies

It is a matter of immense pleasure that Yoga guru Shri Mohan Karki is coming up with his new book "7 SECRET OF YOG SCIENCE" covering Asana, Pranayam, Shatkarmas, Bandhas, Mudras, Chakras and Meditation. I am fully assured that the book will fulfil the yoga needs of society and humanity and the readers will attain physical, mental, psychological, social and spiritual well being which is the real state of health according to WHO.

May all those who read this book be inspired and motivated to discover their dormant and hidden "inner self" and graciously relive the yogic life. I wish him and his tireless effort a great success.

DR. BABITA SINGH
Coordinator, Technical Sessions &
Teaching Programs Ujjain Yoga Life Society

Yoga was really difficult and weird for me initially. Some sort of things was written in unknown words like Sanskrit. After training, I really started to enjoy yoga and finally fell in love with yoga, which made me feel light in my body and happy in my soul. Yogaguru Mohan gave me educated lectures on medical issues and yogic sciences. He is my guru forever.

PROF. DH. KIM—South Korea

Dear Mr. Mohan Ji, Namaskar! You have been doing great work in the field of Yoga and I find you one of promising innovative yoga guru. It is my pleasure and privilege to write about 7 SECRETS OF YOG SCIENCE book. Being a yoga guru I congratulate you for writing this book covering all the aspects of Yog science. I pray all homes have this book and utilize the knowledge given to maintain good health. Guru Mohan ji has been awarded for his contribution to Yoga and meditation, and over the years he has trained thousands of people. I hope and wish this book will be translated into all Indian languages.

SUNEEL SINGH—Yoga Guru, Delhi

I have gained all the positivity and peace from Yoga. May others benefit from your teaching. I am sure this book will be one more step in this journey of life transformation for the readers.

NEERU NARANG—Pitampura, Delhi

I have had the best opportunity to learn Yoga from you. You have been a very inspiring teacher, making even the difficult asanas easy to perform and have always encouraged putting in extra effort in achieving perfection. I wish you the very best for your book. I am sure it will help the novice to understand yoga much better.

NEHA SINGH
Teachers' Training Participant—Delhi

Respected' Mohan sir' I know you from (little) long time. You are really a yogi person, very calm (sthita-pragya) and when you teach, one can easily make out about your knowledge. I know you love reading moreover knowing and learning. I hope and wish that your book will make wonder and satisfy hunger of pupils. Best wishes for you. Hope to see your book soon.

SANGEETA SHARMA—Yogaguru, Delhi

My best wishes to Mohan Sir. I recommend this book to all the yoga gurus, yoga therapists and true seekers of authentic yogic wisdom. You can easily understand how yoga can help each one of us to evolve so that we can achieve the ultimate.

ASHISH SINGH
Yoga Guru

This is the book you want if you are serious about beginning your yoga practice. Pictures of Yoga Poses are well illustrated and instructions are clearly stated. This is an extremely helpful book in gaining an understanding of the varied characteristics and functions of yoga as a total physical and mental practice.

PRIYANKA VERMA
CA, Indian Oil Corporation
Teachers Training Participant

I congratulate you sir on completion of your book! I hope that it will benefit many people with your vast knowledge on the subject as it helped me as your student!

RITU ARORA—Sector-15A, Noida

I had sinus, headache and some fever related problem from my childhood. I tried all types of medicine like allopathic, Ayurveda, Homeopathic etc. The problem used to come partly under control and again used to appear with added symptoms. I had to stop going to school. Luckily Mohan Guru Ji came to our contact from yoga camp in temple of our colony. He gave me just 15 sessions within that time with some pranayama, asanas, and Kunjal it went all right. Now, I am going to school without any problems. I thank him very much.

ANSUL AGRAWAL
Student, Kohat Inclave,, Pitampura, Delhi

Yoga practice with Yogaguru has helped me not only in weight loss and better energy but more importantly positive mind set for the whole day. These days my colleagues are more happy with me. A book from my guru, a real Yogi will surely help the readers to achieve transformation.

VIVEK SINGH
Marketing Manager—Moserbaer, India

The Yogaguru workout is a nice combination of warm up, exercise, stamina building and relaxation. Also personal attention is given to all. Best part of Yoga Guru is the nature and attitude of all trainers. I Achieved weight loss 25kgs, 7 inches in 7-8 months. It gives immense pleasure to know a book coming from Yoga Guru. It will be surely a great help to the masses.

AMIT KUMAR SAXENA
Yoga Student, Noida

The topics covered in the book are extremely useful. It gives ample opportunity for doubt clearance on yoga. I am sure reading this book will be a life changing experience for readers.

ADVOCATE PREM KSHETRI
General Secretary, Hamara Swabhiman

Many congratulations. I hope that your book will kiss the height of Mt. Everest and depth of ocean. May it be proven Ram Baan for all the human beings and be successful to direct all the people in Yoga. Once Again Many Many Congratulations.

ANJIT BISTA—Kathmandu, Nepal

I feel happier & relaxed after attending yoga workshop with The Yogaguru. I think yoga must be introduced in schools & colleges as part of compulsory curriculum to induce a healthy lifestyle. It is good to know a book is coming from an experienced Yogaguru. Congratulations and good wishes from my side.

AANCHAL CHOUDHARY—Engineer- BHEL,Noida

I am very satisfied with Yoga Guru's power yoga class as I've achieved the expected result. I wonder to see the drastic Weight loss & Inches loss, improved flexibility, Strength & Stamina. I got relief in Asthma as well. I'd joined the Yoga Guru 7 months back and since I joined Yoga Guru I have lost around 15 kgs weight. I wish this book also will benefit more people.

YAMINI SHAH—Yoga Student, Noida

I wish you the very best of luck and success as your knowledge would guide others.

AMY DAVISON—United Kingdom